TO KNOW JOHN LENNON

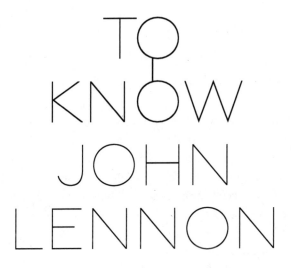

TO KNOW JOHN LENNON

AN INTIMATE PORTRAIT FROM HIS
FRIENDS, COLLEAGUES, AND FAMILY

AIDAN PREWETT

political animal
PRESS

Political Animal Press
Toronto • Chicago
www.politicalanimalpress.com

Distributed by the University of Toronto Press
www.utpdistribution.com

Cataloguing data available from Library and Archives Canada
ISBN 978-1895131-55-0 (paperback)
ISBN 978-1895131-56-7 (ebook)

Typeset in Garamond and Gravesend Sans
Cover images from the Mark Naboshek collection

CONTENTS

for Schy — real love

INTRO

THE BEATLES played six shows in Melbourne, Australia, in mid-June of 1964. The tour had been booked a year prior – pre-Beatlemania – and the Australian public were aware they had scored a major coup. The streets were filled. The airports were surrounded. The Beatles were largely confined to their hotel. The crowds assembled in Australian city streets were the biggest the band had yet seen – or would ever see.

Each of the six shows at Festival Hall, near the Melbourne docks, was sold out. Fans swarmed around the factory and warehouse district, skipping between the train lines that connect the shipyards to the mainland. A sense of camaraderie swept the crowd – especially amongst the Beatles Fan Club members. But as happened with Beatlemaniacs the world over, the kids began to lose their minds in the anticipation. There was screaming and tears – the herd mentality was setting in. Elsewhere, people were getting lost in the crush. Fights broke out. Outside the Beatles' hotel, 300 police officers were called in to help barricade the entries and exits. The police struggled. The army was brought in. *They* struggled.

Even in England, Beatlemania was a new phenomenon. The very concept of popular culture for teenagers was a new phenomenon. And Australian teenagers paid close attention to their English counterparts. These kids knew the Beatles wouldn't be touring Down Under again any-time soon. They had had to get their piece, *now*.

The scene inside Festival Hall was hardly different from the chaos outside. Audience members were fainting; hauled to safety by a small coterie of venue security. As had become the norm, hearing the band was near impossible beneath the piercing screams from the crowd. It didn't matter – they were in the same room as *The Beatles*. Their idols were on stage, right in front of them. Singing just for them. It was a lot to take in. And at the center of this mania – in the front row – was a ten-year-old kid named Michael Pittard.

It was June 16, 1964; Michael's tenth birthday. His seat had been secured by his aunt Doreen, who worked for a local radio station. In the first row, Michael could even hear the music. Occasionally he panned around to witness the teenage girls weeping, pulling at their hair, and fainting. It was unlike anything Michael had seen before. He was coming-of-age at the birth of a new era.

And of course, he knew the songs. He *loved* the songs. But something else took Michael's fancy that night. As he peered over the lip of the stage, at his eye line, he caught the glint of a foil-wrapped bar of chocolate as it bounced onto the stage. The bar had been thrown by a fan – part of a slew of jelly babies and jellybeans that were traditionally hurled at the feet of the Beatles by the Fan Club members. Lollies and sweets were already littering the front row. But this was something else. This was *chocolate*.

The chocolate bar had landed close to Michael. Close enough? Not quite. He reached out across the stage – sud-denly more interested in the chocolate than in the four musicians on stage. He stood on tiptoes, extending his arm further toward his prize. Michael stretched out to gain an extra few millimeters; he was almost at the point of giving up. Then, magically, the shining bar of chocolate began to slide gently towards his extended fingertips. On the low-lit stage floor, a black leather boot emerged, sliding the chocolate toward his grasp. Michael's fingers closed around the chocolate bar. He was triumphant.

Almost in slow-motion, Michael's gaze wandered up into the whirl of stage lights. The boot was attached to a long grey trouser leg; then even further up, to a gleaming Rickenbacker; until Michael's wonder settled on a Beatle face, beaming back at him. It was John.

Michael Pittard is a friend and colleague of mine. When he told me his story, I was thrilled – it's the kind of story that paints John Lennon as a genuine human being. It restores to John some of the humanity that gets lost when a person becomes an icon. So it got me thinking, and it got me started on something. I wanted to find more stories like Michael's. Stories from people who spent time with John, who *knew* him to be a real person. Real – with flaws and foibles like the rest of us. But with something else as well.

Michael Pittard didn't hang out with John Lennon. But his experience illustrated something I hadn't found in the many books and documentaries I'd encountered. I returned to the thought: *What was it like to know John Lennon?*

I was born much too late to ever find out firsthand, but the thought has been chasing me around in some form or another since I first discovered the Beatles' music at age fourteen. I read every Beatle book I could get my hands on, but I knew there were more great John Lennon stories out there. And I knew some of these stories would have their beginnings in John's attempts at leading a more 'normal', everyday life. *What was it like to kick back and have a cup of tea with John Lennon?*

As the occasion of John's 80th birthday approached, I set out to record and document the enclosed collection of interviews with his friends and colleagues. The crux of each interview was: What was it like to know John? To call him a friend? To have him call *you* a friend? We began our conversations with an inquiry: *Is there one moment you shared with John that has really stuck with you after all these years?* It turned out there were a great many stories waiting to be told. The conversations took interesting and unexpected turns, from accounts of falling asleep on the London Underground with John, to memories of hiding in a closet with John to escape the followers of the Maharishi Mahesh Yogi.

And John was no saint – indeed, he'd likely be offended at such a suggestion. So John's friends tend not to shy away from the less savory moments, from John's temper to his relationship with alcohol and drugs. He was a human being, after all, with his own weaknesses and failings – but we're not here to entertain speculation and rumor. We touch on these subjects only in the interest of a deeper exploration of John's character.

This is a celebration – and in that spirit, this is also a portrait of the people John chose to surround himself with. Each character we meet is preceded by an introduction. How did they come to know John? What was their background at the time? What have they achieved since? What unfolds is a story of professionals at the top of their game: Grammy winning musicians and industry icons; film and theatre directors; television executives; award-winning actors, authors, and journalists. Each interview has been approached as a conversation, allowing some ebb and flow in an attempt to draw out the most wonderful, interesting, and insightful John Lennon stories. In each case, interviewees went into great detail and revealed telling, poignant moments that have seldom – if ever – been brought to light before. Many of these stories have remained untold simply due to their qualitative – rather than quantitative – nature. They deal more in emotion than in the detail of dates and times.

These interviews have been arranged chronologically – that is, in order of when each subject first met John. While many of John's friends throughout this book knew him over a period of years, for each the most wonderful and amazing moments seem to have happened early on. This is a common phenomenon in many friendships – they are cemented early and then carried on over a longer period. Some of John's friends speak of times spanning ten years or more, so our chronology is not a strict one.

I have included some relevant background information at the beginning of each chapter, illustrating relevant details about John's life as they relate to his friends. Sometimes I have provided context for an early rock 'n' roll band that John loved, or another area of John's wide span of interests that is referenced more fully within the subsequent interview. Details vary – some interviews were as short as half an hour. Others stretched on for well over two hours, sometimes across several sittings. Each has been edited and curated here to allow the story within to unfold in its most compelling fashion.

This project's main focus is to capture a feeling. What did it *feel* like to ride in the back of a Rolls Royce with John, singing the old favorite rock 'n' roll songs together? What did it *feel* like to be alone in the mastering suite with John, playing back the most recent mixes from *Walls & Bridges* and *Rock 'n' Roll*? What did it *feel* like to hang out at the Dakota building, or at Tittenhurst Park?

What emerges is an intimate portrait of John in his private life, spending time with his friends and colleagues. His sense of humor often comes to the fore. His reputation among journalists for being cynical or scathing is rarely seen. With only a few exceptions, John is described as generous, noble, and charming. This is how his friends remember him. For John's 80th birthday, this book is a celebration among those who knew him.

JULIA BAIRD
CHILDHOOD

JOHN LENNON was born during a lull in Hitler's bombing raids on Liverpool. The city – a major industrial port – was, of course, a major strategic target and suffered the worst British civilian casualty rate outside London. Most Liverpool children born in 1940 share vague memories of makeshift bomb shelters, ruined buildings and panicked faces as firemen raced to extinguish huge warehouse blazes. Amid the chaos, John's mother Julia brought her new baby home to Number 9, Newcastle Road, in the Penny Lane area of Liverpool. This was a house Julia shared with her parents. Together they did their best to shield the youngest member of the family from Liverpool's experience of war.

John's father Fred served in the Merchant Navy and rarely saw John or his wife Julia during the war years. At the end of the war, Fred returned home to find that he and Julia had grown apart. Separation followed, and John – aged five – was asked to make the heartbreaking choice between living with his mother or his newly-discovered father. He had recently spent some enjoyable time with Fred and initially ran to his father, before changing his mind and returning to Julia. Fred left. John didn't see his father again until 1963, when he was 22, and a Beatle.

John soon found himself whisked off to live with his

aunt and uncle Mimi and George Smith. Mimi had made several complaints to the Liverpool City Council and eventually arranged to take responsibility for John's care. Mimi's major argument was that John was sharing small living quarters with his mother and her new partner, John 'Bobby' Dykins. Julia and Bobby were distraught – they were effectively being forced to give up Julia's son. And there is little doubt that Mimi had motives beyond that of John's wellbeing: Mimi and George had no children of their own, and Mimi had doted on John from the moment he was born.

John started school at Mosspits Lane Infants School at a time when he was witnessing major rows between his mother and aunt. Mimi took John permanently into her care in 1946 and withdrew him from Mosspits Lane after just five months. She then re-enrolled him at the more upmarket Dovedale Road Primary School. Unsurprisingly, he presented behavioral issues in his classes. The young John Lennon had little experience of stability.

When John was six, his sister Julia Dykins (now Julia Baird) was born. Two years later, Jacqueline 'Jackie' Dykins followed. The baby sisters grew up looking forward to visits from their brother, as they moved into a larger and more welcoming house – Springwood – on Blomfield Road, Allerton. Springwood was roughly two miles south of Mimi's house, Mendips. Mendips perched over Menlove Avenue in the neighboring Liverpool suburb of Woolton.

John maintained varying degrees of contact with his mother and his two sisters and was able to visit them from time to time, if granted permission from Mimi or if he snuck out. He visited with increasing frequency as he began to approach his teenage years. As often happens, even the strictest rule makers are forced to relax their policies when faced with an impetuous youth.

John could see the injustice of his captivity and refused to be contained any longer. Mimi had to let him go. And so, John would visit Springwood – the home of his mother, her partner Bobby Dykins, and his two sisters Julia and Jackie.

AIDAN PREWETT: What was it like for you and Jackie when John came to stay?

JULIA BAIRD: We just jumped all over him. When John came, because he was a boy, he had Jackie's room and Jackie slept with me. And we used to just run in there in the morning and leap all over him. He did bounces on the bed, and he played with us endlessly, and drew with us and took us to the park and did all the things that you would do with little sisters. We used to go to the pictures with John, and he would go out – leaving Jackie and I sitting in the dark. He'd go out to smoke. But it was a secret.

AP: Is there a particular memory you have of John with your mother at Springwood that has really stuck with you – that you go back to?

JB: From when we were very young, and John would be doing our times tables with us, or drawing pictures with us. Our mother painted and drew – John got that from her as well. So they were doing that for us, and playing the piano and singing and dancing. Children's songs – 'Teddy Bear's Picnic' and stuff like that. And that gradually morphed into my mother teaching John how to play the banjo. I can remember that vividly. John must have been about twelve. She played the piano accordion – she hadn't started to teach him that, or the piano. That all came later. It was the banjo that he wanted to play.

My mother was a bit of a perfectionist, certainly with music. She would be behind him, and she'd have her hands on the frets. And John would be strumming, and learning to pick the strings. And then they would turn it around and they would do it in the opposite way – my mother would be doing the finger work. Then it became very complicated, and John would be doing the frets.

AP: For any family, that's a special moment.

JB: We weren't the only ones with instruments in the house. Music is endemic in a great big port like Liverpool with the ships, the seamen's mission. We grew up on being a port. And music came from all over the world. We got the early recordings of Eddie Cochrane, Gene Vincent… we were getting these things right off the ships, when other places hadn't heard of them.

So music wasn't peculiar to us, if you know what I mean. And people really did sing around the piano. This is pre-television, remember – so people actually talked to each other, pre-digital age.

AP: I'd love to get a sense of what a family gathering was like.

JB: There was a particular birthday of John's. After the war, we were rationed until I was about eight. John was about fifteen or sixteen. So all food was rationed. We had dried egg, two ounces of chocolate a week, two ounces of bacon, two ounces of butter, two ounces of cheese. One pint of milk a day, one pint of orange juice a day, per child. And this was how we grew up. Fortunately, my father worked in a hotel, and great sides of meat appeared regularly and it was divided between all the women in the street. They came in and they took their cut. I'm sure it fell off the back of a lorry or something.

Everyone had allotments, so they were growing their own vegetables. We actually had a very healthy diet in the end. But the chocolate – my aunts had been saving all the chocolate rations to make John a birthday cake. And we all went for the chocolate cake tea, and a lot of it had been eaten. And my uncle Norman – who had been to Burma, and came back with severe Malaria – must have had a moment, 'cos he'd eaten it. Nobody spoke to him for ages.

AP: Your father, Bobby, also played an active role in John's life – is there a particular moment you go back to, between your dad and John?

JB: One time John was smoking in the bedroom. My father hauled him out and said he could have set fire to the mattress. He was about 14 then – 15, maybe – and got him his first job. My father was the manager of the airport restaurant at that time. The old Liverpool Airport restaurant. And he took John down and set him to wait on the tables. Earn his own money – smoke his own money. And he wasn't allowed to smoke in the house. Of course, it wasn't as drastic as that, if you notice he wasn't saying *you'll kill yourself*, he was saying *you'll set fire to the mattress and set fire to the house and we'll all be asleep.*

AP: I'd love to hear about you and Jackie and John at the park, swinging around a maypole on a chain with the other local kids.

JB: Well, John was one of the older ones, so he could pull. The stronger ones went on first. You did it in weight and height, because the last one that took it *flew*. Absolutely flew. And you had to make sure you didn't let go. You weren't manacled to it – you had two bars. And you had one hand above the other. The strong one was leaning up and down at the bottom, swinging you around.

Children's playgrounds were death traps. But we loved them. We couldn't keep away. Nowadays they wouldn't allow a child near anything that we did.

AP: Aunt Mimi and her Mendips house are so firmly ingrained in the folklore – and then so is Mimi's stern character.

JB: Mendips was never the house where John was at his happiest. It was Springwood, the house – that's where he was with us. Or basically, with our mother. Learning to play the instruments and laughing and joking, and he had lots of his friends in. What's strange is that the Beatles fans are fed Mendips. Mimi didn't allow any of that, and yet the house that they're stuck on is the wrong house. And when people go straight to Mendips and say *he never saw his mother*, they miss *all this out* – the relationship.

It wasn't all desperate, obviously. The thing is, there's a Japanese saying *I have to accept this, I have no choice*. John had to accept that he was living with Mimi, because he didn't have a choice. And he never knew the ins and outs.

So there were moments – when Brian Epstein was in Mendips in the morning room – the room that Mimi sort of lived in mostly – leaning on the mantelpiece. With John there, and they're talking about moving to London. This is way later – *way* later. My experiences with John are with my mother, not with Mimi. Because if I was there, then my mother was there.

AP: Among these youthful experiences, you and Jackie caught John 'necking' with a girl.

JB: Barbara Baker. And he gave me two and six to shut up. Again, this is Springwood. He brought Barbara Baker down. They'd gone for a walk and we followed them up the road. We followed them into the park, and then we watched them. What else as a younger sister are you supposed to do? I mean, they weren't *up to anything*. God knows what they would have been doing nowadays. But certainly then, they were fully clothed, rolling around in the grass having a good time.

So he saw us – and I got half a crown. Two and six. It was a fortune.

AP: So that you wouldn't say anything.

JB: And we all went straight to the sweet shop.

AP: And a bit later on, after Barbara Baker, he brought Cynthia home.

JB: He could see the bus from upstairs at Mendips. He'd be eagerly waiting for her bus to come in... and then he'd be whistling around the kitchen – and then sort of casually stroll up to the gate to meet her. And Cynthia did the same. She would watch for him coming back, and then she'd go and lie down on the sofa and arrange her hair over the arm of the chair.

They were besotted with each other. Truly, *truly,* besotted. Call it love, call it lust, call it what you like. It's what teenagers do; it was no different. He was head over heels in love with Cynthia. And I can tell you – she was the most beautiful person, *inside and out.* She had a beautiful soul, and she treated Jackie and I like two younger sisters. If John hadn't become a Beatle, things would have been different.

AP: When John started to get seriously involved with music – could you tell me about a moment where you and your mum were in an audience together, watching one of John's early groups?

JB: Jackie and I had been on a Sunday school outing and mother came to pick us up. The church was literally around the corner – it was almost at Paul McCartney's house – Forthlin.

So my mother picked us up and we went on the bus into town. My goodness – we'd thought we were going home to bed! All exciting. And we saw them on the back of the lorry in Roseberry Street. It was a coal lorry which had not been cleaned. I got up on it and then got down again – covered in coal.

Mother went into the nearest house straight away, because all the mums were having cups of tea and sandwiches. This is classic Liverpool – no beers, no wines, no vodkas: pots of tea. Endless pots of tea and sandwiches.

AP: Perfect.

JB: I went in to find her, and when I came out, the police had arrived because John and some other boy – a bit of jealousy, musical jealousy going on – were verging on a punch-up. So we were escorted back to the bus stop by the police. And that was the end of that. Apparently, there was another concert later but they weren't invited back.

A month later, they were invited to the famous Woolton Fête. We were all there for that too – all of us. It was a pivotal moment in their lives, in their career. The beginnings. Because of course Paul McCartney turned up. We didn't go to the evening do, we went home and went to bed. But apparently John said, "…and he looks a bit like Elvis." So that was it. He was in, wasn't he?

AP: And Paul started turning up at your house to practice.

JB: Yes, he did. He used to come and eat with us. And my mother – the irony – would say, "That poor boy, he's lost his mother," when he went home. "That poor boy. He's lost his mother."

• • •

Julia's story wove itself alongside John's for many years. For that reason, we'll return to Julia again later on. The Lennon/McCartney's story, of course, begins here and remains a constant presence in one form or another throughout John's life.

Julia went on to study languages and later became a teacher and psychologist. While studying in Paris she took part in the 1968 student demonstrations, and has since travelled and worked with a variety of charity organizations around the world. Julia retired to write *Imagine This: Growing Up with My Brother, John Lennon* and is now a director of Liverpool's Cavern Club.

Julia's first book, *John Lennon, My Brother* was published in 1988 and began a shift in the discourse surrounding John's early life. The 'official' story, as it had been told by Aunt Mimi for the previous quarter century, was that John had only reconnected with his mother briefly before she died. Mimi had been interviewed by Hunter Davies for his 1968 book *The Beatles*, which formed the groundwork for so many other Beatle books to follow. Mimi's story largely erased the importance of John's relationship with his mother and sisters. It was like she was trying to keep them a secret.

But Aunt Mimi had some secrets of her own. Those we'll save for later.

MICHAEL HILL

SCHOOL DAYS

LIFE AT MENDIPS wasn't bad for John – it just wasn't with his immediate family. As for any child in that situation, the question *why?* must have played on his mind. He got used to Mimi's strictness and rather enjoyed escaping to the good humor and relative safety of his Uncle George. But he wasn't often allowed to have friends over – instead he relied on visiting others and sneaking out.

John could sit in the branches of a tall tree in Mendips' backyard and peer out over the neighboring fences. A short distance away he could see the imposing Victorian architecture of the Strawberry Field children's home, a repurposed mansion. John would occasionally scale the back fence and run off to play with the Strawberry Field children, and concerts were sometimes held there by the Salvation Army band.

Opposite Mendips, on the other side of Menlove Avenue, was a golf course that stretched most of the distance to John's mother's house, Springwood. Here, John and his sisters would collect lost golf balls and sell them back to the golfers. Sometimes they collected golf balls that weren't lost – only out of sight.

Mischief and disdain for authority were early sources of enjoyment for John, and he soon introduced his school friends to the Lennon brand of civil disobedience. John's school records show an inordinate number of detentions, 'black marks' and canings for a variety of vaguely-described infractions: disruption, rudeness, noise, lacking attention. We're about to hear some of the real detail behind those reports.

John first met his schoolmate Michael Hill when he enrolled in Dovedale Road Primary School. The boys spent twelve of their school years together, starting at Dovedale Road Primary School and carrying on at Quarry Bank High School for Boys until 1957, when both John and Michael left school to pursue different paths. When they found themselves at Quarry Bank, John took up the position of leader of his group of friends. Two pairs of best friends made up the quartet. They were John Lennon and Pete Shotton, and Michael Hill and Don Beattie. This notorious group of boys found themselves in an endless variety of trouble as they moved from class to class. And John in particular was no stranger to corporal punishment.

AIDAN PREWETT: What springs to mind when you hear the phrase '*six of the best*'?

MICHAEL HILL: '*Six of the best*' was being caned. In junior school you'd stand in front of the class and put your hand out, and you'd get a single stroke. This was a bamboo cane, which really hurt and left a red mark. *Whack* – in front of the class. Of course, you'd try not to cry or to flinch. But when you went into grammar school – then you graduated. You might get one, but normally it was six on the backside and in the housemaster or headmaster's study.

AP: And John was caned frequently?

MH: I'd love to be able to tell you how many times. A record was kept – a punishment logbook. People who had access to that reckoned that John was caned more than anybody else in the school. It's probably the only record he held at school, for the number of canings.

AP: Can you think of a specific incident that springs to mind – *John must have been caned for that?*

MH: I can remember one where we were caned together. We all went up, the four of us – John and Pete Shotton, John's best friend, and me and my best friend Don Beattie. We had been caught smoking behind the bicycle sheds by one of the school prefects, and reported. You wouldn't think smoking was such a heinous crime, but it was very serious. It was like the next best thing to being expelled. So we went to the headmaster for that.

But John's worst behavior, really, was terrorizing student teachers. I can remember, even as eleven and twelve-year-olds in our first year at Quarry Bank, two teachers in particular. Both of them short, kind-hearted teachers – one English, one Maths. We saw both of these teachers reduced to tears in front of the class. When you look back on it, you feel quite ashamed.

But John's normal way of disrupting the class was by drawing something or writing something and passing it around. And the ripple would go around the class. Somebody would laugh and they would pass it on. He was very good at getting Pete Shotton into trouble. We always sat together, Don and I and Pete and John, we would all be together at the back of the class. It was easy to make Pete laugh, and he found it hard to stop – whereas John was very good at pulling the shutter down. The teacher usually got a serious-looking John Lennon and a laughing and out-of-control Pete Shotton. So Pete was the one who got the black mark. Two black marks in a week, you had a detention for one hour after school on Friday.

John had plenty of detentions. He wasn't always popular with the rest of the class – the trouble was, he would never own up. If he did something and the teacher said, "Who did this?" He would never own up and nobody would dob him in, so the whole class got punished. Sometimes the whole class might get a detention if it was something serious. Some of these boys had never had a detention, they were perfectly behaved. They were none too happy.

He actually had a good first year at Quarry Bank. But where his behavior really deteriorated was when he lost his Uncle George. Having been brought up from the age of five by Uncle George and Aunt Mimi, and having learned to read sitting on George's knee and reading him the newspapers, George was sort of the father figure. George was the one who comforted him if Mimi was a bit strict. She *was* a bit strict sometimes with John. And with George. So I think they comforted each other.

So when John was 14, with no warning of prior illness, George collapsed, went off to hospital and was dead. And from that point, John's behavior really went downhill. It was like the rope that held him back had been cut. He'd already had very little contact with his mother; he was just starting to get to know his mother – his real mother. Three years after this, his mother was killed.

So he had a lot to be angry about; a lot to be sad about. Which manifested, really, in aggression. But you could see that deterioration. John's last three years at school – he just had no interest in what he was studying, or supposed to be studying. He was just not interested in what was going on at school.

AP: Is there a particular bit of mischief with John that you remember fondly?

MH: In our group, John was the leader. Nobody elected him leader, but we all tacitly accepted that he was the leader – the leader in the sense that he was mostly leading us astray. But I introduced him to the concept of gate-lifting. It must have driven people crazy. You identified these metal gates that you could just lift off; they just sat on the pivot. In those days nearly every house had a fenced front garden with a little gate in front of a footpath leading to the front door. You'd see these same-sized gates, three or four houses apart, and you'd lift them. Two of you would lift one gate, two the other. You'd swap them over. And of course, what made it a bit more exciting was doing it in the daytime – that you didn't get stopped and people didn't come out of the house or look out of the window and see you doing it. So people would come home from work, and – *bloody hell, this is not my gate!*

We often wondered – all they knew was that they had a different gate. Maybe at some point they noticed that three or four houses along – *that's my gate there!* And maybe they swapped them back again. We never found that out.

Gate-lifting – yeah, pretty unusual. But I remembered it particularly, because John was impressed. He wasn't easy to impress, John Lennon. Pretty hard. You tried to impress him, but it wasn't that easy.

But his main claim to fame in terms of misdemeanors was shoplifting. Right up until – the story is – when they were going to Hamburg, that he stole a harmonica in a shop in Arnhem. It's probably true. He couldn't help himself. But kids were bad. If they could steal things, they would.

AP: Was there ever any trouble with the police?

MH: In the early days, there was one occasion where John and I were chased by a policeman. The university playing fields ran from near where I was living right over to where John was living. They were very extensive. They had a pond where you could go and get tadpoles. And somebody had put a big rope up from the tree, so you could swing on the rope right out over the pond and try not to fall off. And they had a groundkeeper who used to come occasionally and tell you off. But on this occasion, he brought a policeman in.

I knew that the way I'd come in there was a rusty railing, and you could slide the railing across so you could get through. A little boy could get through. A policeman couldn't get through.

So we all got chased by this policeman. I said, *"Follow me – I know the way out."* But of course, all the railings look the same – you've only got one chance. If you don't get the right one, the policeman would be right on top of you. But we managed to find it. We all got through. Then you're through; the policeman can't get through. And of course, you're all making rude gestures at him from the other side.

AP: I can picture the bobby's face. What other havoc would you cause?

MH: One of my best memories of John was dressing up. He loved to dress up. He loved wearing hats, funny hats. One of my clear memories – we would have been aged fifteen, probably. During the long school holidays one day, he and Pete Shotton came over. John never came on his own – always with Pete. So they're looking for something to do. And what are we going to do to amuse John Lennon?

"We could dress up."

"Oh, great."

He loved to do that. So we went up to the wardrobe in my mother's bedroom and hunted around the house looking for clothes. My mother had a fox fur made of a whole fox, with a fox's head, with teeth. They used to wear these – they were all the rage in the 1930s. You'd put them around your neck. So John, I remember, wore that: "Fantastic!"

We all dressed up in these weird clothes. And to make them more weird, we had a pair of Wellington boots and a pair of soccer boots. I had one soccer boot, one Wellington boot – John had the other half. So the three of us got dressed up, and we walked a hundred yards or so down the street and joined the bus queue.

The whole thing is you're not allowed to laugh. And the humor is that other people are looking at you – but they don't want to be *seen* to be looking. So they're looking out of the corner of their eye. Or they're trying not to look. And you can see them trying to work out why we're dressed like that – *what's going on?*

He liked to make people laugh, and he liked to dress up. As they say, whenever he had a chance to put a funny hat on…

AP: School uniform might have been a problem, then.

MH: One way we'd get around it, or jazz it up – we'd wear luminous socks, like lime green. Lime green or bright red socks. So you'd have your black shoes, your regulation grey flannel trousers, black blazer, school tie, cap. We'd wear a cap, like a little wolf cub cap.

The prefects would hide behind the sandstone walls. You'd be cycling home, downhill, and they would catch you, 'cos you had to wear uniform to and from school. So if they'd see you coming up or down without a school cap… A lot of bloody spying went on.

So that was John, trying to look like the people that he admired. The rock 'n' roll stars or the Teddy Boys. 'Cos John liked to think that he was tough. He wasn't really; not physically tough. Verbally tough. He could be very cutting. He had a great command of English; a great command of swear words. You didn't have the last word with John Lennon.

AP: Do you ever remember seeing John in a fight of any kind?

MH: No. Oh – yeah, I think at primary school. But that's more wrestling. We all liked wrestling. Kids like getting dirty, rolling around in the dirt. It's pretty natural for healthy boys. But he was – I reckon he was pretty selective. He'd only get in a fight if he thought he could win it.

But John would write. He had his own form of humor, and he had this piece that was passed around the classroom called *The Daily Howl*, which was quite brilliant. Really, the drawings in it are quite amazing. John aged twelve, first year at grammar school, did this project for English Literature. 'Porky' Burrows, the form master, set a project to write and do some illustrations of books and poems that they were reading. And John's is so good. He did four or five pages in an exercise book. Beautifully written and so well illustrated that the teacher kept it. He didn't keep it because he knew John Lennon one day would be super famous. He kept it because it was such brilliant work. But he still had it in his possession years later.

AP: Do you remember any specific examples of John's wordplay?

MH: One that stuck in my mind was a buttered crust – a crust of bread – became a *cruttered bust*. Just swapped the letters. And of course, the famous one – "I hear in the newspaper there's going to be a general *erection*." That's an easy one. Change one letter. He loved to play around with words like that.

AP: And then you, Michael, went off to Holland and came back to Liverpool with a very important record.

MH: Pete Shotton and Don Beattie and I went to Amsterdam on a school exchange when we were fifteen. We were all paired off with Dutch children, and my Dutch friend and I went to a record shop. The guy in the record shop would tell you what the latest hit is you should hear, and they would play them for you. He said, "Oh, you've got to hear this – it just came in yesterday." So we put it on. *Wow.* My immediate reaction when I heard this record was *wow – wait 'til John Lennon hears this.* It was by a singer that I'd never heard of – none of us had heard of – it hadn't been released at that point in England – Little Richard's 'Long Tall Sally'.

You were trying to get a tick from John, you know? So I thought *wow, I've got to buy this.* So I bought the record, but I didn't tell the others. I just put it carefully in my suitcase.

I took this record back and within a couple of days we were at my house. We got our fish and chips and we were going to put some records on. I said, "I've got a record here by a guy I think is better than Elvis Presley." That was deliberately to get John's attention, because John was pretty besotted with Elvis. *Nobody could be better than Elvis Presley.* I deliberately didn't tell them who the singer was, or what the record was, or anything. This was the build-up.

So you put it on the record player, you put the bass on full; you put it on loud. And, well – if you know this Little

Richard number 'Long Tall Sally', it's what I call *in-your-face rock 'n' roll*. *Boom Boom Boom* – saxophones, and he's thumping the piano. It's very, very different from Elvis Presley. Most of the Elvis songs are ballads. This certainly wasn't a ballad – this was thumping in-your-face rock 'n' roll. *Wow.*

So everybody was listening – the four of us. And of course, the record suddenly stops. As they say, the silence was deafening. Everybody's looking at John, for his reaction.

No reaction. Speechless. Unprecedented. John Lennon was never speechless. *Speechless.* So, *wow – I've made an impression.* He didn't know what to say.

So I didn't say anything. I put the other side on; turned it over – 'Slippin' and Slidin' (Peepin' and a Hidin')'. Another...*wow.* So John was impressed, but he didn't say too much after that. But looking back on it, he told the London *Evening Standard* that that was the moment he knew what he wanted to do with his life. He wanted to play music. He wanted to play rock 'n' roll. So of course, he got himself a guitar, and a few weeks after that with other boys getting guitars and banjos they formed a group at school – The Quarrymen.

AP: You saw the Quarrymen rehearse at Paul's house several times.

MH: I remember I went with Don Beattie, we went on our bikes. Don was the one who knew where they were – he knew where Paul lived and he knew where they were performing. It's a small lounge room, and there were three of them. There would have been George and Paul and John, with their guitars playing. No drummer. They didn't have any drums, anyway. There were other people already standing in the room. We couldn't get in – we stood in the doorway. So I couldn't say I even spoke to John on that occasion. We were watching. And it was pretty interesting. I guess we stayed half an hour, and they were practicing different numbers. But that's how it was – people would just walk in. Paul's father worked, and Paul's mother had died. So the house was empty. It must have been a Saturday afternoon. But I think that was a regular thing; people would wander in. The front door was open – *oh, they're practicing.*

AP: So the Quarrymen got together, and that was it for John at Quarry Bank?

MH: We all took the exams. The other three – John, Pete, and Don – failed every single subject. Never passed one exam. And John didn't even pass Art, which was the subject at which he was most accomplished. Despite that, somehow – God knows how – but the school managed to get him into art school. I remember meeting him in town when I was already working.

I said, 'How's the art school?"

He said, "It's great, Mike. I get paid for doing bugger all." He got a small grant. He thought it was wonderful. 'Cos John was lazy. Lazy as. Really not interested, so he didn't work. He was entertaining the art class the same way that he entertained us at school.

AP: Those school years must have meant so much to John. It was the last time he ever had a semblance of a normal life. John must frequently have thought back to his days at Quarry Bank. And to Dovedale as well.

MH: I think so. Because we had a lot of good times. Good laughs. I mean, I had to work very hard for fifteen months, having larked around for three-and-a-half years before that.

But gee, we had some good fun. It was never boring. You'd never be bored with John Lennon around. If John decided something was funny, it was funny within the group. One was earlobes. In a lot of his drawings, he'd have them with elongated earlobes. And you'd be at a serious part of the lesson and John would suddenly whisper, "*Earlobes.*" Uproar.

AP: And there are photos of John wearing the Quarry Bank tie later in life.

MH: Very strange, isn't it? The story is that he got Mimi to send his tie out. Whenever he wore a tie, he liked to wear it. I don't know – it's like the glasses. He hated to wear the glasses. And yet they became his global trademark, the granny glasses.

They were the National Health Service glasses. You got them free. If children needed glasses, you got them free. The round metal frames. So John had them, but you never saw him wearing them, because it was not the image – tough boy. Maybe he wore them at home, perhaps while he was reading, in the privacy of home. But you wouldn't see him wearing them.

And it was very strange indeed to see his book *In His Own Write.* My goodness, when that came out – it was all the stuff he had at school. He said himself that very little of that was original – but Mimi still had it around and he put it into a book.

AP: You're in the book, as the character Sad Michael.

MH: I think, yeah. Going through, you could see. I don't think John knew any other Michaels at the time. Pete Shotton is certainly in the book. And Nigel was a friend of his who lived nearby, Nigel Walley. It was Nigel who'd walked with John's mother to the bus stop. They said goodbye and she was killed a few seconds later.

AP: Another major, traumatic moment.

MH: As John said – he lost his mother twice. At age five, and at age seventeen. That was just after he'd left school. And he said himself that he was drunk for the next two years. I mean, he was a bad drinker. He couldn't handle drink. Easily drunk. And not a pleasant drunk. So those were significant things. By losing, effectively, both parents at age five, and then losing his stepfather, effectively, at age fourteen. Then having rediscovered his mother…I could only think that somehow he was wounded.

• • •

Mike Hill's story remained untold until 2013. While the Beatles were being canonized in the 1960s, Mike was, with two other colleagues from UK, starting and managing the first insurance company in Afghanistan. Many years later, an old Quarry Bank school photograph was unearthed, and Beatles authorities Mark Naboshek and David Bedford encouraged Mike to write a book. *John Lennon: The Boy Who Became a Legend* is a beautiful picture of childhood friendship and of John's early life.

The Little Richard record that Michael brought back to England in April '56 wasn't released in the UK until February 1957. John bought a guitar soon after hearing 'Long Tall Sally', and tuned it like a banjo so he could continue using the same chord shapes he was used to. In July '57, John Lennon was introduced to a young Paul McCartney at St Peter's Garden Fete in Woolton. By this time, Paul was the one singing 'Long Tall Sally'. He knew the words, and he could play it on the guitar with the correct chord shapes. That impressed John.

Little Richard became a great influence on the Beatles. At their first concert in America in 1964, they closed with 'Long Tall Sally'. The final US Beatles concert in 1966 closed with 'Long Tall Sally' too. And at John's final live performance in New York, in 1975, he performed just three songs, one of which was 'Slippin' and Slidin': the record's B side.

ROD DAVIS
THE QUARRYMEN

JOHN WANTED to front a band any way he could. In England in the '50s, the way to get a high school band together was to assemble some friends and play skiffle. Skiffle music had started in earnest in America around the turn of the century, in tandem with the blues. In Britain, the 1950s skiffle revival stemmed from the post-war economic downturn. Most families couldn't afford instruments, so household items were employed instead. Washboards provided the rhythm, and bass was played with a broom handle and string, attached to a tea-chest for resonance. The luckier skiffle groups might have afforded one of the low-quality acoustic guitars that were available by mail-order. The *really* lucky ones had a banjo. In 1955, skiffle artist Lonnie Donnegan had a hit with the old American folk song 'Rock Island Line', and kids around the country leapt for their brooms. The skiffle craze was born.

Rod Davis joined one such skiffle group with some school mates in 1957. The school was Quarry Bank High School for Boys, and the band became known as the Quarrymen. John Lennon was the group's leader. His guitar-playing mate Eric Griffiths recruited Rod on the banjo, and Pete Shotton joined them on washboard. They went through several tea-chest bass players in quick succession;

they could now call themselves a real band. The Quarrymen began gigging heavily around Liverpool, playing youth clubs and any other venues that would take them. One of these was a new jazz club called the Cavern.

John saw the possibilities of skiffle, but his heart was always with Elvis and Little Richard. Rod Davis, on the other hand, was a skiffle purist. Rod was onstage with John on the day Paul McCartney came to see them play. At the time, John meeting Paul was little more than a couple of teenagers sizing each other up. But that day – July 6, 1957 – has entered Beatles lore as an historic occasion, and crowds of tourists still flock to the site on a daily basis.

The celebration was in honor of the crowning of the local Rose Queen, an old Northern village tradition and a big day for Woolton. The Quarrymen spent the early part of the afternoon parading up and down the church road on the back of a flatbed lorry, one of six or seven acts performing from other lorries to entertain the crowds on the street. Once they arrived at the church, the band dismounted and set up to play on a little stage in the adjoining field. The Quarrymen had been invited to play two sets. It was a big occasion – even Aunt Mimi attended this particular gig.

It turned out that Paul McCartney's guitar would later replace Rod Davis's banjo in the group. The Little Richard influence was strengthening – and Little Richard didn't play the banjo. And while the other band members left schooling behind, Rod stayed on and later studied Languages at Cambridge University.

Alongside a career in academia, Rod has continued to play music – particularly bluegrass – and is a member of the re-formed Quarrymen, with fellow original members Colin Hanton, Len Garry, and Duff Lowe. Together they have toured the USA, UK, Germany, Japan, Russia, and

Cuba. While in Cuba in the '90's, they bumped into Hunter Davies, author of the highly detailed and authorized 1968 biography, *The Beatles*. Davies promptly started work on a new book, *The Quarrymen*.

But back in 1957, John Lennon and Rod Davis were just two kids playing music on the back of a lorry.

ROD DAVIS: Every year there was a procession for the Rose Queen. They had the previous year's retiring Rose Queen on one lorry; they had the new Rose Queen on another lorry. They usually had a military band of some kind leading it. One year it was a Scottish regiment in kilts. In '57 it was the Cheshire Yeomanry. There would be a lorry load of brownies; girl guides; scouts; cubs. Youth club members doing silly things on lorries – mock operations, pulling guts out of people and things like that. And this particular year, the last lorry in the procession was the one which the Quarrymen were on. Basically, the Rose Queen was like Carnival in Rio – in Woolton. It was the biggest thing in the year – apart from when a tram caught fire. And bonfire night, of course.

The procession went down a hill and back up... it started outside the Sunday school. The church road is quite a steep road. And of course, the lorries were only going walking pace because obviously you had the band marching along and stuff. But as they took the handbrake off, there was a jerk, and we all stumbled forward. And in 1997 when they reproduced the same event, we were standing on the lorry and it lurched forward like that – and it brought it all back to me from forty years before. The same jerk as – as it happens, it was the same driver. The same driver, in one of his dad's trucks. It wasn't the same truck, but it was the same driver. And in 2017 it was the same driver as well.

AIDAN PREWETT: Were you playing music at the time? Did it upset the tempo?

RD: As it started off, we weren't. But we knew we had to play two sets – we also had to play in the evening. As the lorry was going around, it must have taken about 45 minutes I would think. So we didn't play and sing all the time. There were one or two kids who perhaps walked along beside the lorry, but most of the time you were going past people who'd come out of their houses. So John wasn't going to wreck his voice by singing for 45 minutes in the open air with no microphone.

My dad was a fanatical photographer. In one photograph you can see John singing with his eyes closed. I'd pushed my glasses up my nose 'cos it was a hot sticky day. My banjo's in a case at my feet. I didn't have a chair, so maybe I was already fed up by then of balancing against the back of the cab. The others are all sitting on chairs. All I remember is going around the village. The lorry would come back up and we'd all get off and walk up into the field. A lot of the time, people think that we played on the lorry in the field as well. That's not the case, but I don't remember anything about the actual stage.

AP: Do you recall a moment at the Cavern with the Quarrymen?

RD: I remember arguing with John on stage at the Cavern, when he wanted to play rock 'n' roll. The Cavern was a jazz cellar, based on New Orleans jazz. The owner, Alan Sytner, was a jazz fan. He'd been to Paris, where there was a jazz club called Le Caveau, 'The Cave'.

The first night of rock 'n' roll at the Cavern wasn't until 1960. It had been going for several years and it was only jazz. But because skiffle came out of jazz bands, skiffle was perfectly okay to play there. But not rock 'n' roll. If you played rock 'n' roll in a jazz cellar, you were likely to become unpopular. I don't think you were going to be beaten up, but at the Cavern there was no back entrance – you had to walk through the crowd to get out. And the management obviously didn't like it. I have a very clear recollection of arguing onstage with John.

He said, "Okay, we're going to play so-and-so."

"Oh, for Christ's sake, John – it's only going to cause trouble." But he played it anyway. And at some stage, I don't know whether it was on that occasion, or another occasion – because it happened with George Harrison as well, which was after my time – they got a message from the management which said CUT OUT THE BLOODY ROCK.

We used to rehearse in several places. We rehearsed occasionally at my house. Most frequently we were at Eric Griffith's house, because his father had been a Spitfire pilot during the war and was killed, so his mother was out at work a lot of the time. I remember we were never at Pete Shotton's house, and only once at Aunt Mimi's house. But we used to like rehearsing at John's mother Julia's house, because she would let us play in the bathroom. Obviously, we had no amps or anything, and your voice would bounce off the tiles – acoustically the best place to listen. I spoke to John's sister Julia about this and she said she remembers she and her little sister Jackie being in the bath, and their mum saying, "Come on you two – out of the bath. The Quarrymen want to practice in the bathroom."

I tend to play the guitar very high up, and people say to me – *why do you do that?* I was sort of wondering about that, and I thought – *I* know why I play the guitar like that: Because the place I used to sit to play the guitar – if you didn't hold it like that you got the head of the guitar caught in the toilet roll holder. I can still hear my mother's voice saying, *"There are other people in this house, you know,"* 'cos I used to sit on the toilet playing the guitar. So maybe John did as well. But then again, he was short sighted. And the higher up you hold the guitar, the easier it is to see what your fingers are doing.

We practiced at Aunt Mimi's house only on one occasion that I remember, and that was just after the 6th of July 1957. Our friends often used to come and listen to us practice. It was useful, you could say *what do you think of this?* And sometimes they brought young ladies along as well. I mean, that was the whole point of being in the group, really – trying to attract young ladies. It didn't work for me because I was the banjo player and I used to wear glasses. So I was a bit of a non-starter.

So we turned up at Aunt Mimi's, and there was this lad there and I said *oh, who's this?* And John said, "Oh, this is Paul. He's come to listen to us practice." That's the only time I remember meeting McCartney. So that sticks in my mind.

Another time we were playing in a skiffle competition at the Lacana Ballroom which had red carpet. The ballroom area was wooden, of course, but around the sides was red carpet. And my dad had actually taken us in his car to this. We had the tea-chest bass on the roof, 'cos it was a bit difficult to get to in Liverpool. He was appalled to see John drop his burning cigarette onto this carpet and grind it into the floor. My dad said, "You wouldn't do that at home, John – would you?" And John gave him the death-stare.

AP: I liked to see that the Quarrymen had changes to the lineup, like so many bands – you went through a few different bass players for the early gigs.

RD: Bill Smith didn't last very long. The story is that he didn't turn up to rehearsals – I don't know why. Apparently, he kept the tea-chest bass, but Pete and John went around to his house and allegedly pinched it. So that was the situation, really. Whenever we did play anywhere, there had to be a lead singer. The rest of us just joined in the chorus. There was no attempt at harmonies or anything like that. Usually there was only one microphone anyway, which belonged to the establishment. Nobody had their own gear. We didn't have any amplification, but of course we did have a drum kit, because not long after Bill Smith left, Eric Griffiths had to get the same bus to school as our friend Colin Hanton, who mentioned he had a drum kit.

Eric's ears pricked up because very few groups had a drum kit. Very quickly, Eric recruited Colin. At about the same time, one of Lennon's mates, Len Garry, was pressed into playing the bass. Len had a pretty good voice, but it's difficult to sing into a microphone while you're playing a tea-chest bass.

It was always John's group, basically – although there was no sense of being ordered around. We've discussed this between ourselves a few times in the past. John had the best voice; he was the lead singer. So if he didn't like a particular song or couldn't manage to sing a particular song then we didn't do it. There was no argument. I mean, we pillaged Lonnie Donnegan's repertoire mercilessly. If you went to a skiffle contest – there'd be a dozen groups – by the end of it, you'd be sick of hearing the same song over and over and over again. In fact, ultimately – according to Colin Hanton – that was one of the stimuli for John and Paul starting to write their own stuff. 'Cos later on, when they were playing – half a dozen groups playing on an evening session – inevitably they would play the same songs as other bands. So they said *we'd better write some of our own stuff that nobody else is going to play*. It makes absolute logical sense, doesn't it? You know – if you hear 'Be-Bop-A-Lula' four times that evening, you think *God almighty, they've played most of our set already*. And if you're on later, you've got nothing new to offer to the audience. The same thing happened in skiffle competitions.

So we had a drummer and a tea-chest bass and a washboard all bashing away, over two guitars and a banjo. So John was forever turning around to Colin Hanton on drums, saying, "Colin, for Christ's sake – play with the brushes rather than the sticks!" Other times, he'd say, "Colin, for Christ's sake – hit it! We want to hear the rhythm." 'Cos Colin got into the habit – instead of laying down a rhythm and forcing the singer to sing to the rhythm, he tries to follow the lead singer, which of course is disastrous.

So Colin was forever being told to play quietly in the skiffle group, because he would drown the rest of us. And because we would thrash the instruments as loud as possible, as hard as possible, John would frequently break a string, mid-song. So he'd turn around to me – I was inevitably behind, on the back row. *Stick the banjo player on the back row*. I'd give him my banjo, he'd give me the guitar, and by the time the next song was about to start, I was supposed to have replaced the guitar string and swap it back. An American guy said to me, "Oh, you were his first roadie – his first guitar tech." Well, I never actually thought of it like that.

AP: I have to ask about John's mum – I'm wondering if you could paint me some kind of a portrait of who she was, for you.

RD: Because she was a banjo player, rather than a guitarist, when we went down there to play, she would say to me, "Oh, give us your banjo – give us your banjo," if she wanted to show us something. She'd say, "I hate those horrible guitars." Which, indeed – they were quite horrible. The guitars were really nasty. Really cheap and awful. So she'd always grab my banjo to show us something. I have a mental picture of her standing with her back to the fireplace, playing my banjo.

AP: During the times that you went to rehearse there, you would have seen John with his mum – do you remember any particular moments?

RD: I don't remember any actual incidents, it's just that she seemed to be more like a big sister than a mum, you know? Julia was never like somebody's mum. She never chose to exercise the authority of *somebody's mum*. Julia was very laid back. She didn't try bossing people around or anything. She really enjoyed us going there and playing the music. I can't really remember more than that, so I wouldn't wish to embroider it. She seemed much more like a big sister than a mother.

AP: I wonder – what about Aunt Mimi? Because you were also – you rehearsed at her house that one time. Was she there?

RD: I don't remember meeting Aunt Mimi. I don't ever remember meeting her. It would surprise me if she'd actually been there, because I don't think she quite liked John bringing his friends around. She was a bit of a snob, I think – Aunt Mimi. Not that I had a scouse accent – because we didn't have scouse accents.

AP: None of you?

RD: John Lennon never had a scouse accent. Paul McCartney never had a scouse accent. It's what we call a Liverpool accent. There is a distinction. People who actually know anything about it will make a distinction between the Liverpool accent and the scouse accent. Whereas Ringo was more scouse; George Harrison was more scouse.

If you're in a comprehensive school, you've got to conform. And if you're remotely different, you just get beaten on by everybody else. So I think that peer-group pressure played a great part in John scousifying his accent. I mean, we were grammar school boys in school uniform, so we were natural targets for the teddy boys. So John would put on a scouse accent and act tough. *They don't try to beat us up anymore.*

AP: Is there a moment from your time with John that might illustrate something of this sense of humor?

RD: I mean, we were all mad on *The Goon Show*. The next morning we could practically reproduce the dialogue with all the voices. I can still do Bluebottle, *hello Eccles!* and so on and so forth. We could all do the voices. People in Liverpool are renowned for being funny and stupid. I do remember my dad saying to me once, "You're awfully rude when you speak to people. Are you rude like this to all your friends?"

I said, "Well, they're all – that's the way we are. We're all rude to each other, you know." His humor came out in the *Daily Howl*. I didn't see anybody else doing anything like that. But a lot of it was certainly stimulated by *The Goon Show* – that you could do stupid things. And that's exactly what happens in *The Daily Howl*.

AP: When was the last time you saw John?

RD: Easter of '62. I was back at home in Liverpool and walking through the middle of town in a place called Clayton Square, and I bumped into John. We started talking, and at university I'd been involved in a New Orleans-style band playing rhythm banjo. And we'd made a record on Decca. So I was happy to tell John that I'd beaten him onto record, although it turned out that his 'My Bonnie' recording in Germany had been made before that. I didn't know that at the time. So we started talking about that and other things.

He said, "What instruments are you playing?"

I said, "A bit of fiddle, banjo, mandolin, guitar, squeezebox, autoharp..."

He said, "Oh, it's a pity you can't play the drums, you coulda come to Hamburg and played with us." I actually didn't remember that conversation because it seemed unimportant at the time. But my sister remembered it because my mother was quite pleased that I'd moved away from the pernicious influence of John Lennon – who was known as "keep away from that Lennon" in our house. And the last thing she wanted was – I was two thirds of the way through my prestigious course at Cambridge University – the last thing she wanted was for me to just chuck it all up and go to Hamburg with John Lennon. My mother was doing the washing up, saying, "He's not going to Hamburg with *that Lennon.*"

AP: Were you surprised then, when that previously bad influence, John Lennon, later started campaigning for peace & love?

RD: Anybody who knew him when I knew him – to find that Lennon was *Peace & Love*, you could hardly come up with a bigger joke. "*Lennon?* Peace and love? You must be bloody joking!" I still find it difficult to believe – now – that John changed from the person he was to *peace & love*. I still find that difficult to grasp. I mean he obviously *did*, but I don't know how the transformation took place. I cannot understand how a guy like him suddenly became in favor of peace and love all over the place.

• • •

'That Lennon' had a developed a reputation in Liverpool. From cheap laughs to canings, to cultivating a scouse accent to playing rock music at the respectable jazz club. But John was also developing his passion for music. Music was the only vocation for which he had any drive or ambition – and his ambition was real. He knew that he was the leader of his band. He even had Rod Davis change his guitar strings mid-act. And the sheer concentrated unfiltered *sound* of it all… *"Colin, for Christ's sake – play with the brushes rather than the sticks!"*

Meanwhile, John was so often absent from school because he was sagging off to hang out at his mum's house. He was enjoying the renewed relationship with his mother. Music was their connection, too. Julia had a banjo and taught him some basic chords, and John started spending more and more time at Springwood. John was at Springwood watching television on Saturday, July 15, 1958, when Julia went out to speak with Aunt Mimi. Later that evening, a policeman knocked on the door. Julia had been hit by a car after leaving Mimi's house. She was 44.

John was 17. He was devastated. He started drinking heavily. By this stage he had enrolled at the Liverpool College of Art. His already minimal attendance fell to naught and he dropped out. Music became John's only reason to push on with anything, and the Quarrymen started to pick up more gigs. John had dabbled in teenage romance, and in late 1958 he started dating Cynthia Powell. They stayed together – amid some complications – for the next ten years.

The band that had begun as the Quarrymen changed their lineup and their name several times over the ensuing years. They were at various times Johnny and the Moondogs; the Beatals; the Beetles or the Silver Beatles. A rival band leader, Cass of the Casanovas, suggested the name Long John and the Silver Beetles, which John disliked immensely.

In August 1960, while gaining a following in Liverpool, the boys were offered a last-minute chance to play at a club in Hamburg. They took it. Hamburg became the city that galvanized their musicianship – where they would perform for up to eight hours a night for minimal pay. On their first trip to Hamburg, they performed for 48 straight nights at the Indra club and began to make a serious name for themselves in the Reeperbahn red-light district. They then moved on to the nearby Kaiserkeller for another 56 nights.

While gigging at the Kaiserkeller, the group befriended local students Astrid Kirchherr, Klaus Voormann and Jürgen Vollmer. This trio called themselves *exi's* – a diminutive form of 'existentialists' – and they were talented young artists. All three would contribute to the Beatles' image and sound in later years.

Astrid Kirchherr was unwell at the time of writing this book, and she sent her very kind apologies that she couldn't be available. Sadly, Astrid passed away in May 2020. Klaus Voormann was set to participate, but after Astrid's death, Klaus understandably decided not to be interviewed.

But Hamburg was an important proving ground for the Beatles. It was here that they honed their musical skills endlessly in front of live audiences. They ironed out what worked and what didn't – with instant and sometimes violent feedback from the crowds. To help keep the group awake and upbeat, club owners were quick to offer the amphetamine based 'slimming pill' Preludin. It's been suggested that while they had previously experimented with 'uppers', it was in Hamburg that the group came to rely on the drug.

The Beatles also underwent some changes in their line-up during the Hamburg period. John's best friend from art school, Stuart Sutcliffe, had been playing bass with the group. John and Stu had moved into a flat in Liverpool, where John experienced his first real independence from Mimi. In Hamburg, Stuart started dating Astrid Kirchherr and the pair became engaged in November 1960. Stu then quit the band and enrolled at a Hamburg art school while the Beatles returned to Liverpool. Paul McCartney switched from being one of three guitars in the group – to bass.

The group made another four trips to Hamburg between August 1960 and December 1962, as their popularity – and reputation – grew. But it was after their first trip that they returned to England with a new name. They were now *The Beatles*.

TONY BRAMWELL
BEATLE MANAGEMENT

THE POSTER advertising the triumphant return gig at the Litherland Town Hall read: DIRECT FROM HAMBURG... THE SENSATIONAL BEATLES, which led many of their audience to expect a German group. *They speak good English, don't they?*

That was December 1960, soon after their first lengthy engagement in Hamburg. In the audience at the Litherland Town Hall that night was a young man called Tony Bramwell. He'd caught the bus into town and noticed his old childhood pal George Harrison carrying a guitar case. It turned out that George Harrison was one of these advertised 'Beatles'. Tony soon started working with the group as an impromptu road manager. When the Beatles signed a management contract with Brian Epstein, Brian spotted managerial talent in Tony Bramwell and employed him to book tours.

They signed the contract in January 1962. Brian Epstein was then managing his father's record stores in Liverpool but had always had his sights set on bigger things. He had previously studied acting at the prestigious Royal Academy of Dramatic Art in London, but had dropped out in his first year. The Beatles were undeterred by Epstein's lack of experience; rather, they were impressed with his expensive suits and his car. John was 21 years old at the time of signing. The others were under that age and needed a parental co-signature. Brian Epstein was more senior – 27 – and with the stroke of a pen, he became the group's father figure.

Over the years to come, Tony Bramwell also took on myriad responsibilities for the group, including management of local and international tours, promotional films, and day-to-day handling. When the Beatles founded Apple Corps in 1968, they elected Tony as CEO of Apple Records *and* Apple Films.

After the Beatles split, Tony went on to head Polydor Records, overseeing Brian Ferry, Brian Eno, Slade, the Jam, and many others. Over subsequent years Tony has been a major force at Warner Bros. Records, Decca Records, and PolyGram Records.

But back in December 1960, Tony Bramwell was a kid on a bus, on his way to see an unknown band – direct from Hamburg – at the Litherland Town Hall, just north of Liverpool.

TONY BRAMWELL: I used to go to gigs with Gerry Marsden from Gerry & the Pacemakers. I'd carry his guitar in to get into the venues for free. Gerry & the Pacemakers had gone to Hamburg, so I thought I'd go and see this group called the Beatles, who were playing at one of the venues that Gerry normally played. I just got on the bus to go to the gig, and there was my old mate George Harrison sitting there with his guitar. We started chatting.

"Where are you going?"

"Where are *you* going?"

"Oh, we're both going *there*."

And George said, "Yeah – we're playing there tonight."

I said, "Oh, can I carry your guitar in?"

He said, "'Course you can." And that was like, the *real*

gig, back in Liverpool – Litherland Town Hall. So we got there, and John said, "Why are you carrying *his* fucking guitar? You should be carrying *my* fucking guitar, too." So that's how I sort of became their road manager. That was before road managers really existed.

AIDAN PREWETT: What had changed about them – aside from the band name – since going to Hamburg?

TB: They'd changed in appearance – suddenly they were wearing black leather. And they were playing a sort of different rock 'n' roll to what was being played in the ballrooms in Liverpool at the time. It was sort of an R 'n' B, rock 'n' roll-y mixture of stuff that they'd learned in Germany. And they'd obviously grown up a bit. And they could play a bit better.

AP: Cynthia is somebody I'd love to hear about. Is there a moment with Cynthia that you were a part of that might tell us something about John and Cynthia's relationship?

TB: Cynthia was just lovely. She was really ace. And she loved John desperately – and put up with him. And he just treated her in that North-of-England way. The guy goes out to work and the wife looks after the house. A normal – as it was at the time – northern marriage. But they just seemed to be happily *John and Cyn* for a good few years. Moved to London; bigger flats; bigger houses. She was his wife, and she stayed out of the whole Beatle world in that northern way. The *you wouldn't take your wife to work* attitude.

Beatle wives did not turn up to EMI recording studios every day, and they did not turn up at Beatles press conferences. It was very rare – apart from major functions, premieres and big gigs – that Cynthia would attend. She was just lovely. She wouldn't expect anybody to work for her.

She did the shopping; she stayed with Julian; she did the school run and that sort of stuff. Which John, of course, didn't do.

AP: There are two other people who I would really love to hear about – being of course Brian Epstein –

TB: Well, he's a bit dead.

AP: You knew him quite well, I believe – do you recall a particular moment that's stuck with you?

TB: Brian was *Brian Epstein*. He was a gentleman; he was a lovely guy. He was great to work for. He had this vision of the Beatles being the biggest band in the world, and he *turned* them into the biggest band in the world. Of course, he was gay, which caused a lot of societal and emotional trauma in those days. But he didn't favor any of the Beatles. He did what they wanted – or got them to do what he wanted them to do. Occasionally the Beatles would rebel and say *oh fuck off Brian – we're not doing that, mate*. And he'd say, "If you *do* do that, then *this* happens." So he'd sort it out in that way.

AP: Do you remember the first time you had a proper conversation with Brian?

TB: "Tony, would you like to work for me? I'll pay you to do what you're doing." I'd been fiddling around with the Beatles' instruments and cables, carrying equipment so I could get into their gigs for free. And then sometime in '62 he asked if he could pay me to do it. That sounded good.
  "Yeah, okay – you can pay me to go and see the Beatles."
  And after that he said, "And you can manage one of my

record shops." And I thought, *yeah, that sounds pretty good as well.* That's how it was.

AP: Another person I'd love to hear about is Stu – Stu Sutcliffe.

TB: I only met Stuart a few times. I didn't know him too well. But he looked good. He looked like James Dean – talk about *Rebel Without A Cause.* He just seemed like a nice lad. The last time I saw him, he was standing at the back of the Cavern with Astrid Kirchherr, watching the Beatles on stage. He did seem to be quite a nice lad. But we all were quite nice lads.

AP: Speaking of the Cavern – was there ever a moment with John at the Cavern that you recall?

TB: The Cavern became their home. They could do anything they wanted on stage, because they were – all of a sudden – the Beatles. They were the most popular thing in Liverpool. They'd do silly things, goof around. But I don't remember any specifics.

AP: And suddenly you were off and touring with them – was there a particular moment on the road with John that has stuck with you?

TB: Touring was just touring, but it was very exciting at the time. Initially, when we were going to every city in England, doing proper concert gigs – that was really exciting. That was throughout most of 1963. And then, you know – you go to America. *Yeah! It's America!* But you don't ever really explore anything. It became more a part of the job than a pleasure. It would have been nice to have been able to see the Empire State Building, or in Australia – the Opera

House or Sydney Harbor Bridge. It would have been nice to see where you were rather than being in a venue or a car or a bus or a plane. I love going to those places now.

People say to me, "You were here in 1964."

And you say, "Yeah…"

"Have you seen…?"

"No."

I think it would have been nice to be able to do those things at the time.

AP: Do you have any particular memories from touring in Australia?

TB: Only the fucking crowds. And the weather. The rain in Sydney. And Adelaide, where the crowd went bonkers. There were well over 200,000 people in the streets. An awful lot of people.

AP: I do wonder – there must have been something in America with John that you witnessed, that would have been interesting.

TB: Nothing really springs to mind. Color television – that was quite an *oh wow* moment. *Let's listen to the radio* – flicking channels and speaking to disc jockeys on the air and having fun, which was initially quite a good kick. Watching *Howdy Doody* in color.

AP: We hear all this stuff about how they were locked in the hotel and the only time they got privacy was if they locked themselves in a bathroom. Is there much truth to that?

TB: Oh yeah. In one way it was wonderful. In another way it was fucking embarrassing, because you just sort of *can't* *do anything.* There was no escape from the ever-inquisitive Beatle fan, or journalist, or whoever wanted to get a piece.

You know, there were nice things, like meeting Burt Lancaster or Dean Martin. They were sort of nice. But most of the famous people were a let-down.

AP: Back in England, you were very much a part of the Beatles' day-to-day life – is there a moment in London that springs to mind?

TB: Oh God. Maybe sometime in 1965 – we went out for the night. John said, "Let's pop up to Mick and Keith's." They had a flat up in Kilburn, North London, so we went up there. Mick and Keith were a bit stoned, and boring. They might not have been stoned – or whatever…but it just wasn't that interesting. We got there late at night. We thought, *oh well, let's go back to town.* We walked down to the tube station to go back into London to go to a club. And we fell asleep on the train. Of course, the train went to a terminal in South London – God knows where it went to. We woke up and went, *well, we'll take it back again and get off at Leicester Square or wherever.* But we fell asleep again. And we woke up in Edgeware or Hatch End – somewhere out the top of the North of London. And it was the last train. We looked at each other and went, *"Oh well."* So we just slept there for the night.

AP: Oh my God.

TB: We just stayed in the carriage until six o'clock in the morning. People started getting on board and found us sort of sitting there. So we went back into town and we got off at Oxford Circus, which was next door to the NEMS offices. It was like seven o'clock in the morning. There was no one there. And neither of us had any money or anything, of course. So we went to a café and had some coffee and toast, maybe eggs and bacon. Then John stayed in the café, and I went around to the NEMS offices at ten o'clock when they opened and got some money to pay the café, and ordered a car to take John home. That was just one of those funny nights that we had.

AP: Did anybody recognize John at any point during this?

TB: Yeah – in those days people just used to just look at them with that sort of *could it be? Couldn't it be? Nah – it couldn't be, not under these circumstances – you wouldn't see John Lennon sitting on a tube train at seven o'clock in the morning.* It was beyond any idea that that would happen.

AP: You were responsible for the promotional films – 'Paperback Writer', 'Hello Goodbye', 'Hey Jude'…

TB: Making the little films was caused by union problems. The Musicians' Union in England banned American artists from coming to England and just appearing on television. In America, they banned English artists from going to *America* and appearing on television – *The Dick Clark Show*, or *Shindig* or *Ed Sullivan*, without actually working. The Beatles always did go to work, but it was always a pain in the arse to hang around the studios. We'd be there all day. Rehearse; do a take. And some twat would say, *"Missed that one – do it again."* It was a hassle. So Brian and I came up with the idea – making the clips ourselves.

We explained it to the Beatles. If we'd have just said it was from union problems, they'd have gone on strike – or said *we'll leave the union then* – which you couldn't do, because you couldn't work. So we said *to save the hassle of flying everywhere, let's just spend a day in the studio and make a film. We can do it on our own terms.* So that's what it was, basically. And then it became the normal thing to do. To save faffing around the world and waiting around the studios. And to sell them for a fortune!

While we were doing the films for 'Penny Lane' and 'Strawberry Fields', which I was producing, we were down in Sevenoaks in Kent. I'd booked a little hotel in the High Street called Bright's Hotel, just to use as a base and a changing room if anybody wanted to get some privacy. John and I were just walking down the High Street – and literally next to the hotel was a little junk shop. In the window was a poster: *Pablo Fanque's Circus Royale.* John just stood there reading it. We went in and we bought it for about ten shillings. Within weeks he had turned it into 'Being for the Benefit of Mr. Kite'. And we did find out about Pablo Fanque and what the fair was all about, and his grave and everything, somewhere in Yorkshire. He was quite a famous showman back in the Victorian days.

AP: And of course, George Martin had quite a hand in that song, and so many others. Could you tell me a bit about the studio dynamic under George?

TB: George was a genius. A gentleman and a genius. He knew what the possibilities were in the recording studio – and explored it. John, on 'Being for the Benefit of Mr. Kite', would say, "I want it to sound like a fairground." George would find it and turn it into a psychedelic fairground. George did things which producers and engineers didn't do at the time. He could read music; he could write music; he could play it. He wasn't like one of these kids with iPads. He knew the whole thing. Every instrument. He taught the Beatles everything they knew. Then they went out on their own and worked out how to do it for themselves. 'Cos he was a fucking genius. And a nice guy.

AP: With George – I hope perhaps there's a moment you recall where George had to be a bit strict with the boys.

TB: He wouldn't allow drugs in the studio. It was illegal. And it was also – if you're caught doing anything in the wrong place – it was also the owner of the property who was in trouble. They had to be careful because EMI wouldn't want to be sued for allowing their property to harbor substances. But also – they couldn't play if they were stoned.

AP: On that note – were you ever present when John was on some kind of substance?

TB: You didn't think people were on acid. You'd just put it down to – their behavior was just strange anyway, being a Beatle. Around the *White Album* days, John was sort of only available at strange times. And John was a lazy bastard. He'd rather stay in bed, tripping, than being a Beatle. There was one time when he just turned up at the Apple offices – he had his big beard and a black jumpsuit, and he decided to tell everyone that he was Jesus Christ. He'd obviously taken too much acid or heroin or whatever he was on in those days.

AP: When John and Yoko were busted for marijuana – when that happened, what was your take?

TB: They were certainly pissed off that the Rolling Stones got off fairly lightly. The police just wanted to bust *somebody*.

AP: I'd love it if you could tell me about the *Two Virgins* album cover.

TB: It was a Saturday night in 1968. I was sitting at home and John phoned. I went over and he said, "Can you set up the Pentax so I can take some photographs with the remote control?"

I said, "Yeah, sure – where do you want it?" So I got the Pentax, put a roll of film in, set the light meter and everything; stuck it on a tripod. I connected the remote attachment and showed him – "Where do you want it set up?"

"Oh, just down the hallway here into the back room." He and Yoko stood there, and I set the focus, and it was all set to go. He said, "Yeah – thanks very much."

The following day – Sunday afternoon – he phoned me up and said, "Tony, can you come around and sort some things out?"

"Alright, mate."

I went around and took the film out of the camera. He said, "If you take nude photos – page three stuff, whatever – can you get that stuff developed down at the laboratory? With pictures like that, what are you supposed to do?"

On the Monday morning I took the film into the laboratory. About an hour later they called me: "Tony, you'd better come around and pick up these pictures immediately!" I said, "Alright." So I went around and picked up the prints and the negatives. The lab was all *oh dear...* In those days it was legal to show breasts and things – but it was illegal to show pubic hair. The guy in the art department was horrified.

AP: In 1969, John asked you to put together the musicians for the Toronto Rock 'n' Roll Revival – is that right?

TB: Yeah. It was a Wednesday, I think. John said, "There's a rock festival in Toronto this weekend and I'm going."

"Yeah, *right* – of course you are."

"And I need a band. A guitarist, bass player, drummer."

I said, "Have you asked George, Paul, and Ringo?"

He said, "Find out if Eric Clapton wants to do it. Is Klaus Voorman still in the country?"

Eric lived in Hampstead. I contacted Eric. Eric was always a bit stoned at that time. But he said he'd go. I spoke with Klaus Voorman's wife, Christine. She said, "Oh, he'd love to." Then I was in a club where there was a band playing – their drummer was a really good guy, Alan White. So I asked him, and he said, "Yeah – yeah!"

Then John said, "Can you go and find a list of all the songs we used to do?"

I said, "What songs?"

He said, "The rock 'n' roll songs – you know, those songs on your lists. The old songs the Beatles used to play." So I went down to the music publishers and picked up sheet music for the old Chuck Berry stuff, and Little Richard. In the meantime, a guy at the office had organized the flight to Toronto. And it was like – *off to the airport*. So I got to the airport with the sheet music. Klaus and Alan White turned up. Mal Evans had picked up their equipment. But Eric Clapton hadn't turned up. So I was running around, trying to find Eric. And then the flight was cancelled. I can't remember why. So anyway, Eric turns up in time for the new flight. And I was expecting to get on the flight as well: 'This is going to be fun – *not*'. I can't remember who, but somebody else turned up and went on the flight. So I didn't go.

AP: And the rooftop concert – is there a moment from that that sort of summed up what that was?

TB: A lot of wasted time. It would have been so much nicer to go out in a big way, rather than just *that* – the cold, miserable rooftop. With no audience. Everyone looked miserable. I was running up and down the stairs organizing a playback loop downstairs – then dealing with the police and the press turning up. It was just a shitty day. It was cold and horrible. And we didn't *know* it was the last ever.

AP: Did you have to hold back the police?

TB: No, I just went down and stalled them for a while. They had to get up there in the end. It was just like, "No, you can't come in these bloody offices. *Go away.*" The police station was only two doors away – Savile Row Police Station.

AP: I heard that David Bowie sent a demo tape to Apple around this time.

TB: Bowie used to turn up in the original NEMS offices, not long after we moved to London. His girlfriend worked there. And he used to turn up looking like a schoolboy. He'd pick her up after work and take her home. He was always popping in. He was with his mod band at the time, the Manish Boys.

I ran the Saville Theatre for Brian Epstein, and we had Marcel Marceau – the mime artist – and David asked if he could see him. So I let him stand on the side of the stage.

Anyway, when we started Apple, anyone could come along for an audition. David came in with a tape. The custom was, if a Beatle heard a tape and liked it, they'd get signed. If a Beatle heard the tape and didn't like it, they wouldn't get signed. Anyway, John was the Beatle-of-the-Day when the David Bowie tape came in. He heard it and said, "Nah, nah. Not that one."

John never really involved himself with Apple projects, generally speaking. He was too busy with John

& Yoko projects. He never really brought any talent in from outside. Anyway, a year or so later he said, "Why the fuck have we got all this shit like James Taylor and Mary Hopkins and Billy fucking Preston? I don't get it – why don't we have people like David Bowie?"

"Ahem – excuse me, John. You turned him down."

• • •

Tony Bramwell's experience with the Beatles was immersive – he was on the road with them; in the studio; running errands at their homes and later running their companies. Tony was there from the moment John asked him to carry his guitar, right through to the end. And the promise of the Beatles' early days delivered more than anyone had ever imagined possible. Seeing Stu Sutcliffe standing in the shadows at the back of the Cavern with Astrid Kirchherr. Spending the night stuck on the train with John. Producing some of the first ever promotional music films. Taking the *Two Virgins* film roll to the developer. And keeping the police at bay on that cold, miserable day on top of the Apple building...

Back in January '62, upon signing of the Beatles' management contract, Brian Epstein and Tony Bramwell scheduled tours across England, and the boys and their road crew piled into a van and drove from city to city. Meanwhile, the country was starting to tune in to this new band. People were taking an interest in these boys from Liverpool.

The Beatles returned to Hamburg in April 1962, where they were to commence a two-month run at the Star-Club. A major shock awaited. Astrid met them at the airport in tears. Stuart Sutcliffe had died of a brain hemorrhage the day before.

The loss hit John hard. Stu had been his best friend and his flatmate. Stu's death added to the compounding grief that John had never really dealt with – abandonment and death continued to haunt him.

The Beatles pushed through their grief with the commencement of another 48-night engagement on the Reeperbahn. Brian Epstein continued to market them back in England. When they returned home, the Beatles hype had grown and continued to build around the now-endlessly scheduled gigging and nerve-wracking auditions. And in the middle of it all, John's girlfriend, Cynthia, discovered she was pregnant.

John and Cyn were married on August 23, 1962. A few months after the wedding, the Beatles finally secured their hitherto elusive record deal with EMI's Parlophone and George Martin. They had been turned down by every other major label in the country, and Brian broke the news to the boys with a mixture of excitement and relief. They were on their way.

JULIA BAIRD

BEATLE FAMILIES

JOHN WAS ABOUT TO TURN 22. It was September 1962, six full years after the formation of the Quarrymen. The four boys now known as the Beatles descended the long staircase into EMI's Studio Two on Abbey Road to record 'Love Me Do'. The bulk of the song had been composed by Paul in 1958 – he had skipped school to write it. John contributed the bridge and the soaring harmonica riff, likely playing the harmonica he pinched in Arnhem *en route* to Hamburg. Paul McCartney later told *Rolling Stone*, "John expected to be in jail one day – he'd be the guy who played the harmonica."

'Love Me Do' was released in October, while the band were back in Hamburg. In their absence, it peaked at #17. When they returned to EMI in November, they cut their second single, 'Please Please Me', one of John's compositions. It was written back at Aunt Mimi's house as a Roy Orbison-style ballad. George Martin insisted they up the tempo and change the feel. John's harmonica features just as strongly as in the previous single.

'Please Please Me' was released in the UK in January 1963. Brian Epstein secured them a promotional booking on *Thank Your Lucky Stars*, a Saturday night variety program on ITV. As luck would indeed have it, the country was hit by the worst snowstorm in years. Much of the population was stuck indoors, watching their television sets. This was a major turnaround. 'Please Please Me' hit #2 on the UK Record Retailer charts – the official UK listing at the time. *Melody Maker* and *New Musical Express* independently listed it at #1. Touring quickly recommenced around the country – and venue house capacities were increasing. In America, however, the records were being issued on the budget Vee-Jay label. They weren't widely available. In the States, the Beatles were flopping.

On February 11, 1963, twelve tracks from the Beatles' first album were recorded at EMI's Studio Two. The other two tracks – the singles thus far – had already been recorded. Several overdubs were added a week later, but otherwise, the album *Please Please Me* was completed in just thirteen hours. It was released on March 22 and headed for the top of the Record Retailer LP charts. It reached #1 in May.

Cynthia gave birth to John Charles Julian Lennon in Liverpool on April 8, 1963 – a week before the release of the Beatles' third single, 'From Me to You'. The Beatles were on tour at the time and John was only able to meet Julian three days later. Brian Epstein was named Julian's godfather. The continuous recording, touring, and publicity didn't leave much time for family – especially after 'From Me to You' went to #1 on the singles charts.

In May the Beatles embarked on a new tour supporting one of their American heroes, Roy Orbison. A running theme: the tour had been booked before their explosion of popularity. Audiences were suddenly more interested in the Beatles than in the headline act. On May 26, the tour stopped in Liverpool. Julia Baird, John's 16-year-old sister, was in the audience, about to witness her brother John's now-famous band in a proper concert for the first time.

Julia had no idea what was in store. *Beatlemania* was only just beginning.

AIDAN PREWETT: When you finally got to see the Beatles on stage… I would love to hear of your reaction and surprise in what that experience turned out to be.

JULIA BAIRD: Well, it was what we were hearing in the rehearsals in the kitchen, wasn't it? We were hearing that all the time. And then it was sort of transposed onto the stage.

We saw them at the Empire. Now, if you've been to Liverpool you will know, the Empire is where the opera comes, where the ballet comes. It's the stage that was built that was *big enough*. Big productions. I'd seen them before at village halls and backs of lorries and in a field – but this was like *serious stuff*. Serious stuff. They were supporting Roy Orbison. They were the closing bit of the first act, believe it or not. And we were so excited to be going to see Roy Orbison, believe me.

Anyway, we were all sitting down. They do the concert – somebody on first and then the Beatles, and then the interval, and then the star of the show was to come on. Well, they did their bit, and then people were screaming. We'd never heard this before. Not as madly as it came to be – but they were being stupid, I thought. And then the interval came, and we went 'round the back. We met Roy Orbison, and it was all very jolly-jolly. We went back to our seats. And Roy Orbison came on and the audience were all still screaming for the Beatles. I was mortified. *One* – I wanted to listen to Roy Orbison, and *two* – how rude!

AP: Yeah – wow.

JB: That's how it had got. How rude – screaming though *their* songs was one thing. In fact, it's what stopped them performing. The fans dobbed themselves in by doing it. But to scream through *somebody else*? The screams. I honestly was in a state of shock.

And then we all got in the car afterward. The Beatles came out through the stage door, got in the car, and the fans were – not rocking it, but right up against it. And this was in the early days. It was just like *mad*. Mad.

AP: Did you have any preparation mentally for what it would be – to be in a car that was besieged…

JB: No. It was scary. Now, years later, if you can relate an early stage performance to the last stage performance at Candlestick Park, in late August 1966… So we're now in 1963, aren't we? They ran parallel – because the fans screamed through *their* act, which must have been a bit of a surprise to them too, because you certainly didn't get screaming in a field or in a village hall. But you did get people getting up and throwing the chairs to the side so they could dance.

So they screamed through that, and they screamed through Roy Orbison. And the Beatles didn't like it. I can tell you – they did *not* like that. They didn't want it.

AP: Back in the early days, when John came home with a copy of the vinyl pressing of 'Love Me Do', you got to hear that before…*anyone*. Could you tell me about that – was he excited to share that with you?

JB: Yes. By that time, my mother had died. We were living with her next sister, Harrie. And cousin David and Jackie and I at that time shared a room. It was a big room, and we demanded to be together. I mean, we used to go to bed and then get up and start playing darts. So we had the record player up there. And John brought this record.

I just said, "Hmm... I don't think much of that." I was a bit derogatory. Because we'd heard them all over the place, singing. And that was much better than the record. We all sort of burst out laughing. Of course, it got to number 17, didn't it? It was 'Please Please Me' that really did it, the following February in '63.

AP: You mentioned earlier that Brian Epstein came to Mendips. So you were there, and Brian was there leaning on the mantelpiece...

JB: On the mantelpiece over the fire, talking to Mimi. Mimi liked him because he was very posh.

AP: What sense of character did you get from Brian?

JB: He was a gentleman, an absolute gentleman. We knew nothing about any other side of his life. Obviously, we didn't know he was gay. We wouldn't have known what being gay was at that time. Neither did anybody. It wasn't common knowledge. I mean, to be Jewish and gay, must have been very, very difficult for him. Nowadays he'd be in a different life, wouldn't he?

AP: Oh yes, of course.

JB: He'd be accepted, it'd be fine. There'd be no skulking or hiding – or anything. Another tortured man, because he couldn't be who he was. Desperately sad. He was an absolute gentleman, believe me.

AP: Do you remember anything specific that he said to John or to Mimi? Or to you?

JB: No. he was just lovely to Jackie and I. But that particular time on the mantelpiece – they were talking about moving to London. They were going to have to move to London.

AP: What did Mimi have to say about that?

JB: Well she wasn't keen, but she didn't have a choice because all the contract work – everything – was going on in London. And in fact, George Harrison was the last to leave. He was still going up and down on the train. He didn't want to leave home. And John – it was 1963, in about October, they borrowed a flat until they got somewhere of their own. 'Til they moved to Kenwood – John, Cynthia and Julian.

AP: Speaking of Julian – that's a really interesting and delicate time, because the Beatles were really taking off and Julian was born right in the middle of it. What was – I mean, you met Julian before John did, is that right?

JB: Yeah – we did, actually. 'Cos he wasn't there.

AP: Please tell me about that – and you would have then seen John with Julian. In the first days of them meeting. Could you paint me some kind of portrait of that time, and that scene?

JB: Well, it was just – it was big excitement, as a baby always produces in any family. He came back to Mendips, and everybody came. My aunt came down from Edinburgh, and another one from Cheshire. We all just got together to welcome the baby.

He's actually John Charles Julian Lennon. He was known as Julian from the start, but he's John Charles. John for John, of course. Charles for Cynthia's family. And then Julian, blatantly, for my mother. I was for my mother, my niece for my mother, and my granddaughter is for my mother.

AP: When John was with Julian in those early moments, was he a doting father?

JB: Yeah, he loved it. It was sort of new to all of us. He loved it. You've got to also remember that when – because the Beatles had started and everything that was going on – I remember the sisters saying, "John, you do not have to marry her."

And he said – he swore, and I can't tell you what he said – "I want to marry her. We are getting married. Can't you get it into your heads? I want to marry her. I love her and we're *getting married.*" So he was actually given a way out – if he'd have wanted it. He wasn't doing it.

AP: A bit later on, you were at the Liverpool premiere of *A Hard Day's Night*.

JB: And we're giving John sandwiches. We're giving him sandwiches, and he can't eat. We all thought *oh poor John – he's not eating.* And we were stuffing ourselves, of course – tables full of classic sandwiches, sausage rolls, you know – basic stuff.

We were on the balcony at the town hall, and it was only the second time *ever* that they'd closed the city down. They closed it down once for Dixie Dean in 1922 – the Everton player, when he won just everything in sight. They closed it down for him. And then they closed it down again in 1964 for the premiere of *A Hard Day's Night*. And do you know what? It took something like two letters and five phone calls to organize the whole thing. Can you imagine now, how many layers of emails and non-entities receiving emails – can you imagine what it would take now, to close the city down?

AP: It would be endless. That is amazing. What happened at the premiere?

JB: We'd been taken off to the Odeon cinema, where *A Hard Day's Night* played. Anyway – John appeared on stage and came out through the curtains before it all started, and said, "Where's my family? I've lost you all!"

And we all stood up and said, "We're up here, John!"

We were sitting with the mayor. And we all got chocolates – a beautiful box of chocolates to sit with. And my cousin David – we lived with him by then because my mother had died, as you know – he became our brother. And he fancied the mayor's daughter like mad. They were sitting behind us, and he kept taking our box of chocolates and offering it to her. She had her own!

AP: There was a point at a later concert where you were in the dressing room with the Beatles before they went on stage. Could you talk me through – what was that scene?

JB: It was very exciting. John and Cyn had bought Kenwood – it was in 1964. Jackie and I went down. Straight away he said, "I want the girls to come down and see it." It wasn't built – there was no kitchen, nothing. We went to stay.

Julian was a baby – he was about eighteen months old. And we took him to Harrods and bought him loads of clothes. Cynthia bought him a black polo neck and little black jeans. And she bought us clothes. Jackie and I couldn't look at anything – Cynthia would just pick it up and put it on the counter.

Then we went to the Finsbury Park Astoria to see the

Beatles' Christmas show, and we were in the dressing room with John, with the others. They were drinking what we thought was Coca-Cola. *Not.* We were drinking Coca-Cola. We were drinking our *own* Coca-Cola, isn't that funny? "That's *your* bottle, girls."

And the Rolling Stones were in there, 'cos they were coming to see the show. And then it was all – *"Knock-knock, five minutes..." "Four minutes...three minutes..."* And then the Stones disappeared. And they said, "Come on, you have to go and sit outside now." So we went out.

The first four rows were empty. Now, that had not been the case at the Roy Orbison concert. Presumably, this was a device that had happened in the meantime, because of the screaming. You see, I thought initially it was only because it was Liverpool – and it was a sort of *pride.* But obviously, it was everywhere.

So the first four rows were empty, and we're being put behind the first four rows. And I said to John, "We want to go down there, we want to go down there."

He said, "You can't. You can't. You've no idea what it's going to be like."

I said, "*John,* we want to go down there."

They were ready to go, and they were saying, "Come on, come on, come on..."

And in the end, I just said, "*Please,* let us sit down there."

He said, "Alright, then!"

So we jumped off stage and went and sat in the second row. So there was one row empty, then Jackie and I, and then two rows empty – and then everybody else.

So – safe. From *what,* you would wonder. As the curtain drew up, and 'She Loves You' started, the screaming started, louder than it had ever been in Liverpool. It was quadrophonic. And everybody – all the fans ran down to the stage. And these security people arrived from absolutely nowhere. I hadn't seen them; I hadn't been looking – we were just excited to see the concert. They arrived to push them back. It was just like utter mayhem. If it had been a school, you'd have said, *"Right. Closed for the day. Go home. We've got to re-issue all the rules and regulations here, nothing is working."* You can't imagine it anywhere else.

AP: Absolutely.

JB: And they were trying to sing 'She Loves You'. Well, they did sing 'She Loves You'. And John, out of the side of his mouth, said to the security at the bottom of the stage, "Get the girls – *get the girls."* And we were hauled ignominiously on our stomachs under the curtain on the right-hand side. So we had to watch from the wings. And John turned around and said, "Told you so!"

We had no idea it was going to be like that. Really and truly. No idea.

• • •

In later years – post-*Sgt. Pepper* – John gave Julia and their cousin Liela a key to one of the London flats used by the Beatles as a bolthole and for storage. Julia and Liela would crash there while in London and borrow outfits to wear around town. George Harrison was the smallest Beatle and Julia found that his collection of rather fabulous jackets fit her quite nicely.

Back in 1963, the Roy Orbison tour continued until May 9, and was immediately followed by a long string of dates and media appearances that continued until the end of June. On July 1 they were back at Studio 2 of EMI to record 'She Loves You' and its B-side, 'I'll Get You'. The next day they commenced a two-day BBC radio session, which was immediately followed by back-to-back tour dates and media appearances throughout July, August, and early September, between several recording sessions for their second album, *With the Beatles*.

In late September, the Beatles were granted two weeks off. George Harrison visited his sister in the USA, enjoying his freedom to travel unnoticed in this region where the band wasn't yet famous. Paul and Ringo went to Greece. And, a year after their wedding, John and Cynthia got their honeymoon in France. Baby Julian stayed with John's aunt Harrie – also guardian to John's sisters Julia and Jackie.

John and Cyn were able to see the sights of Paris largely without interruption from fans, and they squeezed in as many tourist traps as they could. They could feel their anonymity was fast disappearing.

TONY PALMER

ALL MY LOVING

Please Please Me spent an unprecedented 30 weeks at #1 on the UK album charts. In November 1963, it was finally replaced in the top spot – by the Beatles' second album, *With the Beatles*.

Later that month, the group held a press conference at Cambridge University to promote their performance at the local Regal Cinema. They had been touring almost non-stop throughout the year, performing more than 200 concerts around the UK, with a brief run of Swedish dates thrown in for good measure in late October.

It was a chaotic time, and a time when the Fab Four were grappling with their newfound fame. These young men were defining themselves, and quicker than most. Their characters were being forged in the pressures of fame and their frantic life on the road: in the midst of their celebrity, they were coming of age. But – at this time – the Beatles were still reasonably accessible to those who were able to keep a cool head. And at the Cambridge appearance, John Lennon befriended a university student named Tony Palmer.

Tony Palmer went on to make two pioneering music documentaries with John Lennon, among other works featuring Jimi Hendrix, Cream, Frank Zappa, and Eric

Burdon. More recently, Palmer has directed works for theatre and opera, with further documentaries focusing on classical performers. Palmer's films have been honored with BAFTAs, Emmy awards, New York Film Festival medals and two wins of the Prix Italia, among myriad other accolades.

One of the first steps on Palmer's filmmaking and literary journey was at Lennon's recommendation: the world needed a TV program that painted the music scene as it really was. The resulting product was *All My Loving* (1968), an exploration of popular music amid the politics of the day. The film was deeply controversial. It ruffled feathers at the BBC and cemented Palmer as a new wave filmmaker with a serious edge. But back in 1963, Palmer was a Cambridge student reading History and Moral Sciences. And he was about to meet John Lennon – in disguise.

TONY PALMER: I first met John at a press conference in Cambridge where I was a student. He came up, talked to me, and said he wanted to be shown around the university. And I said, "I'm not going to do that, 'cos you'll be mobbed, and that's not my idea of fun." I mean, they were famous at that point, but not *mega* famous.

But I eventually agreed, and he said, "Come and meet me at the hotel at two o'clock." So I turned up at the hotel, and there was this ridiculous figure in a huge fedora hat, a false beard and a dirty Macintosh – trying to escape from what was then thought to be his image – that of a well-cut, clean-living, slightly nasal singer.

AIDAN PREWETT: As you were walking John around the campus, what was he most interested in seeing, and talking about?

TP: He often said it to me subsequently, that he felt – as did many of those of his time, who were kind of swept up in the rock 'n' roll business – that he'd somehow missed out on the education to which he quite rightly aspired, and quite rightly deserved. So the place I couldn't get him *out* of, almost, was the big library in Trinity College, built by Sir Christopher Wren. And of course – it's books! He was fascinated by these. And he kept taking books off the shelf, and I said to him, "Please be careful with them, my university career is on the line here."

And he said, "Oh, don't worry about it."

The Wren Library has tables where as a student you're supposed to sit down and study. So he sat at one of these tables, opposite me, desperately looking around to make sure that we weren't going to be arrested. But nobody took any notice of him, even if they knew who he was – 'cos he'd jumped the disguise by now. I found that absolutely fascinating. He knew that somehow in his upbringing, he'd missed out on an education. That was something that he felt, absolutely to his dying day, that that was an area in which he was lacking.

AP: To think that somebody like John, who achieved everything that he did – it's mind boggling to me to think that he felt as though he'd missed out on anything. But at the same time, I can really see where he's coming from. It's so interesting.

TP: By about 1966 they had fame and they had money and they had the leisure. I'm absolutely sure at that point, that John bought every book he thought he ought to read. Because when you start to look carefully at the lyrics of his songs, they're littered – as are Bob Dylan's – they're littered with references to James Joyce, to Pushkin, to T.S. Eliot, to Yeats – particularly Yeats. I mean, they *read*. When you go to 'Strawberry Fields Forever', for example, if you look carefully at some of those images that he's using, *where did they come from?* Either the guy's imagination is diseased, which it clearly isn't. Or his antennae are working full time. He's picking up on *everything*.

And the two books that he wrote – *In His Own Write* being the better of the two – that again is full of references to James Joyce. I mean, he clearly had looked at Joyce's short stories, and looked at *Ulysses*, even if he didn't grasp the full significance of it. I'm not saying that he *didn't*, but it would appear to be unlikely, because after all, as he frequently said, "I'm just a rock 'n' roll guitarist." Which is nonsense, of course – any rock 'n' roll guitarist could not have written things like 'Strawberry Fields Forever'.

AP: Would you say that he was warm toward you?

TP: Toward me? Yes, very. I never had a cross word with him, ever. I mean, he was generous to a fault. I have discovered since he died, lots of people who were in trouble financially – a relative was ill, so on and so on – John just very quietly intervened and settled the bills, if you see what I mean. So I think his generosity – we don't really know about yet. I'm sick and tired of reading biographies about him which don't pay enough attention to that. But I'm absolutely sure that was the case.

And of course *that*, in the beginning, but also in the end, was the motivating factor for Apple. I'm not talking about the record label, but Apple the office in Savile Row. You know – any lunatic could come through the door – "I've got this great idea…"

So the lads between them – would say, "Well, here's a few bob, maybe ten thousand. Go away and do it."

And of course, it was McCartney, and McCartney's new girlfriend-later-to-be-wife's brother, John Eastman – who put a stop to it crying, "Nonsense, you're just pouring money away for nothing."

AP: Is there a moment that you can recall that would sum up that warmth that John had?

TP: At one point I was the music critic at the *Observer* newspaper in London for about seven years. It wasn't my main job, but it was just something I did for fun. Derek Taylor, who was their great publicist, rang me up one day and said "John's got this new girlfriend called Yoko Ono. Nobody wants to touch her because they think she's bonkers. Would you like to interview her?"

And I said "Of course – I'll be straight down there." So I went down – I spent an afternoon with them at Abbey Road, in Studio Number Three, and in the canteen, talking to Yoko. And I found her very interesting. I didn't think she was bonkers at all. I thought she was rather unusual, but certainly fascinating. I printed a long interview with her in the *Observer*.

That of course further endeared me to John when the two of them started to get together, and as a result of that, John rang me up one day and said, "Would you like to write the biography of me and Yoko?"

AP: Wow.

TP: And I said, "Well, sort of..."

So he said, "Come over and stay." That was at the big house they had near Ascot, Tittenhurst Park. And I stayed there – it was meant to be just for an afternoon, but it turned out to be a very long weekend, where I interviewed Yoko at length. I didn't need to interview John because I knew pretty much what he would say. But what was fascinating was – this is the answer to your question – he was very concerned that as they'd only just moved in and they were re-building the kitchen, *what do we do about breakfast? What are we going to do about lunch?*

I said, "John, lunch, I know, is going to be brown rice. I'd rather not have brown rice for breakfast."

He got very worked up about this, and said, "I can have breakfast brought in."

I said "No, don't bother, I'll go down the shops, I'll get a couple of eggs – I'll fry up some eggs. I'll be perfectly happy."

"Oh good," he said. But it was the extent to which he *cared*. I was quite taken aback.

John and I were also involved in the Richard Neville trial – involving the publication *Oz* – because I was Richard Neville's bailee. Richard needed someone to guarantee with a sum of money that he wasn't going to flee the country. Richard asked me, "You know John Lennon – can you get John to kind of do something to raise the profile of what's going on?" Because it was really thought to be a trial all about the freedom of speech. So John turned up outside the Old Bailey, waving a placard, claiming to have written a song about it all – 'God Save *Oz*'. So that's more typical of John than just *he was just one of the Beatles.*

AP: Is there anything, in all of your encounters with John, that has really – something he said or a conversation you had that really stuck with you?

TP: Oh, that's interesting, because they all merge from one into another. At the end of this tour in Cambridge, John just scribbled a telephone number and gave it to me and said, "After the concert tonight, we'll be taken away immediately." As I said, they were famous then – I think they'd had two or three number one hits. But they weren't the mega-famous that they later became.

I said, "But I'm not coming to London, I think I'm destined to become an academic. But thankyou thankyou thankyou, it's been wonderful to meet you." So two-and-a-half or three years later, I came to London and started work at the BBC. And I still had this bit of paper. So I thought, well, *nothing ventured, nothing gained. I'll ring the telephone number.* It surely can't be still connected.

To my amazement, a girl answered the phone. I could tell from the tone of her voice that I was the four hundredth person that morning who'd rung up to say *John Lennon said to call.* And I said, "Well he really did, this is my number at the BBC," and I put the phone down expecting to hear nothing more.

Half an hour later, Derek Taylor calls me. And he said, "I've got a message for you from John," and I thought *Christ, what's this going to be, then? Who the hell are you? What do you want? Leave me alone? Talk to somebody else?* I couldn't think what it could be.

So, very hesitantly – and I didn't really know Derek at that point – I said, "Mr. Taylor, what is the message?" He said, "John wants to know why it's taken you two years to ring him up!"

So we then met for lunch – inevitably brown rice – and he gave me the idea, and almost the scenario, for the first film that I made about rock 'n' roll which is called *All My Loving.* When it aired, John himself said, "You changed rock 'n' roll on BBC television *overnight.*" 'Cos, you know, we had let these guys talk and play, and respected them as human beings.

Anyway, after that film, he sent me a telegram, which

I've got in front of me. And I've worried about it ever since, because it doesn't quite mean what it says. It says:

IT IS IMPOSSIBLE TO OVERESTIMATE
THE UNIMPORTANCE OF PRACTICALLY EVERYTHING.
LOVE, JOHN.

And I thought that was wonderful. *It is impossible to overestimate the unimportance of practically everything.* And in a way, that is so typical of him. That was his mantra through life. And I think that was why he influenced so many people. It wasn't just that he wrote 'Give Peace a Chance', or 'All You Need Is Love'.

Much later on, I did this huge series called *All You Need Is Love*. A seventeen-part series on the history of American Popular Music. And that *again* was his idea. He said, "We all talk about these things — blues, jazz, rock 'n' roll, ragtime, swing — but none of us really knows where it came from, how it developed, how it influenced the other strands of what we now call rock 'n' roll." He said *do it*. And I said *yes sir, anything you say* — never realizing how complicated it would be. Anyway — this was, again, over lunch. Over brown rice, in New York. When we finished, he shot off. He said, "I've got to get off to a meeting now," and he got to the door of this tiny little restaurant, and he turned around and he said, "By the way, I've got a perfect title for you."

And I said, "What's that?"

"Call it *All You Need Is Love*."

I said, "Hang on — I think there's some group whose name I can't remember who wrote a song by that name." And he laughed, and out he went. He eventually sent me a note giving me permission to use the title.

When the series came out in a big box set in 2006, the

American distributor insisted that we do a title search. I said, "It's common parlance – everybody says *All You Need Is Love*, or *Love is all you need*," or some such combination. They said *no no – must have a title search.* So I then found out that the Beatles themselves had never copyrighted or trademarked *All You Need Is Love*. But two people had – one was a brothel in Amsterdam, the other was a manufacturer or risqué lingerie in Hong Kong. And unfortunately, John was then dead, but I told this to McCartney, who thought it was the funniest thing he'd ever heard.

But you see, that was their attitude. They did make a lot of money – of course. But they weren't interested in property. What they were writing was not a commodity – not something which was there to be bought and sold. It was an outpouring of what they felt. And that again goes back to John. *It is impossible to overestimate the unimportance of practically everything.* That was – I'm sure – the mantra that guided his life. Hence the *Oz* trial. Hence all the other strange things that he got involved in. He was a major political force, without wanting to be so – or without seeking it. It was just that he was an example of what youth could do.

AP: I'm interested in exploring the difference between *John Lennon: the man*, vs. *John Lennon: the image*. Was there anything in your mind that changed in terms of your perception of him?

TP: That's a simple question with a very complicated answer. I mean, from a very early time all four of them got very confused about what the public thought they were like, and what they *knew* they were like. So, to some extent that made them closer-knit than they otherwise would have been. I mean, Ringo was always thought to be the joker – for example. I always found Ringo very bright, very intelligent, very knowledgeable. Paul was always portrayed as the group's PR. Which of course he was, but a much more complicated person than that. John – because partly, oddly enough, because he was married – was always sort of the odd one out. Which he never was. That simply wasn't the case. He was more abrasive, and more aggressive than the others. Personally, I'm talking about. And also, he was the one who most frequently changed his hairstyle, his clothes, his glasses – until quite late on. So he was the one who was trying to escape, I think, from what the perceived image of what being a Beatle was. I mean, the simple illustration of that was the haircut.

I mean, that haircut – nowadays, you wouldn't take any notice of it. But of course, at the time, it was thought *that was their trademark*. Their Beatle Mop haircut. So, as the Beatles became associated with the Beatle haircut, John did everything – you know, grew a beard, got his hair longer, grew moustaches, often came to a meeting almost in disguise – to get away from what the perceived image of these nice, clean cut mop-topped young men was.

And of course, that again was exacerbated by the rise of the Rolling Stones – and they definitely saw themselves as the good side of the coin. If the Rolling Stones wanted to behave badly – you know, take cocaine, and get up to all kinds of sexual shenanigans, well that's fine, but that's not *them*. So again, they got tar-brushed – I think is the right word – with an image that wasn't really them. That was the point.

And so John, who was, in a way, a kind of free spirit in every sense – I mean, that's the only simple way to describe his relationship with Yoko. They undoubtedly, certainly at the beginning, found each other fascinating, and found a kind of love between the two of them. But you can't imagine *Ringo going off with Yoko*, if you see what I mean. So John was much more of a free spirit. The image he wanted to put out was, in a sense, a rebellion against what other people thought his image was. So – simple question, complicated answer.

AP: You've mentioned brown rice a couple of times now – I'd like to hear a little bit about that.

TP: It's a kind of running joke – I think he discovered brown rice in India when they went off with the Maharishi. He always thought that was just a holiday – he never saw any significance in that. It was a holiday to get away from people like me, I suspect. But in India they convinced themselves that brown rice was better for them. So it was a joke, you know – *you're coming to lunch? Well, brown rice first course, brown rice main course, brown rice for dessert.* I mean, that isn't what you got, but we had a running joke.

AP: Tony, is there anything that I've missed that you feel that I should know about John?

TP: I don't know – as you can tell, he was a hero of mine as well. But someone who one knew *warts and all*. He wasn't a perfect human being – no human being ever is. But he was someone who was courageous. That's the important thing about him. He was intellectually and creatively courageous. And if you think of the milieu from which he came – lower middle class. It's always described as working class – it wasn't working class – lower middle class background and his dysfunctional family. And his mother being killed almost in front of him. It's a remarkable achievement, somehow. There must have been something very special about him, to have escaped from all of that, and put his stamp very firmly on the time of his life when he mattered. And he did matter.

The famous definition of Bobby Moore – the English captain who won the World Cup. Jack Charlton said "The thing about Bobby was, he was one of us. He was one of the team. But he wasn't *like* us." And that was a perfect description of genius, I think. One of us – did all the things that we did – farts, goes to the lavatory, etcetera, but they're not *like* us. They're different. There's something about them which is different.

• • •

John's interest in educating himself in the canon of classic literature proved to hold a strong influence over his song-writing. This interest was made clear in his time spent at the Trinity College library, and later buying up all the books he could find. By devouring books, John afforded himself a vantage point from which to develop an understanding of the wider arts. In 1963 he was a more mature John Lennon than the Quarry Bank schoolboy had been.

And so he arranged to tour Cambridge with Tony Palmer. In characteristic Lennon style, John attempted to disguise his recognizable outward appearance. Two years later, Tony finally called the number John gave him and was thrown into the deep end of the rock 'n' roll world. By this stage, John had also developed his social conscience. And he was pushing Tony to make honest films about the real world of music.

IT IS IMPOSSIBLE TO OVERESTIMATE
THE UNIMPORTANCE OF PRACTICALLY EVERYTHING.
LOVE, JOHN.

But back in 1963, despite their string of UK hits, the

Beatles were not yet the international stars they would prove themselves to be on the *Ed Sullivan Show* in February 1964. Before they agreed to tour America, they wanted a US #1 single. The throngs of fans were being noticed by the international press, but the American public couldn't buy the albums yet. Where were the American records?

Capitol Records finally yielded to pressure and signed the Beatles' catalogue for a proper American release. 'I Want to Hold Your Hand' was launched in the US on Boxing Day 1963. This was the big moment, and Capitol had five million bumper stickers printed, reading THE BEATLES ARE COMING. Hype was building all over the country. On January 25, 1964, they reached the top of the charts.

Three weeks later – February 7, 1964 – the Beatles arrived in New York and set about the conquering of America. 3000 screaming fans greeted them at the newly renamed John F. Kennedy airport. Two days later, Ed Sullivan introduced the band to 73 million viewers. They then caught the train down to Washington where they gave their first concert on American soil. They closed the show with Little Richard's 'Long Tall Sally'.

While in Washington, they attended a charity ball at the British Embassy. At the party, the Beatles found themselves treated as sideshow amusements. To Ringo's horror, a lock of his hair was snipped off by a young woman. John walked out. Who would want to hang out with a bunch of toffs, anyway?

The next day they played two sold-out shows at New York's Carnegie Hall. Police had to barricade parts of 7th Avenue and 57th Street. It was here that a young songwriter and record producer named Phil Spector secured some time to hang out with the band. Mutual admiration was noted – the Beatles had recorded a version of Spector's 'To

Know Him Is to Love Him' for their Decca audition. Spector would turn up again later in their lives.

After just a handful of American appearances, the Beatles returned to England. They were now the biggest band in the world. They had made England cool. They had made *Liverpool* cool. And they would never again know the normal life that they longed for in so many of their lyrics.

Two weeks after returning from the States they began production on their first film, *A Hard Day's Night*. The album of the same name would be recorded sporadically throughout the first half of the year – whenever there was a spare moment in the hectic schedule provided by Brian Epstein.

In March, John's first book, *In His Own Write*, was published by Jonathan Cape/Simon & Schuster. It comprised a collection of drawings and short stories drawn largely from his self-devised school publication *The Daily Howl*. Foyles booksellers held a literary lunch in his honor at the Dorchester Hotel, where John embarrassed himself – not realizing he was expected to make a speech. Cynthia later stated that they were both hung over from a night out at the Ad Lib club, and John began to panic when suddenly faced with a room packed full of the aristocratic literary establishment. He certainly wasn't expecting a huge crowd and imposing television cameras. After being introduced to the microphone John managed to utter, "Thank you very much, and god bless you." As he sat down, he turned to the aging gentleman next to him and said, "You've got a lucky face." That meagre utterance constituted the entirety of John's formal Literary Luncheon address. His audience was not impressed. Brian Epstein came to John's rescue and took over the proceedings with a short speech, in damage control mode.

In June 1964, the Beatles embarked on the tour that had been booked well in advance of their worldwide fame: Denmark, the Netherlands, Hong Kong, Australia, and New Zealand.

John's Aunt Mimi joined the tour in New Zealand. Her own aunt, John's great aunt Harriet Millward, had emigrated there and Mimi had maintained written contact with the extended family. John invited his Kiwi family to the Wellington concerts, where he met some of his second cousins for the first time. Mimi then accompanied the Beatles back to Australia for the final few dates in Brisbane.

On the flight, Australian television reporter Bob Rogers conducted a mid-air interview with John. Rogers asked, "How about your Aunty Mimi – how's she enjoying it?"

John: "Oh, she likes it 'cos she's never been this high before."

After Brisbane, Mimi returned to New Zealand to stay with the extended family for a couple of months. While Mimi was away, the seventeen-year-old Julia Baird – then Julia Dykins – found a key to Mendips. Julia was able to use the house as she pleased in Mimi's absence. There she experienced blissful solitude for the first time in her life, devouring books and staying overnight whenever she pleased. Mimi never found out.

IVOR DAVIS

BEATLES USA

THE BEATLES arrived back at Heathrow Airport on July 2, 1964, in time for the London premiere of *A Hard Day's Night* on July 6. Only four months had passed since filming had begun. On July 10 they returned to Liverpool to accompany the film's release, where more than a hundred thousand people crammed the streets outside the town hall just to wave at the boys who had been local kids only a year or so earlier. To the Beatles, these crowds were the same people they'd grown up around, and they regarded them fondly. But to the people of Liverpool, the Beatles had morphed into deities. They were untouchable, and they were no longer relatable as ordinary people.

The difficulties of being in the most famous, most adored band in the world were just beginning. In August they would return to the USA for a proper tour – 32 performances in 24 cities over 34 days. The American fans had been holding their breath since February, and for the Beatles, life was about to be heightened yet again.

In 1964, a young British foreign correspondent called Ivor Davis was covering the West Coast of the States for the London *Daily Express* – circulation four million daily readers. As was the lifestyle, one day in August he got a call: *Go to San Francisco and follow the tour with this new rock 'n' roll group. You'll be travelling with them and staying on the same floor of their hotels. It's all arranged.* Ivor Davis performed this duty and kept the Beatles company from the first day of the tour until they returned to England five weeks later.

Ivor witnessed the height of Beatlemania – travelling in the second limousine to-and-from each concert, where he had a reserved seat in the press area at the front of the stage, and where he dodged the volleys of jellybeans hurled toward the band. The Beatles couldn't leave their rooms, and naturally befriended those few journalists who shared the hotel floor with them. Sharing these same hotels, limousines, and private jets were Brian Epstein, their publicist Derek Taylor, and various road managers including Mal Evans, Neil Aspinall and Tony Bramwell.

Ivor Davis's book *The Beatles and Me on Tour* covers the fascinating events of the Beatles' experience in America in meticulous and personal detail. While on the tour, Ivor ghost-wrote a weekly column in the *Daily Express* for George Harrison, for which the touring lifestyle served up a plethora of surreal moments. In Seattle, the Beatles extended fishing rods out a hotel window into a nearly stream – catching nothing. In Cleveland, panicked police officers stormed the stage and stopped the show – sending the Beatles back to their dressing rooms until the uproarious crowd returned to their seats. And Ivor was there for two of the most iconic moments in Beatle lore: when Bob Dylan introduced the Beatles to marijuana – and the following year, when the Beatles met their hero: Elvis Presley.

IVOR DAVIS: The first time I met John was in early August 1964. I'd arrived in San Francisco at the Hilton hotel and I had to fight my way through about 200 young women.

When I got to the desk they said, "No – we've got no accommodation."

I said, "I'm with the Beatles."

"Oh – sorry!"

So I went to my room and I called Derek Taylor – the Beatles' press guy. Terrific guy. He used to work for the newspaper I worked for, the *Daily Express*. Derek took me into a big suite, and the Beatles were there. I remember this because they were watching themselves – on television – arrive in San Francisco. And the other exciting thing was they all had remote controls. Back in '64, they never had remote controls in England.

Derek said, "John, I want you to meet Ivor." And John kind of grunted.

Oh, thank you – nice warm welcome.

The same happened with George, Ringo, and Paul. Paul smiled and shook my hand, but the rest of them were just completely glued to the telly. And I thought, *what the hell?*

You've got to remember that they'd just arrived from a long transatlantic flight. They were jetlagged and tired; they'd had a couple of drinks. I think they were feeling no pain. And so from that welcome I thought *wow – this is going to be a grind.*

But fortunately, once they saw that I was part of the family, and I was going to be with them for five or six weeks, they started loosening up. Because they were trapped in hotels—and of course on the charted jet—we quickly got pally with them. Also we often had adjoining hotel rooms with them on the entire tour.

AIDAN PREWETT: So they warmed up nicely.

ID: Once they all recovered from their jet lag we bonded pretty well. While I could leave the hotel, the Beatles couldn't. There were young women parked outside the hotel day and night. So in a way it forced them to talk to me and the handful of others covering the tour. There were few constrictions; I could wander into their next-door suite—and John was hospitable.

There was a running joke—he would drink rum and Coca-Cola. I told him that it makes me vomit. So he said, "Raid the mini bar—but don't tell Brian…he's always moanin' about our mini-bar bill."

John loved nothing better than to provoke people. When we first met, I told him my first name was Ivor—but he insisted on calling me Ivan—then Ivan the Terrible. I didn't know at that time but apparently he had a schoolboy friend named Ivan.

Much later Paul warned, "Don't take John too seriously – you have to take everything he says with a pinch of salt."

AP: In all of the time that you spent, specifically with John, is there one moment that has really stuck with you over the years?

ID: There were two things. John would call me at two in the morning and say, "We're playing Monopoly, come over."

So I'd go over there, 'cos I was two rooms away. We went into the suite; I'd raid the minibar. John would have his rum & coke. He didn't drink that much – didn't drink wine or beer or any of that stuff.

He wanted to play Monopoly and he needed somebody else – and another regular player was Arthur Schreiber. Schreiber was an American political reporter who'd been dragged away from the political campaign to cover the Beatles. And he wasn't too keen. He thought, *why the hell am I covering this pop group?*

So we started playing Monopoly with John. It was about

two in the morning. We sort of had fun, although John did cheat a bit. He'd just shout, "Wrong number!" and roll it again. What – are you going to argue about a silly game of Monopoly?

In the middle of the game, he'd say, "Hold off a minute, I've got to call home." And he'd pick up the phone and call Liverpool. And he'd talk to Cynthia. What was funny about it was that after a great long conversation, she'd put the baby Julian on, and for about a minute, John would make baby noises into the telephone. He'd say, "Miss you. Bye everybody." He'd hang up, and we'd finish playing Monopoly.

John was great fun. He was outrageous – he had a brilliant brain. He just said what he thought. He had no connection between his throat and his brain. He just let it out.

One time we were in Key West, Florida. We weren't supposed to be there. What had happened was there was a hurricane – we were on our way to Jacksonville, Florida, and the private Electra jet that we were travelling in had to divert. So we landed in medium weather in Key West and we had to get a hotel. We got a bungalow hotel in sort of lush foliage. Because the weather was bad, we all showed up at John's big bungalow. By that time we were pretty friendly; we were part of the family.

We started watching television – I remember this because there was Fidel Castro, live on television. Cuba was just 90 miles away. And so John – seeing this big bearded guy spouting his political speech... John didn't know what he was saying, but he sat there listening. I remember John popped a few 'prellies' – Preludin. They were pills. He did it openly, he didn't make a big deal about it. It was kinda to keep him awake. I think they got used to them when they were in Hamburg.

So he took some of those and he was suddenly very animated. When the two-and-a-half-hour speech by Castro finished and we flicked the TV off, John suddenly jumped up and started doing an absolutely brilliant impersonation of Fidel Castro. I mean, it was kind of Mickey Mouse Spanish – garbled stuff. But we were rolling about – it was hilarious. Absolutely hilarious. I always remembered that because he was able to mimic Castro, the inflection of the voice... Castro was like a 300-pound guy with a big beard.

John had a warp speed mind—and the only other person I ever met who thought and spoke so swiftly and with such humor was the late comedian Robin Williams. And like Robin he could switch accents and jump from subject to subject—with lightning speed.

AP: Is there a conversation between you and John that you specifically recall?

ID: He told me that he would never have joined the British Army if they had called him up to do national service. "I would have run away to Ireland," he said. "Look what happened to Elvis when they dragged him into the Army... it destroyed his career. I wouldn't want that to happen to me."

And John hated the Beatle merchandising. So did the other Beatles. Of course, they never realized it was such a huge money maker. One day I walked into the Lennon suite and showed him a Beatle wig I had bought for a couple of dollars—or even less. John took it from me—walked to the hotel window – and tossed it out.

AP: During the tour, was there a moment between John and Paul that you witnessed that might provide some insight into their relationship?

ID: Well, I must tell you that I never saw them arguing. I know this sounds crazy – it sounds almost fairy-story. But they never did – at least not in front of me. I mean, they were funny – they exchanged sharp comedy stuff – not just at the press conferences. But every city seemed the same. We did the same thing – we arrived, we took a police escort to the hotel, we went up to the hotel, they did a press conference, had a meal, and we went off to the concert. Sometimes they did one concert in the afternoon and then another concert in the evening.

So one day I walked into the suite. It wasn't, *may I come over?* The doors were open. We'd walk in. And there were John and Paul sitting on the floor, surrounded by sheafs of yellow pad notepaper. And I could see that they were engrossed in a conversation about songs and lyrics. You know – it was a mess, because they'd taken these yellow pieces of paper, aimed at the wastepaper basket and missed. To this very day I regret that I didn't pick up some of those, because I would have been a rich man.

Anyway, I said, "What are you doing?"

And they said, "Well, we've got two albums to do, we've also got a Christmas album to write…"

So when I heard that I said, "Okay! Excuse me," and I left. I mean, they wrote in hotels – on one occasion they were on a plane, another in the back seat of a car and I knew they were writing. So they had an amazing timetable. Just horrifying. Brian Epstein – I mean, every year they brought out two or three albums and about six singles. Every year. So the pressure was on. But the great thing about it was that they could write very quickly. And I remember Paul said to me – I met him years later when he wrote 'Live and Let Die' for a James Bond movie. And I said, "Great song – you could win an Oscar for this." It didn't win an Oscar.

He said, "It took ten minutes to write!"

So those guys wrote quickly. That was always an interesting thing to see – the relationship between the two of them. As I say – I'm not Pollyanna. But I never, never, saw them fighting.

AP: I'd love it if you could tell me about the most terrifying moment that you experienced in terms of that crowd mania.

ID: It was always a bit of a joke because we came in two limousines, and we left – I left in a limousine, they left in a meat truck or an armored vehicle or an ambulance. But I know how scary it is, because this really happened: In Cleveland or somewhere, the Beatles had taken off. They'd made a getaway in an armored truck and they were long gone. And I was sitting in the second limo and about 30 young women descended. The limos were tinted, so they couldn't see inside. I was never so scared in my life because the young women started – it was almost as though they lifted the limo up. But they didn't – they just started shaking it. It was terrifying. They were able to rock the automobile so violently.

I wanted to say, "Open the fucking window and show them that I'm not a Beatle." It was like an earthquake. Fortunately, the driver took off and the girls kind of fell off. It was crazy. And that's the kind of things the Beatles were going through – everywhere. They really could *never* leave the hotel. I mean, I don't think they would have been *killed*... but they could have been torn limb from limb. The girls – these young teenagers were pretty fierce.

At the Hollywood Bowl there was an artificial fountain before the stage. The girls used to run and jump into the water to swim to the Beatles. Now – bedraggled young women climbing out of the water – what would have happened to them if they'd touched a Beatle with an electric guitar? Fortunately, security was heavy and they kind of fished these bedraggled young women out. They would have done anything to get to touch a Beatle.

AP: How did John cope with all this external pressure?

ID: Since they were all trapped in the hotel room for hours on end, John liked to go to the drawn curtains—and dramatically open them. When screams came from below from the waiting fans who saw this, he shut them. He did it a few times. Then got tired of it.

I saw, from time to time – amid the dull screaming from street level – he walked around in his hotel room doing the Adolf Hitler salute. It was his way to let off steam—black humor-- because he didn't like the adulation of the fans. At the end of the tour he said something like, "We're like performing fleas—everyone comes to see us but not hear our music." True. Although I sat in the front row at every concert and I could hardly hear the Beatles—because the girls screamed from start to finish.

AP: Can we jump now to the Riviera Idlewild Motel, when Bob Dylan showed up?

ID: It was the end of the tour, and we were in a fairly modest motel. As I was going up to their room – because there was going to be a party for all of us to say goodbye – I saw a scruffy-looking guy. He had a backpack. And I said, "Hey, that's Bob Dylan." And it *was* Bob Dylan. He could have been a European guy hitchhiking across Australia – or anywhere. I saw him go into the larger suite. I was sitting outside. They had a couple of sliding doors. And somebody – one of the roadies – put a wet towel down across the door. I wasn't sophisticated in the use of – quote – 'drugs', but I did know what was going to happen.

We were there drinking, and after about an hour the door opened and there was Ringo giggling on the floor. So I said to Mal Evans, "Why is he rolling around giggling?"

And he said, "Bob gave us a wonderful, fat marijuana cigarette." Bob had lit it and handed it to Ringo. And Ringo, not knowing the diplomacy involved in sharing marijuana cigarettes, kept it to himself and smoked the whole damn thing. So no wonder he was a bit... he was giggling on the floor – but he could have been on the ceiling.

Everybody was mellow. I mean, Brian Epstein was in there. All the Beatles were very mellow. And thanks to the generosity of Mr. Dylan – and of course, as you may know, John and Bob Dylan had a great relationship. Even though, at one time, John – as he was wont to do – made a little pass at Joan Baez, but then realized that she was off-limits.

So they got really high, thanks to the good graces of Mr. Dylan. Bob left – I think he was living somewhere in New York. And the next morning, the slightly hung-over Beatles – we went to the airport with them – and they got on the plane and went back to London. And Bob Dylan gave them the perfect finale – deserved – for their trip home.

AP: Was that really the very first time they'd tried marijuana?

ID: I think it was the first time that they'd tried a good grade of marijuana. I believe in Germany – in Hamburg – I don't think they had marijuana. They had pills. They had uppers, to keep awake. But I believe this was their first experience in the ceremonial use of marijuana, which Dylan very generously provided them. And of course, after that it was a necessary accoutrement in the armory.

AP: Now John, obviously, was a big Elvis fan. So for John to meet Elvis – what was it like for him?

ID: They tried to meet Elvis in 1964, but it didn't work out. Elvis was making movies, the Beatles were harum scarum all over the country. And then the next year, in the summer of '65, I got a call. I knew that Brian Epstein and Colonel Tom Parker had gotten together several times at the Beverly Hills Hotel to try to make the meeting happen.

So, finally we show up in the limousines at Elvis' house. Apparently, they'd had a few puffs of marijuana just before they arrived, by the way. I think they called it *cups of tea* or some euphemistic phrase. So John bounds out of the limo, goes straight in and says, "We're here to see the owner," or some silly thing like that.

By the way – I saw a letter that Brian Epstein wrote. He said in the letter, *no press – no tape recorders – no photographers*. Ridiculous – the biggest meeting in pop history.

We all go in there, and I know I have to keep my mouth shut, because the press are not allowed. And so I just sort of sit back and watch. And the amazing thing, that even today stuns me is that nobody there said, "John, Paul, George & Ringo – I'd like you to meet Elvis." There were a couple of people kind of just sitting on the couch in a fairly tight outfit, with the shag carpeting. And there was Elvis.

Now, I believe that the Beatles were in awe of meeting Elvis. And Elvis kind of had mixed feelings. But what happened was that nobody said *anything*. So they sat around watching Elvis clicking on the television with the remote. And finally, Elvis – much to his credit – jumped up and said something like, "If you guys are gonna just sit around, I'm goin' to bed – unless you guys came here to jam." That broke the ice. So they pulled out the guitars, they plugged them in – mostly R'n'B stuff, Fats Domino and stuff like that. But none of the Beatles songs. That eased things up a bit, and they started conversing. It wasn't a huge room – a medium-sized room. We could hear what they were saying – it was like they were center stage, and we were all looking. They were talking about Buddy Holly – Paul McCartney was a great fan of Buddy Holly.

They talked about that and then Paul said something like, "Elvis, we wish you'd make music kinda the way you used to." I think Elvis took that the wrong way – that they were criticizing his current music. So Elvis took offense. Elvis was making three shitty movies a year – at least. I mean, he made thirty-odd movies in double-quick time.

Elvis said to them, "It's the same movie each time – different leading lady. I beat the bad guy up and sing the same songs."

The thing I remember they laughed about, was that they both – the Beatles and Elvis – liked the Stanley Kubrick movie *Dr. Strangelove: Or How I Learned to Stop Worrying and Love the Bomb.* Which had Peter Sellers playing three different roles. John *loved* Peter Sellers, because he was a fan of *The Goon Show.* So from that point of view, they hit it off. Elvis had a good sense of humor. He liked that film – it had just come out, maybe the year before. So that was the only real wavelength that they were happy about.

We had finger food, pizzas – a help-yourself buffet. I think Ringo went in the other room to play billiards or snooker or pool or whatever they call it in America. And then after about an hour-and-a-half they broke up. They said – you know – *we'll get together again* – but they never did.

• • •

Ivor Davis spent the following four decades reporting

major American stories for the *Daily Express,* the *London Times*, and the *New York Times*, including the assassination of Robert Kennedy and the trials of Sirhan Sirhan, Angela Davis, Patty Hearst, and Daniel Ellsberg. Ivor also covered the infamous Manson Family trials as they unfolded throughout 1969 and 1970. Prior to the trial, Ivor wrote the first book about the Family, called *Five to Die* – for which he interviewed those members who hadn't yet been arrested and investigated their Spahn Ranch home. Ivor's research was so detailed that the Los Angeles District Attorney came to rely on his book for their prosecution case. Ivor has recently turned his focus solely to books, including *The Beatles and Me on Tour,* and *Manson Exposed: A Reporter's Fifty-Year Journey into Madness and Murder.*

John Lennon, meanwhile, had met his idol. He must have been disappointed that he and Elvis hadn't connected on anything more than a superficial level. The next day a couple of the Presley entourage attended a party at the Beatles' rented villa, and John asked Elvis' friend Jerry Schilling to convey his real feelings to the King: "Please tell Elvis that without him, I'd have been nothing."

1965 saw more endless touring, the film *Help!*, the Shea Stadium concert, their first taste of LSD, and the awarding of MBE's for each Beatle. The Membership of the Most Excellent Order of the British Empire had never been awarded to anyone under 25 before. At Buckingham Palace, the boys were nervous and snuck off to the lavatories for a secret smoke. "I don't think it was a joint," says McCartney. When presenting the award, Queen Elizabeth asked John if he'd been working hard. "No, we've been having a holiday," he replied. It was a lie to the Queen: they'd been recording *Rubber Soul.* John sent his medal to Aunt Mimi, who displayed it on her mantelpiece in the new seaside home he'd recently bought for her.

Rubber Soul was released in December, and shortly afterward John gave a lengthy interview to Maureen Cleave, a friend from the London *Evening Standard*. Buried in the transcript were the words, "We're more popular than Jesus, now." These words were dug out in August 1966 by the American press, taken out of context and re-released just in time for the Summer '66 US tour. John faced the press in New York and apologized. Maureen Cleave released her own statement to clarify the issue, but it was too late. The press swarmed on it, and some radio stations began organizing mass burnings of Beatle memorabilia. KLUE radio in Texas was struck by lightning the day after it staged just such a burning and was unable to broadcast again until some expensive technical equipment was repaired.

The tour was distressing. Protestors, including uniformed members of the Ku Klux Klan, picketed outside the stadiums and waved placards that read GO HOME BEATLES and other less savory remarks. Airport ground staff in Memphis discovered several bullet holes in the underside fuselage of the Beatles' touring plane.

Candlestick Park, San Francisco, marked the end of the tour. It would be the Beatles' last formal concert. They had no desire to return to the road.

LESLIE CAVENDISH
BEATLE HAIR

IN NOVEMBER 1966, John attended an art show at the Indica Gallery, for which Paul McCartney was a financial supporter. The exhibition John came to see was by a Japanese artist called Yoko Ono. Here, John was invited to climb a ladder and use a magnifying glass to inspect a piece of installation art on the ceiling. It was a tiny word on a small, white canvas. The word was:

YES

"It was positive. I felt relieved. It's a great relief when you get up the ladder and you look through the spyglass and it doesn't say *No* or *Fuck You* or something. It said *Yes*," John told *Rolling Stone* in 1970. By this stage, John and Cynthia's marriage was faltering, and John had admitted to Cynthia that he had been unfaithful through many of their years together. Even so, it took about a year for John and Yoko to officially get together.

May 1967 saw the release of *Sgt. Pepper's Lonely Hearts Club Band*, which ushered in the Summer of Love. George's wife Pattie signed the Beatles and a significant entourage up for a transcendental meditation course with the Maharishi Mahesh Yogi, who was conducting a retreat at University

College in Bangor, Wales. As the Beatles and friends swept through the overcrowded Euston Station to board the train to Bangor, Cynthia became separated from the group. She was prevented from boarding the train by a police officer, who didn't believe that she was Cynthia Lennon. The train pulled away from the platform moments later. John opened his window and called out to her, but it was too late. Cynthia was distraught. She'd been left behind so many times before. And this time – on a platform crammed with onlookers – felt more public. And more final.

While in Bangor, Paul's longtime girlfriend Jane Asher answered the phone and was asked to get Paul on the line, urgently. It was a call that would upend the Beatles' entire world. Brian Epstein had died – the cause was later ruled an accidental overdose. Brian's death left the group rudderless, grieving, and in need of a new management plan. Every aspect of the Beatles' direction had been overseen by Brian. Suddenly, it was all left solely to them. And John had lost another parental figure.

"Best carry on," was the message from all commercial interests, and in September 1967, the Beatles were touring again – this time in a fictional sense, with the filming of the television special, *Magical Mystery Tour*. Upon their return they founded a new company, Apple Corps, to consolidate all the Beatles' interests into one company. They would be their own managers. This added further stress to an already untenable workload, and the pressures coming from interested parties – and each other – were immense. The Beatles held themselves together in the studio, but relationships were fracturing.

The year before Brian Epstein died, a promising young London hairstylist named Leslie Cavendish – trained by Vidal Sassoon – was working at Sassoon's new Grosvenor

House salon. As a junior, Leslie had the good fortune of having a boss who frequently ran overtime. Leslie soon found himself stepping in, to style some of the most high-profile heads in the world.

One of these last-minute clients was Jane Asher. Jane immediately approved of Leslie and asked him to drop by the house to cut her boyfriend Paul McCartney's hair that very evening. And so, on September 3, 1966, Leslie Cavendish rang the buzzer at Paul's house and went up to deliver the haircut that would change his life. Paul took a liking to Leslie, and Leslie remained Paul's hairstylist for many years to follow.

Leslie became a regular face at the Apple building and was soon cutting the hair of the other Beatles and their colleagues. Leslie was granted an all-access pass to the Beatles' empire, which included EMI Studios – later known as Abbey Road, the Apple offices and Trident Studios. In September '67 he was invited along on the *Magical Mystery Tour* coach ride – a week-long trip with the Beatles around Devon and Cornwall. When Apple Tailoring opened in May 1968, Leslie's personal salon opened in the basement. Leslie was in the Apple building at 3 Savile Row when the Beatles gave their impromptu rooftop concert. And Leslie was privy to several moments in the recording studios – including one tense occasion with John's new partner Yoko Ono. Leslie's stunning recollections are chronicled in his book *The Cutting Edge* – a thrilling insight into the private world of the Apple Corps universe and the real swinging London.

LESLIE CAVENDISH: When Paul came into the Apple offices everything was sort of nice – "*Morning!*" I couldn't imagine anyone getting uptight, 'cos Paul was always walking in with a sort of easygoing way about him. Ringo was the same. George would float in – he was always floating in. Everything was relaxed. And I always had this thing when Lennon came in – it was like the headmaster had arrived. *What mood is he in today? Is he on edge? Had some-thing happened to him? Or was it peace & love* John? There were so many different aspects to Lennon that were a bit different to the others.

I just remember, you got to know the people in the office – you would see them all the time. And I was a new face as far as he was concerned.

John said, "Who's he?"

Mal Evans said, "Paul's hairdresser."

John just looked at me for a moment, and then went: "Come and cut my hair, will you?" And he just walked down the corridor and into the boardroom, which was pretty large. It was a typical boardroom with a high chair. You know – the executive's chair that you can look down importantly from.

His hair was sort of longish. I started cutting his hair, and there was a journalist there. They were just talking, it was a normal conversation about music. So I was cutting his hair and doing it – didn't take much off – and that was that. I'm not even sure if he said *thank you.* I'm not even sure if he noticed. I'm not even sure if he knew I was there.

Another time he was talking to a lady who was wearing all black. To me she was a journalist – she could have been a journalist from the Far East. Why not? The Beatles were big in Japan and all those places.

I'd take a little cape and put it around the back of his neck and put a towel there – just a routine thing. As I'm doing it, he's moving his head. I kept saying, "John, could you just – just one second, I just want to do this to you."

He was saying, "But I don't understand!" He kept

leaning forward. "I don't understand what you're talking about…" to the person sitting there.

I thought *that's strange. What's she saying that he doesn't understand? She's a music journalist – what could he not understand?*

The conversation got a little more interesting as well, because he kept moving his head all over. That's the worst thing for someone cutting hair – moving. As I had his hair in my fingers, he'd move, so I'd lose the bloody hair! I'd say, "John, could you please keep your head still for a moment…" I was just taking the ends off his hair. But he kept on moving. It was like a silent movie, for me.

I kept thinking – *what are they talking about? This lady's intriguing him so much – what's he want me around for?* He could have been speaking to her for an hour already – two hours. I've got no idea. For somebody – for me – to be there 25 minutes, standing over his chair, observing this – made me think, *he's going to tell me to go in a minute.* But it was me who said, "Okay John, I've finished up."

He looked up like, *oh – are you there? I forgot all about you.* So that was the second time I cut his hair. It was a very interesting situation.

AIDAN PREWETT: How long after that did you read the paper and go, *oh – that was Yoko?*

LC: She got publicized – a great friend of the Beatles was a guy called Robert Fraser. He had a gallery in London. He was into heroin; he introduced them to the heroin scene. He had a very avant-garde sensibility. He was the type of guy who would bring over Andy Warhol. Yoko's work was presented to him, but he decided that it wasn't for him, but he knew a guy called John Dunbar, who was married to Marianne Faithfull at the time. John Dunbar was in partnership with Peter Asher – Jane's brother – in an art gallery called Indica. Indica is a type of cannabis.

So I'd got to know about Yoko because she was in the papers. She's a talented artist, actually, if you're into that type of thing. My mind's always open to that type of work, even though I don't understand it. She obviously engaged John to be inquisitive. And suddenly this lady, and him – it was always *John & Yoko*. You couldn't go anywhere without hearing *John & Yoko*.

John – living out at Kenwood – was probably a bit starved of what was *going on* in the art world of London. Yoko filled that gap. She was the person that introduced him to the art world in terms of the depth of how he perceived things, and questioned things. Which obviously, for a songwriter, that's got to be amazing – for someone to explain to you *their artform*, and you can write it down – it may just dig at something deep inside you.

For example, 'Glass Onion' – there was a top restaurant in London called Parkes, in Beauchamp Place. My girlfriend at the time was a waitress there. Every time she used to go there – she'd get there at six o'clock of an evening – and she had to put fresh tulips on every table. Other people had roses, they had tulips.

Now – Lennon used to go to Parkes. My girlfriend used to say to me, "Oh, all these people came in today…" The Beatles would go; Lennon would take people there.

She'd say to me that she'd have to get in early to put the tulips on the bloody tables.

I used to say to her, "What are you talking about, Tulips?"

So, Lennon was there: *Looking through the bent-back tulips, to see how the other half live…*

AP: And you got to see the Beatles recording at some studio sessions.

LC: I used to see them at Abbey Road Studios – then called EMI. That was interesting, to be able to watch Lennon and McCartney and the others all work together. They used to have a four-track recording studio there. So you'd have booths for the drums, the guitars in one booth, the singer with the mic... Then they would come up into the engineer's room. I can remember Lennon and McCartney talking to George Martin and Geoff Emerick. They were fiddling around with things. That was interesting to see – because people in the music business hire a record producer, and they'd leave it largely to the record producer. In those days, I don't think they thought that musicians were able to deal with technology or knew how to play around with it. But that's the great thing about the Beatles. *Who cares?* If there's 20 knobs up there, *what happens if you just turn 'em?* Noise. *So what? We just want to hear how it sounds.*

"It'll sound awful," George Martin would say.

"Good," said John. "We just want to hear how awful it sounds."

And also, you don't speak. You're in such a privileged position to be able to be in there. You don't speak. But to watch that – it was absolutely fascinating.

The Beatles always recorded late at night, so their sessions started at eight or nine o'clock at night and they finished at six or eight o'clock in the morning. The rules were – for them – no girlfriends. That's the way it was. But I went down to Trident Studios that day, and who's sitting down on the floor? John and Yoko. And Yoko's stroking John's hair. How nice is that? The others were all playing around, and he's lying there having his hair stroked – which I thought was strange – and it did cause a bit of tension. Obviously that tension had been building up, 'cos it couldn't have been the first time John had been down there with her.

Ringo wasn't there. There was George, there was Paul, and there was John. Normally, in a studio environment like I saw over at EMI, they would come together and talk together. I would have imagined that in a confined place like Trident, it would have brought the three of them closer. It was like an L-shape, basically. It was small. I was sitting in the corner. It must have been about 11, 12 o'clock at night – and I remember George Harrison came over and just said, "Does anybody want a cup of tea?" He said, "Leslie, do you want one?"

And I said, "Yeah – that'd be nice."

It was a bit like that. He went and made me a cup of tea, he made Paul a cup of tea. But I didn't see him make John a cup of tea, or Yoko. I didn't know whether he wanted to get away from them, or what the reason was. But you felt that unit was broken.

AP: Was there a particular moment between John and Paul that you were there for, that might give us some insight into their relationship?

LC: I was on the *Magical Mystery Tour*. Brian Epstein had died two weeks before. He'd been their manager... he was their father figure. The guy that got them where they are. They may have outgrown that relationship eventually – that we don't know. But he died, and the next thing – they're on a coach.

When Paul came on to the coach, we were told we had to go and pick the other three up at Virginia Water. So the filming wouldn't start until they got there. There was no sort of depression *outwardly* for Paul. He was full of beans, with the director, sorting out what they were doing. When we got down to Virginia Water, I remember it was like going to a bus stop – for John Lennon, George, and Ringo. *Hello!* And they jumped on the bus. There were only 43 of us there. And four of us were the Beatles.

For a lot of that film, I was sitting behind John, who was next to George. They did not look like happy buddies. They didn't have the enthusiasm of Paul. While John was on the coach, he was a bit subdued. He used to fall asleep a lot. Sometimes on purpose. He didn't really have a role to play on the actual coach. You see it in the film, where they sing and record – that's what they're there for. But Paul was co-directing. They went along with whatever the director – and Paul – said. I saw no input from John or George on the coach. Maybe they discussed it late at night. Maybe they'd said *Paul is a load of crap.* I don't know what they were thinking. But I didn't see John or George say *actually I don't like that. Let's change this, Paul.* I never saw that.

I think Lennon was bored. I'm sure that with Brian it would have been more of a business thing, to say *look guys – we get out, it's gonna go out at Christmas time and the audience is going to be brilliant...* On the business side, I'm sure that was the sell. But it didn't seem to be of any interest to those two, at all.

I had quite a few laughs with them, 'cos I used to look after the little girl – little Nicky. So when you hear the song 'I Am the Walrus', you hear a little voice going "No you're not!" That's little Nicky Hale. She was five years old – grown up now, obviously. My job was to look after her. John used to put little Nicky on his lap. He played with her – bouncing up and down. But when she was with me, sitting behind him, she would pull his feather from his hat.

He'd go, "Oof! Leslie, will you control that little girl,

please." He was actually being nice about it. So then you saw a little bit of humor come out from him.

AP: Is there any other particular moment that springs to mind in terms of John's humor?

LC: There was an occasion where I did an interview about the texture of the Beatles' hair. A lovely lady called Caroline Rouger, who worked for *Disc* magazine. She'd been a client of mine and she asked me if she could interview me about the Beatles' hair. Which I thought – considering I'm their hairdresser – why not?

I went and had coffee with her. I'm about 21 at this stage – *I've seen the world* – *I've cut the Beatles' hair. Nothing's gonna get past me.* But she was clever, this journalist. She said, "Leslie, you've been doing the Beatles' hair for a while – can you give me a feeling of what their texture is like?" That would be a question that *Hairdresser* magazine would have asked me. For a journalist – is that the main question you would ask? She obviously wanted to know that – but she had something else on her mind.

She said, "What's George's hair like?"

I said, "George has got really lush, thick hair." I used to hand-dry it, flow it through. Same with Paul. And Ringo – he just had to shake his head and his hair would fall into shape there. And I said, "and John's is okay."

That was the hook, wasn't it? That's what she was waiting for.

"Oh – so John's is just *okay*, is it? Not as thick as the others?"

I haven't sussed it yet. I'm falling right into it.

I said, "Well, no – he hasn't got as thick hair as, say, George."

She said, "Ah, interesting. So would you think that

maybe – let's just push it forward a few years, let's go twenty years, thirty years later – do you think that of all the Beatles, Lennon would lose his hair first?"

"No, no – I didn't say that at all."

"But you're saying his hair is the thinnest."

"Well yes, it was."

"So it makes sense," she's feeding me now. "It makes sense that in years to come, if they've got three luscious heads of hair – as you put it – and John's is *okay* – as you put it – is it possible that he could lose his hair before the others?"

"Yeah, I suppose you *could* put it that way. I suppose you could. I mean, he wouldn't end up bald – but I suppose there's more chance of him losing his hair than the other three."

We left it at that. I didn't think there was much wrong with it, actually. We had another coffee and I'm sure she asked me a few other questions to distract from what she'd got out of me, and went home.

Disc magazine came out on a Friday, and they started advertising the article on the radio. Derek Taylor, being the Beatles press officer, rang me up in the evening. He said to me, "You did an interview the other day, about John Lennon?"

I said, "No-"

"You've done something about their hair?"

"Oh, yeah – yeah, yeah."

"Why did you say John Lennon is going bald?"

I said, "I didn't say John Lennon's going bald."

He said, "Well, they're advertising that the Beatles hair-dresser, Leslie Cavendish, is saying John Lennon's going to go bald."

I said, "Oh my God – I did this interview…" And it all twigged. "Oh my God."

He said, "You'd better sort it out, okay?"

So here I am – the Beatles had backed me for a hairdressing salon. They'd paid to put a hairdressing salon in the basement of Apple Tailoring in King's Road. It's their money – part of Apple branching out. And I'd talked: their main man is going to go bald.

I'm thinking *oh my God – this is it. They're going to bollock me.*

So I go down to the shop in the morning. The phone rings – straight away you know it's John Lennon.

"Hello Leslie," he said. "What's going on?"

I said, "John – I really do apologize." I was groveling. "I really am sorry." I'm stuttering – picturing him on the other end of the telephone going *this is just crap.* "She took me out and she asked me. I never said anything about it. I was just talking about textures, and I told her these things, and she took me out of context-"

And he stopped me. "Okay – enough, enough." I was expecting him to slam the phone down. He said, "Don't tell me about being taken out of context – look what happened to me! I gave a bloody interview and they ended up saying I thought I was bigger than Jesus Christ." Then he laughed. And I thought to myself – *oh, he understands.*

And I went, "Oh."

Then there was a break in the conversation. It could have been three, five seconds. It felt like a lifetime.

Then he said, "Leslie, I want to ask you another question."

"…what's that?"

"Am I really going fuckin' bald?"

I said, "No – you're not, actually."

"Good," he said. "Come over here now. If you see any hair on the floor, pick it up and stick it back in my head again."

AP: Skipping forward a little bit – I'd love to get a really nice visual image of the rooftop concert. I'd love to get a kind of play-by-play of what that *day* was.

LC: My day was different to what basically happened. I had no idea that was going on. It was also a very cold day – it was a blustery day. My girlfriend – friend, by the time this all happened – Chris O'Dell, ended up working for the Beatles and became George's PA. She knew everything that was going on at Apple. And she rang me up.

"Come over to Apple today."

I said, "What for?"

"*Come over* – something's happening."

It was like a *calling*. So I said okay. 'Cos if my friend Chris tells me to come over, she knows what she's talking about. So I go over there, and there were a lot of wires downstairs, and there was a lot of movement going on. I had no inkling what that was about. I went through reception, said hello. It was crowded. I walked upstairs to the first floor which I think was the press room. Lots of movement going on there – people buzzing in and out. It didn't seem normal, but it looked like maybe they were filming part of their documentary. It wasn't until I was trying to find Chris that I realized what was going on.

They had spiral staircase going up to the rooftop. Trying to go up the stairs, approaching the staircase, Mal Evans, who was a very big guy, said, "Can't help you, Leslie, sorry."

I said, "What's going on? There's all these wires and cables going up there, and cameras and people carrying equipment." I had to stay downstairs. And I couldn't understand what Chris was talking about – why should I be here?

Suddenly – I'm not sure how long after it was – we heard: "*JOJO WAS A MAN...*"

It was coming up pretty loud, you know? I'm thinking, *What the hell? What's this all about?* It took a little while to realize – *they're doing a bloody concert on the roof!*

They were playing on the rooftop. And – *where's my friend Chris?* She was sitting next to Yoko on the floor, on the roof. She'd worked her way up there. It was so blustery that Yoko gave John her fur coat. You see him wearing it in the film.

The amazing thing about it was looking out the window. Savile Row is a very narrow street in the middle of London, just off Regent Street. You've got pavements either side – it's the place with all the tailors – *by Royal appointment.* Where the aristocracy would go and have their hunting jackets made. There were businesspeople just walking up and down. Suddenly this music was playing. You looked out the window, and – if you can imagine: on the street, if you looked up, you couldn't see the roof. It's not like a big roof. But you could hear 'Get Back' beaming out there. So you saw all these people craning their necks, just looking up – *what's going on?*

The whole point of this was that they were going to cause a public disturbance, and they were going to get the police to come along to arrest them, to take them down to the police station – and the publicity would be *worldwide.* That didn't quite happen because the policeman was a Beatle fan. At the end – he was up there – and he turned around and just said, "Mr. McCartney, have you finished yet?"

• • •

In the years that followed, Leslie's celebrity client stable continued to grow. To this day, he remains chief hairstylist to a select few of the world's most famous and influential heads. But in September 1966 he was the luckiest hairdresser in the world. That luck – in the form of Jane Asher – combined with his talent, charm, and Vidal Sassoon training, thrust him without warning into the intimate world at the core of Apple.

At the height of the 'Paul is dead' media frenzy, Leslie was called upon to confirm or deny the rumors. He was happy to report that the break in Paul's hair had not changed in the slightest – the cute Beatle was very much alive.

John, meanwhile, was re-evaluating *everything*. The Beatles were without a manager; their guiding force had disappeared – so they went searching for a new guru. In February 1968, the Beatles, accompanied by their partners and friends including Mia Farrow, Donovan, and the Beach Boys' Mike Love, travelled to Rishikesh in India to take part in a full course of transcendental meditation with the Maharishi Mahesh Yogi.

Cynthia accompanied John and later wrote that she had hoped the trip would help to strengthen their marriage – but it was not to be. After a week or so, they found themselves sleeping in separate cabins. Ringo had trouble with the food and stayed only a week; Paul followed after two weeks. George and John stayed the longest – nearly two months – before leaving hurriedly when the Maharishi was accused of sexual misconduct.

But the India trip was – more than anything – a period where the Beatles could take some time out from the eye of the hurricane. It was a creatively rich period, during which the bulk of material for *The Beatles* – or the White Album – was written. Donovan's fingerstyle guitar picking influenced John's compositions 'Julia' – about his mother, and 'Dear Prudence' – about Mia Farrow's sister Pru, who was intently focused on meditating in isolation.

George penned 'While My Guitar Gently Weeps'. Paul wrote 'Back in the USSR', for which Mike Love suggested that Paul reference different geographical regions as the Beach Boys had done with 'California Girls'. John also wrote 'The Continuing Story of Bungalow Bill' after an incident involving an American guest at the camp – and the shooting of a tiger, which had dismayed him.

Pattie Boyd's younger sister, Jenny, had just turned 20 and initially had a difficult time in Rishikesh. After a misdiagnosis of tonsillitis and nearly two days of suffering, she was finally diagnosed with dysentery. With the proper treatment, Jenny's condition soon improved. The ordeal led to her favorite moment with John, as she writes in her book *Jennifer Juniper*. Jenny graciously allowed for this excerpt to be reprinted here:

Jenny Boyd: As I was sitting up in bed the following morning, leaning against my pillow and still feeling weak, John and Cynthia walked into my room. John handed me a picture he'd drawn of a man sitting cross-legged with a turban on his head. He was playing a flute and in front of him was a snake, coiled up in a basket with his hooded head peeking out. The inscription underneath read:

BY THE POWER THAT'S IN AND THE POWER THAT'S OUT, I CAST YOUR TONSIL-LIGHT-HOUSE OUT.

LOVE, JOHN AND CYN

TWO MONTHS of the 'summer camp' lifestyle was enough for John and George. They were starting to feel that they were being used by the Maharishi for his own publicity. The allegations against the Maharishi were the final straw. They came from a questionable source – Alexis 'Magic Alex' Mardas, who seemed intent on shifting John's focus from the Maharishi to himself – but the two Beatles were concerned enough to leave immediately. John's original lyrics to 'Sexy Sadie' were: *Maharishi, what have you done?* John wrote these lines while waiting for the taxi out of Rishikesh.

John and Cynthia arrived back in London in mid-April. John and Paul took a quick trip to New York to promote their new Apple venture. Cynthia went to Greece for a real holiday.

On May 19, 1968, John invited Yoko Ono to Kenwood while Cynthia was away. They made a recording that evening in John's home studio which would become their first experimental album, *Two Virgins*. Their relationship was cemented. Cynthia returned home to find John and Yoko wearing only bath robes. She packed her bags and left. John and Cynthia were divorced six months later.

In the public eye, however, the Beatles were still on top of their game. The *Magical Mystery Tour* album had been a major success, despite the criticism that was heaped on its televised counterpart. The animated film *Yellow Submarine* gained buoyancy in July 1968, and it was followed by the release of the *White Album* in November. The fans were reassured. But by early 1969, amid sessions for *Let It Be*, John and Paul seemed to agree only on the fact that their partnership was coming to an end. A major factor was an impending new business management deal with Allen Klein, also manager of the Rolling Stones. Paul McCartney had refused to sign the deal but was outvoted by the other Beatles. They quickly moved onto their final recorded album, *Abbey Road*, with the tacit assumption it would be their last.

John and Yoko married in Gibraltar on March 20, 1969, eight days after Paul McCartney married Linda Eastman. The location was a technicality: John and Yoko had tried unsuccessfully to get married on the cross-channel ferry. John later recalled, "That was the romantic part: when we went to Southampton we couldn't get on because she wasn't English and she couldn't get the day visa to go across. And they said, 'Anyway, you can't get married. The Captain's not allowed to do it anymore.'"

They flew to Paris, only to be told that they needed to give prior notice of intent to wed. So John called Peter Brown at Apple. Brown did some research and came back with the news that they could get married in Gibraltar – being a territory of Britain. They stayed in Gibraltar for only a few hours; the ceremony lasted only ten minutes – after which John and Yoko jumped on their chartered flight back to Paris. A few days later they were driven to Holland.

Their Amsterdam honeymoon would be a bed-in: Seven days tucked into a king-sized for peace, with the world's press welcome each day from 9am to 9pm. The media were bemused, but almost universally accused John and Yoko of naiveté. Not to be deterred, John and Yoko started mailing pairs of acorns to world leaders, accompanied by a letter:

> Enclosed in this package we are sending you two living sculptures—which are acorns—in the hope that you will plant them in your garden and grow two oak trees for world peace.
>
> Yours with love, John and Yoko Ono Lennon

Many of these world leaders wrote back personally. Some even detailed the location of their planted acorns.

In May 1969, a second bed-in took place in Montreal. Here they invited celebrity guests including Timothy Leary, Allen Ginsberg, and Petula Clark. While in the room, they recorded John's newly composed anthem, 'Give Peace a Chance'. Tommy Smothers, of the comedy duo the Smothers Brothers, joined John on a second acoustic guitar. The percussive sounds heard are thanks to a hotel closet door being opened and closed in time with hand claps from the seated participants. The track became John's first single as a solo artist and was a major hit, despite its use of rudimentary recording techniques.

Then in August 1969, John and Yoko moved to their new home, Tittenhurst Park. Situated in Ascot, an hour west of London, Tittenhurst is a sprawling, 72-acre property that includes several additional houses, separate from the Regency mansion. One of these houses bears a striking resemblance to the Mendips house John grew up in with his Aunt Mimi. John insisted that a lake be dug on the property, complete with an island in the center – reportedly inspired by childhood memories of performing in *Treasure Island* at Dovedale Road Primary School.

The main Tittenhurst house was later immortalized in the video clip filmed for 'Imagine': a huge white mansion with white rooms, white bi-fold shutters, and a white piano. It was to become the archetype for all rock star mansions to follow.

RAY CONNOLLY

FIFTEEN AGAIN

THE TORONTO Rock 'n' Roll Revival, in September 1969, was Canada's answer to Woodstock – with a nostalgic twist. It was a day-long festival themed to celebrate the early days of rock 'n' roll. The bill featured Little Richard, Chuck Berry, Bo Diddley, Gene Vincent, Fats Domino, and Jerry Lee Lewis. John's interest was sparked by this lineup of heroes from his teenage years, alongside up-and-comers the Doors and Alice Cooper. John signed himself on at the last minute with the Plastic Ono Band, a musical ensemble that didn't yet exist.

With Tony Bramwell's help he recruited Klaus Voormann on bass, Eric Clapton on lead guitar, Alan White on drums, and Yoko on backing vocals. When they arrived at the gig, John threw up before going on, and struggled to perform. In D.A. Pennebaker's film of the concert, titled *Sweet Toronto,* John seems nervous, scattered and emaciated, with unkempt hair and a giant beard. His vocals are notable for their strained, unnatural vibrato. Heroin had entered the picture, and it had become a major problem. John and Yoko had started snorting it during sessions for *The White Album* and *Let It Be.* By the time of the festival in Toronto, they had already failed in several attempts to quit the drug.

John and the Plastic Ono Band played some old '50s standards, and also premiered 'Cold Turkey', a song detailing the throes of heroin withdrawal. John later said that he nearly vomited again on stage while performing the song. Eric Clapton – who had his own experiences with the drug – was aloof, standing stock-still for most of the performance. Yoko, however, was bursting with enthusiasm and chose this moment to showcase some of her signature vocal stylings.

John was already flirting with the idea of leaving the Beatles, but on the private flight to Toronto, with his new band rehearsing around him, John made the decision to formalize his resignation. He informed the other Beatles and their business manager Allen Klein at a meeting shortly after his return from Canada. Klein and McCartney urged John not to inform the public, as it could be disastrous for the impending release of *Abbey Road*. John almost kept his mouth shut, but he had already informed one journalist, who he had invited to join him in Toronto. That journalist – and friend – was Ray Connolly.

Ray Connolly's career began at the Liverpool *Daily Post* and soon led to the London *Evening Standard* in 1967, where he was sent to interview all the big names: Elvis Presley, Muhammad Ali, Jimi Hendrix, Bob Dylan. He got to know each of the Beatles and continued his friendship with John Lennon until December 1980.

Over the years, Ray Connolly's body of work has included novels, biographies, documentaries, and feature film scripts, centering largely around music. In the 1990s he collaborated with Sir George Martin to write the music history documentary series *The Rhythm of Life*. His most recent books include *Being John Lennon: A Restless Life* and *Sorry Boys, You Failed the Audition*.

Ray was one of the first people to learn of the Beatles' impending breakup. Ray was also the first person John called when he sent his MBE back to Buckingham Palace. Ray was there for the founding of the Beatles' new company Apple, he followed the *Magical Mystery Tour*, and he witnessed some of John's early days in the United States. And in September 1969 John invited Ray to join him in Toronto, where John was about to perform in his first live concert independent of the Beatles.

RAY CONNOLLY: I was on the phone to John one day, and he said, "We're going to Canada. Why don't you come with us?"

So I said, "Well, yeah – okay. When?"

He said, "We're going next week, but you can come a couple of days after." So I went over and he was staying at Ronnie Hawkins' house just outside Toronto. When I got there, he said, "Come upstairs, quickly."

So I said, "Oh – what is it?" And he took me to his bedroom. Whenever you talked to John, you always talked to him in his bedroom. Always. If you're by yourselves, you know – the little secret bits. You're always in the bedroom.

He said, "I've left the Beatles."

I said, "*What?*" I'm thinking: *This is the best story of my entire life*, as a young journalist. And at the same time, I'm thinking: *No no no – don't break up the Beatles*. I'm a huge fan, you know.

So he said, "Don't tell anybody – I'll let you know when you can put it out."

So that's how it went on for the next few months. That's how it was. And of course, I didn't put it out, 'cos he'd told me not to. But Paul did put it out eventually. And Paul got all the blame.

So I then rang John, and he said, "Yeah, I've heard the

fuckin' news." He said, "Why didn't you write it when I told you?"

"Well, you told me not to."

"You're the journalist, Connolly – not me." So there you go. You couldn't win. But yeah, we stayed friends.

AIDAN PREWETT: Is there a poignant moment in any conversation you had that you really recall vividly?

RC: I remember when we were talking about his parents, his mother being killed. He certainly mentioned his uncle, with whom he'd lived – Mimi's husband. And he just suddenly said, "I've had a lot of death in my life." And he was only 29 then. *I've had a lot of death in my life.* And he's talking about Stuart also, Stuart Sutcliffe. So that was a sort of sudden – one of those bleak moments, you know. It was like a shadow had passed over him.

He usually was either ranting – and he would go on these long rants which were a lot of exaggeration and half self-mocking. Which *Rolling Stone* – the American interviewers never got. He was mocking himself half the time. And laughing at himself, and laughing at Yoko, and making jokes and things. But they printed it verbatim. And on paper, it sounds really angry and vicious – but when you listened to him, the way he told it – it wasn't angry and vicious, it was often very funny. But that was John.

AP: In all the time that you spent with John, do you remember any particular instance of mischief?

RC: Everything he did… If John hadn't been a rock star, he'd have been a great stand-up comedian. He was actually very funny all the time. For journalists, he was a great person to interview because he spoke in headlines. They weren't necessarily true, but they were funny. There's the time when the

Hare Krishna people were down at Tittenhurst Park, and he let them hang around, they seemed harmless enough. There was a group of them – they were painting this sort of nineteenth century temple thing, down in the grounds. And when they'd go past, they'd say, "Peace man, peace."

And I'd say, "Okay, peace man – yeah."

That was what they said then – '69-'70. *Peace man, peace.* I went there quite regularly. Then one day they weren't there. So I said, "What happened to your Hare Krishna mates, John?"

He said, "Oh, I had to show them the door – all that saying "peace" all the time, I couldn't get any fucking peace!"

Things like that. He'd always see a joke. He couldn't resist saying it. Now and again he would upset some people. But he'd still say it.

But mischief – well, when he sent his MBE back to Buckingham Palace, he rang me to tell me what he'd done. I'm thinking *oh crumbs,* "What did you say?"

He said, "In protest of the war in Vietnam, and that Cold Turkey's slipping down the charts."

And I said, "I'm not sure that's a good idea, you know, to put the two together."

He said, "Well, it's too fucking late now anyway. It's on its way."

He looked for a joke in things all the time. Which may have been a kind of nervousness, I'm not sure. Not knowing how safe he was on certain ground – he'd always make a joke.

AP: So he called you up to explain the MBE stuff, he let it be known to you that the Beatles were breaking up before that was going to go out. Your bond with John was quite substantial – what do you put that down to? Why was he drawn to you?

RC: Well, we were exactly same age. We came from the same part of the world. I know that Yoko liked me, we got on. And also, I could talk to him about rock. Most people covering the Beatles in those days were showbiz people, or people who weren't real fans.

One time we were in a car in Upstate New York. We were going along in this limousine, and John and I were singing all our old favorites — 'Ain't That a Shame', or 'That'll Be the Day' or whatever — the two of us, you know. And then we'd go — *if you knew, Peggy Sue...* and then we'd go to another one. Eventually I could see Yoko getting really bored with these two old rockers, going on about it. And suddenly John stopped. And I probably said, "How about one more — *think it over...*" One of those.

And John said, "You're not a fuckin' jukebox, Connolly."

He'd have to end it with a joke, you know?

What it is, you know: you're suddenly fifteen again. And it's just a mate singing the same songs. As we had. That's what it was. They were no longer big stars. They were *other fans.*

Now, the point is that all rock stars — they start off as fans. And they stay fans all their lives. Because once you're a fan, you can't *not* be a fan. Of a certain period. I mean, I'm not a fan of the Elvis films, but I'm a great fan of the early Sun recordings, and the early RCA ones, you know? And you stay a fan for life. And that takes you back immediately to the most impressionable time of your life, when you're fifteen, sixteen — when you get involved in these things. And so those were the times I remember, with John particularly. Talking, not about the Beatles — never about the Beatles. It's about what it was like to be fifteen or sixteen.

AP: I want to know — could you give me a kind of portrait of the very first time that you met John?

RC: I got this incredible job in London, as a feature writer and reporter, covering this area of music for the London *Evening Standard* – and virtually the first thing I'm asked to do is to get in my car and follow the *Magical Mystery Tour*. I didn't know anybody, and I found out where they were staying the very first night – down in Devon.

I go to the hotel, and I'd seen them at lunchtime where they'd stopped. And I thought – how do I get to know them? It's very difficult. So I'm down in Devon, and I go into the bar. And in the bar, everyone's there – John and George, probably Ringo – and all the journalists who knew them, who were mainly, virtually in their thirties. To me they seemed middle-aged. People who were on the *Daily Mirror* and *The Sketch* – those sorts of things. So I sit down at the back, near the door, and think *how do I get to know them? How do I break in?* And suddenly someone sits down in the chair next to me. And it's Paul McCartney. And I thought, *well I've got to say something! What am I going to say?*

"I know your dad," I said.

"Really?" And he wanted to know why.

"I know your Mike." And then he took me up.

I'd been a subeditor at the Liverpool *Daily Post* – a graduate trainee thing. And I'd interviewed Mike McCartney – Paul's brother. And I met his father, Jim McCartney, who was really a very, very nice man.

Over the next couple of days, Paul would be very nice to me. And I was scared of John, because he was meant to be quite fierce and frightening and all these things, and have a sharp tongue. And then bit by bit I'd go into Apple. I interviewed Paul first, I did a big interview with Paul at his house. It was when *Magical Mystery Tour* went on television. And I thought it was terrible, to be honest. And I rang him up. In those days, you couldn't ring a Beatle. I mean, you still can't. But anyway, I rang him up. I had his phone number – I don't know how I had it.

And his father answered: "Hello, Ray."

So I said, "I want to talk to your Paul, please." His father was staying with him over Christmas.

So his father said, "Oh, he's still asleep. I'll tell him you rang."

I said, "Well, what shall I do?"

He said, "Ring back a bit, later on." So I rang back in an hour's time. And he's still asleep. I was writing a big piece for the *Evening Standard* about *Magical Mystery Tour*, so – *I've got to get Paul.* So I rang a third time. On this occasion, Mr. McCartney said, "Listen, son. I'm going to go and wake him up for you." So he went upstairs, and he went into Paul's room and he said, "Listen, you've got to talk to Ray Connolly on the phone, from the *Evening Standard.*" He knew I was from Liverpool. And Paul gave me a front-page lead.

So we did that – and that sort of led me to Ringo. But I'm still nervous about John. Finally, Yoko gets involved – I want to interview her, and I go to Abbey Road where they're just mixing the *White Album*, and John is in with George Martin, mixing. Yoko's sitting outside with me – a very long interview. Very good. And then I sort of said hello to John, and he said "Hi! Alright. Everything okay?"

I said, "Everything's fine." And then I think they finished mixing 'Cry Baby Cry', and as they left, Paul turned up and took me into the band room there. He began to play me this new song he'd written, which is all about *Mother Mary come to me.* And I thought *this is a great song – like a hymn.* But he hadn't got all the words. He kept going, *speaking words of wisdom...* and then he hadn't finished it.

And I said, "Oh, this is good." But first of all, he played me 'Lawdy Miss Clawdy' and 'Money Honey', all those rock 'n' roll things he used to play. So that was quite a big night for me.

I don't know when it was, but I began to see more of John. And then the really big moment came when the stories about Paul being dead began going around in America. I got a phone call in the middle of the night – late in the evening anyway, from some US *Today Show*. They wanted to talk about *is Paul dead?* And I said, "He's not dead." And they said there was this story that Paul *is* dead. But I'd seen him at Apple all the time – in and out.

And then I wrote a big piece in the *Evening Standard* about how the Beatles weren't really playing much together anymore, since they stopped touring. And the subeditor put on it: *The Day the Beatles Died.* Well I hadn't quite said that. I'd implied it; that they weren't really together. And the next day, when I saw it in the paper, I thought *oh crumbs, I'm going to be in real trouble from the Apple lawyers.* And what happened instead was that on my desk that morning, was delivered a rose wrapped in cellophane with a message:

TO RAY, WITH LOVE FROM JOHN & YOKO

So I thought, *ah, I'm onto something. I've got it right.* So from that moment, John became my man on the inside.

AP: Would you describe him as charming?

RC: He could be extremely charming. He was incredibly articulate. He was well-mannered. All these things about him being this Liverpool scruff – it's all bollocks. He was no more working class than I was. He lived in a very nice semi-detached house near a golf club. So he wasn't working class. He'd been brought up very nicely to use knife and fork very well – all these things, you know – when he had to.

One example was when we were in New York together once, he and Yoko were going to go and look at an apartment in the Dakota building. This is before they lived there. And it wasn't the place they finally got. But he'd heard it was a great place to live. And I had a friend who lived there anyway, so I knew about it. So I say, "Oh, it's a very posh place, the Dakota."

So, being John, he got dressed up in a suit and tie. Because he knew he had to go and meet the social conservative people who ran the place, you know? They had a committee to make sure that no scruff got in. So Yoko came out in a pair of hot pants and a very low-cut blouse, and John went mad. I mean, he just went *mad*. It was really embarrassing. He said, "You can't go like that – you look fuckin' terrible, like a fuckin' whore." You know – awful. "Tell her, Ray – you've been there. You know what it's like. Tell her."

And you think *oh God. I don't want to get involved in this* – you know, in a marital row. Yoko didn't say a word. She didn't argue in front of me. I'm sure she did later. But she went back into the bedroom, got changed, came out in a long skirt. But he saw it as *they were going to be with smart people. I'm going to dress smartly. I'm going to do the social thing*, you know? He wasn't going to go as a sort of ranting anarchist.

AP: Speaking of anarchy – did he talk about politics with you at all?

RC: He talked about politics in those vague ways that people do who are not really following it that carefully. Obviously, he was against the war in Vietnam, but everybody *was* that we knew. Everybody. In America, the Beatles hadn't mentioned the Vietnam war, and they were embarrassed that they hadn't. They hadn't done it because they were told not to by Brian Epstein. But when they finished touring, they couldn't shut up about it. Everyone we knew felt the same way about that; it was those vague politics of protest. Mainly about the Vietnam war. And against the laws about marijuana. Where people he knew got locked up and things like that. He never discussed in any great detail. But what he liked – he liked to ally himself with students, and people who he thought were – I imagine – intellectually important.

When Robin Blackburn or Tariq Ali said *What should we do to start the revolution?* John didn't want to know. He'd never thought further than singing 'Power to the People'. Which is an easier thing to do. Or wearing a little sort of military uniform. But he got over that very quickly. He forgot all about that and went on to feminism. So there's this myth about John being this great rebel, but he wasn't. He wasn't a sort of political leader, *ever*. Obviously, he would be against the unfairness of the situation, just like you and me. But by no means – he was never a Marxist.

There's a very funny story about – by the time he died, he owned all these apartments in the Dakota building, one of which was stuffed with fur coats, refrigerated. And Neil Aspinall, who worked for the Beatles, whom he'd known since even before the beginning – even before they'd made a record, Neil had been with them. And he'd become the managing director of Apple. Neil goes over to see John, and he looks at all the fur coats and says, "Yeah, imagine no possessions, John."

And John said, "It's only a fuckin' song, you know."

• • •

To be fifteen again – where it all began for John. Sagging off school to listen to the old records with his mother, or at Michael Hill's house. Picking up a guitar for the first time. Forming the Quarrymen. He'd started out in music as a fan – a teenage kid set on Elvis Presley and Little Richard. He'd reconnected with his mother through these songs. Feeling fifteen again must have been a lovely escape from his Beatle reality.

At the end of 1969, the news of John's departure from the Beatles sat with Ray Connolly. Ray waited patiently for several months, checking in occasionally with John to find out when he could break the story. The answer was always *not yet*.

A lot was happening for John and Yoko. When they moved to Tittenhurst Park, they decided the time had come to kick their heroin habit. This was a much more difficult process than either of them expected.

John later publicly stated that he and Yoko got into heroin quite deliberately because they were feeling increasingly ostracized from the Beatles and from the outside world. They wanted some form of emotional shield – an attempt at self-medication. They were both hiding from significant, unresolved trauma in their lives. John's was family & loss trauma. Yoko's trauma stemmed largely from war and its aftermath. Seven years older than John, Yoko was twelve by the time the second world war ended. The Ono family lived in Tokyo throughout the extensive fire-bombing, and Yoko was old enough to be deeply affected by her experience of the horrors of war. In any case, heroin only added to their misery.

'Cold Turkey', John's withdrawal treatise, was recorded in September and released in October 1969. The Plastic

Ono band reconvened to record the track at Abbey Road two weeks after the Toronto festival. John had previously offered 'Cold Turkey' as a contender for *Abbey Road*, but Paul McCartney didn't like the idea of it as a Beatles song.

In November, the single inched up the UK charts to number fourteen, then began its decline. The following week, John chose his moment to send his MBE back to Buckingham Palace.

To close out the year – through the Christmas period, 1969 – John and Yoko purchased billboard space in eleven cities around the world:

WAR IS OVER!

IF YOU WANT IT

Happy Christmas from John & Yoko

Over the new year into 1970, John and Yoko spent time in Denmark with Yoko's former husband, Tony Cox, and Yoko and Tony's daughter Kyoko. Cox was interested in alternative philosophies and was espousing a new concept called *instant karma*. John loved the idea as a social commentary and quickly turned it into his next single. George Harrison played on the track and suggested that his producer friend Phil Spector come along – Phil was slated to produce George's first solo album later in the year. True to its name, 'Instant Karma' was written, recorded, and released to stores in just ten days. By February it was a major top ten hit around the world.

But then in April 1970, in a press release for the new *McCartney* solo album, Paul stated that he and John had no further plans to write music together. The press ran with it – PAUL QUITS BEATLES. Ray Connolly – and John – had been scooped.

DAN RICHTER
TITTENHURST PARK

THE RELEASE of the *Let It Be* album and film quickly followed Paul's break-up announcement. The documentary provided fly-on-the-wall access for cinema audiences to witness the group's acrimonious recording sessions. The fractured relationships within the Beatles were suddenly brought into the public sphere – they were imploding in the most public way.

Amid the recording chaos back in early 1969, the *Get Back/Let It Be* tapes had been abandoned. George and John had brought Phil Spector in to salvage the project in early 1970. Phil sorted through the hours of tapes and added orchestral arrangements. George and John liked Phil's work. Paul McCartney did not. Paul didn't even know about the changes until it was too late. EMI removed George Martin's name from the sleeve, even though he had produced the original recordings. George Martin asked why this was the case, and EMI explained that he hadn't produced the final product. George suggested the label should read: *Produced by George Martin – Over-Produced by Phil Spector.*

John and Yoko went into therapy soon after the release of *Let It Be*. They spent several months of 1970 in London and Los Angeles with the American psychotherapist Arthur Janov, undergoing his experimental treatment, 'Primal

Therapy'. Out of this period of intense and difficult focus on childhood trauma – and heroin withdrawal – came much of the material for the next album, *John Lennon/ Plastic Ono Band*. It features some of John's most personal, introspective songs: 'Mother', 'Working Class Hero', 'Isolation', 'Love'. In a 1970 interview, John told Ray Connolly that the treatment required him to unpack his past and encouraged him to write about the most important incidents in his personal history. By comparison, he explained to Ray, many of his early attempts at writing poetry were 'gobbledegook': "Because I was hiding it from Mimi, or perhaps hiding my emotions from myself."

John and Yoko produced the album in London with the help of Phil Spector. Yoko simultaneously prepared material for her own album, *Yoko Ono/Plastic Ono Band*. They were released concurrently in December 1970. John had just turned 30 in October.

Paul McCartney filed a lawsuit against the other Beatles on December 31st. He was only able to exit the Beatles' partnership – and Allen Klein's business management – through legal action. In March 1971 the judge ruled in his favor and the Beatles' associated companies were placed in receivership. This created a legal minefield which effectively locked away the rapidly accruing monies from Beatle recording and publishing royalties. It would be another four years before a final settlement could be reached.

Throughout this period, Dan Richter was a major part of John's life – and Yoko's. Dan had first met Yoko in Japan in 1964, and by 1967 his family was living opposite Yoko and Tony Cox in their spacious London apartment building. At this time, Dan was working with Stanley Kubrick on the film *2001: A Space Odyssey*. Dan was a professional mime and Kubrick hired him to choreograph the film's unforgettable 'Dawn of Man' sequence. He also played the lead ape character in the film. Dan subsequently enjoyed a career in Hollywood as a studio executive.

When John and Yoko bought the mansion at Tittenhurst Park they invited Dan and his family to move into one of the other houses on the property. The two families lived in tandem during the making of *Imagine*, and later spent a considerable time together in the US as well. The Richter/Lennon families shared much with each other and Dan became indispensable in the lives of John and Yoko. Dan saw John in unfiltered light, away from the music industry and away from the seething throngs of fans. John's singular persona – as a non-Beatle – was being redefined.

While John and Yoko were in Los Angeles with Arthur Janov, they asked Dan Richter to supervise the installation of a state-of-the-art recording studio into the basement of Tittenhurst Park. When they returned in late 1970, John christened it Ascot Sound Studios – otherwise known as ASS. It was here that they started work on *Imagine*.

DAN RICHTER: I first met Yoko in Tokyo in the spring of '64. I was studying the Noh theatre – basically coming out of a mime discipline. I was stuck in Tokyo with no money and I was doing street theatre to support myself. A fellow I had met on a boat, Jed Curtis, had done some performances with Yoko and he said, "You and Yoko will love each other. You've got to meet each other." So he introduced me to Yoko, and Yoko and I became friends.

Later, when I was working for Stanley Kubrick in London, she turned up on a grant to do a series of performances on destruction in art, and we got together again. And we ended up getting apartments side by side. We took over a floor.

Later, John became her patron. They became involved

and he started coming around. I was between projects, and I was a little bit down-and-out. I was trying to get another film job. And Yoko and John had just bought the Tittenhurst estate. Yoko was being treated terribly by everybody at the Apple office and everybody associated with the Beatles. I mean, they basically were *after* her – so she wanted some of her friends around to back her up a bit, to give her some cover. And so she invited my wife Jill and I, and our baby Sasha, to come out and live with them on the estate. So we said *sure, that sounds great.* Because – you know – they'd provide a car to go in and out of town and whatnot. They had more money than God.

Their assistant at the time, Anthony Fawcett – he had stopped working for them; Yoko wanted me to work for them. She said, "I know you're an artist, but can you help us out?" So – short term I said yes. And then I got sucked in, so I ended up living at Tittenhurst for three-and-a-half, four years. By the time they left, I was so involved in their life. It was like a monster – a gigantic baby you could never feed enough. It just wanted more. And so, I would fly to New York every week to meet with them and to take care of things and to make sure everything was cool. So I kept on working for them.

Finally, when they moved to the Dakota, which I guess was around '73, beginning of '74 – something like that – they wanted to shut down all their film business and whatnot so that Nixon might let them stay – to send the signal that they might stop being political and stop meeting with Jerry Rubin and Abbie Hoffman and all these people and trying to overthrow the world.

They were making films – a John Sinclair film and a number of political things. I was pretty much supervising all of that, and I was making a film – and they shut it all down. They wanted me to stay in England and look after their affairs there. They wanted to buy me a house, blah blah blah. And I said, "You know, I'll make it easy for you: Go fuck yourself." And I left. But we remained friends. And Jill and Yoko remained very close and still are to this day.

So anyway, I'm this guy where if John asked me what I thought, I would tell him what I thought. I wouldn't try to figure out what he wanted me to say so I could suck up to him and get closer. So he used me as a sounding board a lot of the time. I was in a unique position in that I hadn't wanted to be there in the first place. I'm not a rock 'n' roll person. I certainly appreciate it, but my tastes went more to Bob Dylan and folk music, jazz and classical music, things like that. I was more Yoko's friend – I knew more about the arts, and the people in the arts and my contact with the people in the art scene. 'Cos most of John's friends were the rock 'n' roll people.

John pretty much wanted to get away from the rock 'n' roll world. He wanted to break the Beatles thing, which he felt – again – was like this giant baby that you couldn't feed enough. You know, it was just devouring him. And in order to be free of that, he wanted to get away from a lot of the rock 'n' roll associations. So he would rather meet with Andy Warhol or Miles Davis; people like that.

AIDAN PREWETT: You must have been there when certain hits were written. Do you remember any of those?

DR: Well, yeah – 'Imagine'. I heard bits and pieces of the song – I had no idea. *No* idea. I mean, we recorded the album in – I don't know – five days or something. We had built a studio at Ascot. In the morning I'd look at the mail and stuff that came in and try to get through it, 'cos there was so much stuff. We had an office there with secretary Diana Robertson and a couple of assistants. We'd go through stuff that was coming at us all the time. And I'd try to make enough sense of it. So once I knew that the breakfast had gone up and they'd probably had half an hour, I'd go up and knock on the door and say, "Hi guys, do you mind if I come in?" They'd say *yeah come on in* or whatever. I'd say, "I just want to bring you up to speed on some stuff…" And we'd talk.

On this particular morning, John said to me, "I'm going to record tonight."

I said, "I'm not sure the studio's ready, John."

He said, "I don't care if it's ready or not, I'm recording tonight. I'll call Mr. Harrison, and you call everybody else, and lets all meet at nine o'clock, ten o'clock tonight." They always liked to record at night. So we went nuts that day trying to get everything ready – get the studio ready – I'm lying on my back with a soldering iron, making the last connections in the board. And John turned up; some of the guys were there. Klaus Voorman showed up first. Alan White was there 'cos Ringo wasn't available. I forget who was the keyboardist – it wasn't Nicky Hopkins that first night. Anyway, the guys were showing up. John came down – Phil Spector of course hadn't turned up yet. And George, who was supposed to do lead guitar that night hadn't turned up yet.

So John said, "Alright guys, we can at least do some of the backing tracks and whatnot." And they just *started*. He not only had all the songs in his head, he had all the arrangements in his head. He knew all the parts. He knew what the bass had to do. So he would say to Klaus, "Okay, I want you to go *dom dom dom boom*, here, and when I do this on the rhythm guitar, you're gonna go to *ba dee dom*

bom, ba dee dom bom. "You know, he had it all worked out.
Every bit of it.

And they just started laying down backing tracks, and
then suddenly there's a ring at the front door, and I figured
it was probably George or Phil. So I went out, and it was
George Harrison, and he's all sheepish and shy. And he's
nervous – one thing about people who are great musicians
and performers is that they're always nervous before they
go on because they have such high standards to live up to.
You know what I mean? If you've made major hits all your
life, every time you go out, you're scared you may not pull
it off; that you can't do it anymore.

So anyway, George says, "Listen – I don't want to go in
right now. Is there a room I can just go and an amp so I can
just warm up on?" I said *sure, no problem*, and he took his
guitar into the dining room and some guys brought him an
amp. And then soon he wandered in and it was *hi – what's
up man?*

"Okay, we've already laid down these backing tracks
here…" And it just progressed. And Phil Spector, who
was producing it, hadn't even turned up. And suddenly at
about one in the morning, a limo pulls up and it's Phil and
Dennis Hopper – who's passed out. Phil instantly sobers
up, sits down behind the board and it's like he – he just
knew what to do, he just synched up with what John was
doing. And the songs just came out. And Yoko had musical
paper – staff paper – and so she's writing everything down
because she actually had some education and knew how to
write music and stuff. And we just made *Imagine*. It just
took a few days. And meanwhile we're shooting everything.
We had a film crew there.

I'd heard bits and pieces of the songs. But there was
one song – I remember it later became that bit *love is the*

answer... I think it was in 'Mind Games'. And that riff – I heard that one riff *da, da, da da da* – I heard that for two years. Every time we'd be walking down a hallway backstage someplace and past a piano, John would stop and – *love is the answer*. You know – he was trying to fit it in. He could never get it into anything. But finally he got it into 'Mind Games'. So he had all these pieces going in his head.

Can you imagine not only writing a piece of music, but understanding the orchestration of it – what all the parts are doing. You listen to so much of his work – the things work because the bass is doing *this,* or the drums are doing *this*. You know what I mean? It's just so good.

AP: With Phil Spector – with everything that happened with Phil in years to come, was there any inkling then that something was wrong?

DR: Oh yeah. Oh, he was bat-shit crazy – to use a technical term. He was nuts. He had guns and things like this. He had a guy, an ex-cop I think, or an FBI guy – some guy named George, in a black suit with a tie, who was there just to try to keep him from going too crazy. He was like his security guy. Phil was just crazy.

We were doing a concert at Madison Square Garden in New York; it was a fundraiser for the One to One Foundation that this crazy television news guy Geraldo Rivera was putting together. One of his breakout moments was that he had snuck into a hospital over on Staten Island or something, where they were keeping disabled people in really terrible conditions. He had founded the One to One Foundation as a fundraising organization for these people, and he had talked John and Yoko into doing a fundraiser at the Garden. And we had sold the idea to ABC television, so it was also going to be a television show. We had a bunch of cameras there – a *bunch*. We mic'd everything separate to the PA system, so we could get voices clean and each instrument clean, and we wired them all back to a truck – a recording truck that had a multi-track recorder in it. The whole idea was that Phil was supposed to produce the music.

So here we are, and I'm supposedly running all of this – I'm the poor bastard in charge of everything. So I'm backstage, the concert's going on and all these guest artists – Stevie Wonder and Melanie all these people – and John and Yoko are up on stage, we're nearing the finale. And Sha Na Na, this band that played stuff from the '50s, rock 'n' roll, wearing zoot suits and cool clothing... So anyway, I'm over by the recording vehicle, and Phil's not in there. So I say, "Phil, aren't you supposed to be in the fuckin' vehicle listening to the music and figuring out what to do?"

He said, "No, no, no – they'll just get it raw and I'll deal with it later."

At this time, George McGovern was running for President, and his wife was there as a guest of the mayor. So the Secret Service was there, and some FBI guys were there because they were watching John and Yoko. It's creepy. They're all backstage. So Phil starts shouting at one of these guys: "You fuckin' sons of bitches, you're real bastards." And he tries to take a swing at one of these Secret Service guys. And of course they grab him – as they do with people like that. So, all of our roadies were these big monsters with beards and ripped t-shirts and muscles and whatnot. They jump in and this mêlée breaks out – everybody fighting. So I figure my job is to protect Phil. He's bat-shit crazy but I'm gonna protect him anyway. So I grab him by the scruff of the neck and the back of his belt, and drag him up to the stage and throw him on stage – because I figure the Secret

Service guys won't go on stage. He whirls around – he sees an empty keyboard; he sits at it and starts playing. So that's the life I was living.

AP: So in amongst all of this – a question I've asked myself so many times – what was it that made John keep going back to Phil Spector in subsequent years, all the way through to *Rock 'n' Roll*?

DR: Well, Phil *is* a genius. Like most geniuses – just because you're a genius doesn't mean you have to have any other good qualities. You know what I mean? He's in jail now. He murdered a woman. But he was a great producer. The thing about Phil is, he created the Wall of Sound. He also – early on – understood that 95% of the rock 'n' roll that was being made was being listened to through a little car speaker with two kids necking. So he filled that space. He understood that the highs and the lows that were being picked up by expensive stereo systems – most of the audience wasn't going to hear that. In fact, when we were mixing, he would say, "You got a car speaker?" We got a car speaker which we set up on top of the board, and we could channel the mixes back through the car speaker, so you could listen to it the way the kids would hear it.

In those days, he was walking around with a button that said **BACK TO MONO**. He didn't like stereo. But he was brilliant. He could see *there's an empty space in here* – and then he'd put in a tambourine or a maraca or something just to fill that sound. Because if it was down in a range that was being used already, you wouldn't hear it. So that was one of the ways he created the wall of sound. And also – he'd do things like in the *Plastic Ono Band* recordings, there were two drums and two pianos. He'd double up on instruments. He knew what he was doing; he was a great producer.

It's just like the Stones, their best stuff is with Jimmy Miller, who did 'Sister Morphine' and 'You Can't Always Get What You Want'. That's great stuff, but that's the result of a producer. In fact, most music today − as far as I can make out − the producer is almost more important than some of the artists. Especially with sampling and all this other stuff.

AP: Is there one particular moment you experienced with John that has really stuck with you over the years?

DR: The thing with John, like all very famous people... he was more than famous. I mean, he was at the top of the heap. Now, this means that the reality around him was distorted by his presence. What that means is: Imagine you're John Lennon. You're looking out through his eyes. The whole world is looking at *you*. Every face is in adulation; is drooling, almost. It doesn't matter what you say, they're going to say *yes*. And all of them are going to want something from you. So this is this world where these poor people who are that famous have to live. And it affects all of them. I've known a number of very famous people in my life, and it's this distortion that they suffer from − it really dominates their life. They can't trust anybody. They can't trust their banker; they can't trust whoever is in the bed beside them. They just can't trust anybody because what's going on is so much bigger than everything else. It colors and distorts everything.

So you get these moments where that goes away. The façade melts for a moment. And I had that a couple of times with John. I remember those, because I was with − sort of − the real guy.

One that I remember pretty well: Yoko had a daughter, Kyoko, with her second husband, Tony Cox. Tony was pretty much a hustler – he had hustled *for* Yoko, when they were together. Yoko would want to wrap up a lion in Trafalgar square and do exotic performance pieces, and he'd hustle to make it happen. So she needed him. And once she and John fell in love – and they *really* fell in love. It was like *Romeo & Juliet* – she could have anything she wanted. She wanted to cut a car in half: *okay, we'll buy a car and we'll cut it in half.*

So Tony Cox not only lost his wife, but he had lost, almost, his purpose. Because he wasn't needed by her any longer. And the fact that he had been a hustler, he had run up a number of dubious debts and other things. And he was stuck with them. And John and Yoko pretty much took care of things for him and straightened things out. But he didn't want to give up control. And the last thing he had that was a source of control was Kyoko. So he started disappearing with Kyoko and going off places – to a commune in Scandinavia, you know. And Yoko would follow with John. She didn't want to give up custody of her daughter. Once custody battles started, she would either win custody or have joint custody – because Tony was going nuts and running away.

So anyway – he had disappeared, and we found that he was in a commune down in Majorca, with a bunch of the Maharishi's people who had taken over a hotel complex that was partially finished. And Kyoko was there. John wouldn't let Yoko go out there alone, so John and I drove Yoko out there. They said to Yoko, *"Okay – go to this particular room and we'll contact you when you get there."* So we drove her out, and the three of us snuck into the room. And as the people knocked on the door, John and I climbed inside this closet and hid. Some people came and took Yoko, and the Maharishi's people sat down in the room. So we had to remain in hiding. And so we spent a couple of hours stuck inside this closet.

AP: Wow.

DR: Yeah, it was really weird. Now – the point is this: You reach a certain point. You can't be in a closet with somebody, trying to not let anybody know you're there – with a bunch of crazy people outside… What happens is – suddenly it was just me and this guy in a closet, hoping we wouldn't get caught. You know what I mean? And John was a funny guy. He had a tremendous sense of humor. Like many very intelligent people, he could see the humor in everything. And he loved to play practical jokes. So we're giggling, and we're trying not to let them hear us. And the longer we're trying not to let them hear us, the more we wanted to laugh. So that was probably the first time that I got close to John, and that sort of opened the door. And I think he started trusting me more. 'Cos he realized I really didn't want anything from him.

So anyway, Yoko came back, and we climbed out of the closet and we went back to the hotel in Palma. We had figured out that during the day Kyoko was in this daycare center. And we knew where it was. And we also knew – Yoko's pretty smart – we figured out what their schedule was, and that Kyoko would be outside playing with the kids between 10 and 11am, or whenever it was. So we got in touch with the British Consul. Yoko had legal custody of Kyoko, so they said, "You should have no problem if you want to pick her up. She's your daughter and you have custody – you can do it."

So the three of us drive out there. I'm driving – they're

in the back seat. I pull up to the daycare center. Yoko gets out, picks up Kyoko, puts her in the back seat of the car and we drive away. Soon, there's a roadblock. Tony's called the police. So they hide under a blanket in the back seat and we just drive – a big smile on my face, and we drive through. We get to Palma and we get to the hotel. Kyoko doesn't have any shoes. So I drop John and Yoko off at the hotel, and I said to John, "Don't open the door to anybody. Call the British Consul, have his representative come over – and I'll go get some shoes for Kyoko." So I went and got some shoes, and I came back – the lobby was full of the Guardia Civil or whatever they're called – guys with guns; stooges with suits. So I called the room. John answers.

I say, "The place is crawling with fuzz."

He says, "I know, they're already in the room." *Click.*

So they busted them and took them down to the police station. And I followed. They wouldn't let me talk to them. I said I wanted a lawyer in there. *"No, no, no – we're just talking."* Anyway, we finally got him out in the middle of the night.

Tony Cox came out and was absolutely nuts. *"I've got John by the balls, this is going to cost him millions..."* Awful. Just awful. So we got back to the hotel. In the morning we were meeting with lawyers. I bought tickets for Mr. and Mrs. Smith and friend. You could do it in those days – on about five different flights out of Palma to places like Paris, Rome, and whatnot. So that nobody would quite know what was going on. We got in the car down to the airport, and the three of us are walking in.

Suddenly a guy comes running up: *"Mr. Lennon! Mr. Lennon!"* Oh shit. Here we go.

I jump in front and go, "No, no, no – this is Mr. and Mrs. Smith. My name's Dan."

They said, "No, no. That's John Lennon."

I said, "No – this is Mr. Smith."

He says, "No, that's John Lennon. Follow me." So we start walking. He takes us into a back room with a couch; it's very comfortable. He says, "You'll be safe here 'til the flight leaves. People won't bother you."

AP: Thank God.

DR: So we got on a plane to Paris. They put us on beforehand. I said to the stewardess, "Do you have a bottle of champagne we could buy?" We're sitting up in the first class.

She said, "Yeah – you can't open it 'til after we take off."

I said, "We don't want to."

As we took off, we opened the champagne. We knew we were outta there. I remember John saying, "What do we do next?"

I said, "Let's go to the hotel in Paris and we can talk about things."

But also that morning, Allen Klein had sent Peter Brown in a chartered plane, and Peter and I had given a press conference. So here I am giving a press conference and representing them, and I wasn't working for them. You know – I'm refusing to work for them. I'm refusing to take any money. I said, "The minute I start taking money I'll be like all the rest of the toadies, you know?"

I remember on our way down to the car to the airport, John says to me, "Are you crazy? You've got to work for us. I mean, you're representing us at press conferences and things like that." So I agreed to it. And then it got ridiculous. He had this power over me at this point.

He said, "Well, if you're going to work for me, I want to get you some nice clothes."

I said, "John, for Christ's sake…" And he started pulling out all this clothing. He had all this stuff. People would send him things; people would make him things. There was a group of designers led by Simon Posthuma and a group of Dutch designers called The Fool, and they had made all the clothing for the Apple boutique.

John had said, "I want a coat with hundreds of pockets so I can hide things. I want pockets inside pockets. I want pockets hidden in seams." So they made him this coat. It was like a frock coat. It was all different colors of velvet, with silk linings. It was just gorgeous. Very exotic. So he said, "Okay, how about this?"

I said, "I can't walk around like this."

And he'd pull out beautiful silk shirts and all this stuff.

And then we would play games. We would play one game when we were down at the Cannes Film Festival. We were trying to find – *who could find the biggest ash tray?* They were being interviewed by Al Aronowitz or one of the music guys, and John had bought me this big pink jacket… it was just ridiculous. I saw this *big* ashtray. So I put it under the jacket and I walked out where they could see me. And I opened my jacket so they could see the ashtray. John said, "Uh, Al – could you excuse me for a second? I think I have to go to the bathroom. Can we just cut here, and start again?" He disappeared for about ten minutes. He came back with a bigger ashtray and handed it to me. So that's John. We played. He was like a puppy sometimes. There's a photo somebody sent me of him doing this crazy almost-like-a-duck walk; him, me, and Yoko walking through Cannes and John is goofing off. We were just playing all the time.

AP: Do you remember any specific practical joke that John would play?

DR: You know, I don't remember – they weren't so much practical jokes as horsing around. Making faces when somebody's trying to be serious – trying to throw you all off, that kind of stuff. The way he made up words – we'd fall into that. He'd always have a name for me, and for the life of me I can't remember specifics of it, it was so long ago and there were so many drugs involved. It's hard to remember a lot of that.

AP: Let's just say there's a quiet moment – it's just you and John, there's time available to kick back. What do you talk about?

DR: It could be anything, Aidan. We could be talking about Andy Warhol's work, or where to get the best pair of cowboy boots in New York. *Where did you get those shirts?* Do you think Leonardo was gay? I don't know. Just *stuff*. The thing is – you could talk about *anything*. It's not so much the stuff you're talking about, it's the fact that you're with a friend. And you're just letting stuff come out. Gently; easy flow; the give-and-take that you have as you talk about the things that happened today. *Remember this guy? Or that guy? Or this thing that happened? Or that thing that happened?*

I mean, John would periodically – one of the things he had with me, he said – after that thing in Majorca with the cops and us getting out of the country and whatnot – and me finally agreeing to formally work for them – he said, "You don't know enough about rock 'n' roll."

I said, "I know rock 'n' roll. Little Richard and things like this..."

He said, "No, no. Do you know who Rosie and the Originals are?"

"No, I don't know Rosie and the Originals."

"Okay," he says. He bought this old jukebox – a Wurlitzer. We got it in New York. He said, "Your job is to fill it up with all the greatest 45s in the history of rock 'n' roll. All the *original* stuff." Not the later stuff after the British invasion, the real down-home early stuff. And then he would say, "You know what the key to rock 'n' roll is? It's because they could only hear that middle range. Suddenly, the rhythm guitar became much more important than it ever was. Because it's right in the middle of that middle range. That's how important it is. So the rhythm guitar is at the soul of rock 'n' roll. And it's true. When you look at the Stones and look at Keith Richards. He's not playing the lead. The lead guitar isn't the most important guitarist there. And John, of course – the rhythm guitar of the Beatles. If you listen to all the Beatles stuff, the rhythm guitar is setting up *so much* on all the songs. So those are the kinds of things we would talk about.

AP: When the façade melted with John – do you remember perhaps what he said during any of those moments?

DR: Yeah. I think the last time I saw him was a year or so before he died. I had gone up the Dakota so many times when he wasn't there, to see Yoko for something and he just didn't happen to be there, or maybe he was off with May or something. So this was the actual last time I saw him. He was in the middle of a lawsuit with Allen Klein. The first thing – when I left John I got a call from Allen Klein saying, "*You gotta work for me, now that you're not working for John – and I'll pay you a lot of money.*"

I said, "Allen, I can't do that. The reason you'd pay me a lot of money is because you and John are going to be suing each other and you want dirt on him. And I can't do that. I wouldn't do it to you, and I can't do it to him. I don't want to get involved in that."

So anyway, further down the line, I'd gotten a grant to go back to the American Mime Theater. I was trying to go back to my roots and get pure again, etcetera etcetera. This attorney turns up – this young woman in a pinstripe suit – and says, "I represent John. We have a bunch of papers we'd like you to look at and see if there's anything in them that you think might be incriminating for Allen."

I said, "Well, there won't be anything in there, but I'll look at them." So I look at all these papers. There's nothing in there.

So they say, "Okay, can you come up for a meeting with the attorneys?" I said sure. So they sent a limo down and a guy to pick up the boxes. I go up there. They line up all the boxes in the middle of a conference table. I walk in there. There's more attorneys – at least ten or fifteen of them. And there at the end of the table, quite dramatically backlit by a big open glass window – we're forty stories up or something – is John, singing 'Danny Boy'.

So I walk in and he says, "Well, it's about time you turned up," or something like that.

I said, "I was hoping you'd be here."

He said, "Dan, is there anything here we can use against Allen?"

I said, "No, I told them there wouldn't be, John."

He said, "I didn't think there would be. They said we had to ask you."

So he then turned to one of the head attorneys and said, "Is there somewhere where Dan and I can go talk, without people around?" They said yes, and they got us a room, this little side office someplace. And we went in that room, and suddenly John stopped being John Lennon and turned into *John*.

We sort of made an awkward hug and he said, "How're ya doin'?"

I said, "I'm doing okay, how about you?"

"Yeah, I can't complain. Everything's okay." And he asked after Jill, we went through the *how's all the family members?* kind of thing. We talked for a while, just like old friends. He wasn't like John Lennon at that point. It was just John.

I had a white button. He had done a show at the Robert Fraser Gallery – it was kinda the first art show he'd done. I think *This is Not Here* was the show, where he'd been influenced by Yoko. And he had these buttons that had nothing on them. Just a plain white button. And I was wearing one of them.

He said, "Wow – I'd forgotten all about those. I never kept one!" So I said, "Well, why don't you take this one, then?"

He said, "No, no, no – that's yours, I can't do that."

I said, "Yeah you can – it's your creation. You should have *one* of them. Come on – take it, man." So I gave him the button and he put it on.

Then he said, "I guess we've got to go back out again." And almost – you could see he was just like – *I've gotta go back, I've gotta be John Lennon again.* And then he did something that I'd seen him do so many times before he stepped through a door where people were going to be looking at him or he knew there were going to be photographers. He reached up to adjust the front of his hair. You know – the little bang area, over the forehead. He always did that – the minute he knew he had to be seen, he'd do that. And literally, before my eyes, he changed into John

Lennon again, and we walked out. And that was the last time I ever saw him.

To become that successful, you have to sacrifice a lot. Not only do you have to sacrifice a lot, you have to be *prepared* to sacrifice a lot. Because you consciously have to know *I'm giving up something.* You have to be driven – and sometimes you have to turn your back on people you love , because they just can't go on the trip with you. And the trip is going to be over if you don't let go of them. And a lot of people can't do that. So you pay a tremendous price. And he paid it.

But he was still this funny, bright, really intelligent, really funny, ridiculously creative guy from Liverpool. The music was just coming out of him all the time. He was writing music all the time. On the back seat of the limo. On the plane. Endlessly in his bed. Sitting in his bed, smoking dope with a guitar, watching television because it was one of the only ways he could actually see the world without being attacked. It reminded me of when I heard about Mozart who couldn't write it down fast enough because the music was just coming out so fast. John was like that. He had this gift; it was there all the time. And it was always original.

AP: Dan, is there anything I've missed? Is there anything about John that people should know, that maybe they don't know?

DR: Well, in spite of the fact that he was one of the great geniuses of the 20th century, he had almost an awkwardness about him. Almost like he didn't know how to move. He didn't know how – everything, he did his own way. Not the way other people do it. He saw things in his own way. He had his own vision all the time, and it's not something – he didn't say, "I want to have my own vision." He *had* his own vision. It dominated. It wasn't something he was trying to get or develop. It was almost a burden he had to carry. And he just saw things uniquely. And it turns out that his vision was pretty good.

You have to remember, a lot of the things he said and talked about and did, back when he did it, people would say, "What the fuck are you talking about?" And he's proven to be – when we were doing those first recordings that he and Yoko were doing, people were calling me up from the Apple office all the time: "You've got to tell them to stop doing this shit. Tell them they can't do this – they're not only destroying the Beatles, they're destroying themselves." But they weren't, you know? They weren't.

I saw Yoko last spring, there was a concert at Walt Disney Concert Hall, where the stars were singing her music. It was a magnificent evening – a standing ovation for everything. I went backstage after, and her friend and press agent Elliot Mintz got us some time alone together before all the people got in. And we were sitting there just holding each other's hands and looking at each other. We both started crying. I said, "We've come a long way. You made it, Yoko."

She said, "I know – I couldn't stop crying all through the evening." 'Cos you just don't know what she went through. And John believed in her from the very beginning. Because she gave him so much. Everybody says *oh, she got money from him, he legitimized her* – I think she gave him more than he gave her.

• • •

Dan Richter found himself uniquely positioned during an extraordinary period of music history. His front-row seat provided full access to some of the most incredible moments of John's career, from his earliest days with Yoko to the recording of *Imagine* to the *One to One* concert at Madison Square Garden. And through it all, John was besieged by the onslaught of the outside world: everybody wanted a piece. The very world around John seemed to warp in his presence.

But Dan Richter wasn't interested in celebrity. When John recognized this, he accepted and welcomed Dan into his life. And John loved to play – but the shutters had to go back up, as they did each time he had to step outside and again become John Lennon.

KIERON MURPHY

IMAGINE

IN MAY 1971, John launched himself into the recording of *Imagine*. He assembled the written material for the songs and gathered his musicians at Tittenhurst Park. With his studio-at-home, John was able to teach the band his arrangements and get straight to recording. Phil Spector was brought in again as co-producer, along with George Harrison's lead guitar, Klaus Voorman's bass, Nicky Hopkins' keyboards, and drums from Andy White and Jim Keltner.

John filtered much of his resentment toward Paul McCartney into the new album. The track 'How Do You Sleep' is a direct dig at his former bandmate. 'Imagine' itself sprang from words in Yoko's book *Grapefruit*, where she wrote, '*Imagine the clouds dripping. Dig a hole in your garden to put them in*'. These words also feature on the album's back cover. John later said he regretted not crediting Yoko as co-writer on the title track. Yoko took polaroid pictures of John which feature on the front and back cover; he stares upward at the sky.

Witnessing the first session of recordings for the new album was a young photographer called Kieron 'Spud' Murphy. John took a liking to him and invited him back to be one of the first members of the public to hear the album.

John wanted to hear Kieron's feedback. It was on this second visit that Kieron Murphy captured one of the most enduring images of John: light streaming from behind, hands clasped in front of him, a pensive expression, and sunglasses. This image became the cover art for the album *Lennon Legend* in the 1990s.

Kieron Murphy started his photography career in Dublin in 1968, photographing bands and musician friends like Henry McCulloch, later of Joe Cocker's Grease Band and Paul McCartney's Wings. With a growing reputation, Kieron quickly moved to London and took up a photography position with *Sounds* magazine. Over the years he has worked with Rod Stewart, the Rolling Stones, Carly Simon, Joe Cocker, and Marc Bolan among many others. But upon arrival at *Sounds*, one of his first assignments was to photograph recording sessions for *Imagine*.

KIERON MURPHY: Tittenhurst Park had a kind of gravel car park at the front of the house. The house is very near the road, which wasn't very busy – there wasn't a big long driveway. It was on a country road, in deepest leafy Surrey. The house doesn't look as big from the front as what you see in all the films. That's actually the back of the house – it looks ten times bigger. From the front it just looks like a very nice Georgian country house. But not like a rock star mansion.

I was brought into the kitchen where there were a bunch of people milling around. John and Yoko weren't there yet; they were still getting out of bed even though it was five o'clock in the afternoon. They tended to stay up working all night and to sleep during the day. I just sat around talking to some people for a few minutes. And then John and Yoko appeared down this spiral staircase into the kitchen. I remember metaphorically – or actually – holding my breath when John and Yoko descended.

They seemed to suddenly appear in the room. They didn't seem to walk in; suddenly they were there. *A puff of blue smoke* and there they are. They both looked like they just got out of bed. John was very scruffy. He hadn't had a shave for days. His hair was all over the place. He looked like he needed a shower very badly. But he was already *on* – let's have a cup of coffee and breakfast and get started. We all sat there for half an hour or whatever it was, until Phil Spector wanted to make a start. I remember being in the kitchen, because I drew breath and sort of sat down and had a coffee that someone made.

When you see the film *Above Us Only Sky*, which is obviously a much fuller picture than I got at the time – I recalled when watching the film – he was right in the middle of a massive creative process. And I just happened to glance into it for a few hours. I realized what a privilege it was. In retrospect, I recognize it now. And being older, and what he's going through, putting an album together. I found it very moving watching – in film – watching him teaching all the songs. 'Cos that's what he was doing when I was there.

AIDAN PREWETT: And then you started taking pictures.

KM: The first time I was there, I didn't know if I'd even get five minutes with them. I ended up being there for about eight hours. But I thought *this could end at any moment. I can't go back to the editor of Sounds empty handed.* So I just literally – after the initial formalities of getting introduced and so on, I said, "Do you mind if I start taking pictures now?"

John said, "Fine." And he happened to be eating his breakfast.

Looking back now, it looks very intrusive, actually. But the first ten pictures or so are him eating his breakfast, drinking coffee, drinking a glass of milk. But looking back at it I thought, *Murphy, that's a bit cheeky, photographing the man having his breakfast.* But it didn't bother him. He'd had cameras pointed up his nose for so long it didn't bother him at all. The next thing – I look around and I'm sitting beside George Harrison, who had just materialized. And it was like, *what the fuck?* You know? I'm now sitting at a breakfast table with two ex-Beatles. Alright – I can die now. *Lord, take me now. It doesn't get any better than this.*

AP: Do you remember anything they said to each other at this juncture?

KM: No – looking back on it, I was so focused on getting the pictures, I was really *in the zone.* Partly because of time pressure. They might say at any moment, *that's it, everybody out now.* So I was gobsmacked when John said, "Do you want to come into the studio and have a listen?" Uh, is the Pope a Catholic? "Yes – that might be nice, actually, thank you very much." That was just mind-blowing to hear him playing and singing. Playing that famous old white Epiphone. Which I assume – I never asked him, but I assume it was the one that he played at the last concert on the rooftop of Apple. So it was all very emotionally laden.

AP: Do you recall what piece they were playing – or were you shooting and they were recording all kinds of different stuff?

KM: They were only working on one song while I was there, which was 'How Do You Sleep'.

AP: Wow.

KM: I know!

AP: So you're there with two ex-Beatles, singing about another ex-Beatle.

KM: Yes – because it was a studio setup, they were all listening on headphones, so they could all hear each other through the mics. And the people in the control room could hear what Lennon was singing. But because I was in the room, it wasn't amplified for me. So I couldn't hear what he was singing a lot of the time. Everybody else could hear him through headphones – I didn't have any headphones. I could hear the guitars and piano very loud, and I could see him singing into the microphone. But I didn't know what the song was about. And eventually, as he was teaching bits of it to people – he might be just singing and playing guitar to George or to Nicky Hopkins or whatever – I began to piece together the lyrics. *Fucking hell – is this about Paul McCartney?*

It kind of gradually dawned on me when he sang the lines 'the only thing you done was Yesterday'. I thought, *hang on a minute – that sounds very familiar.* The opening line of course is, 'So Sergeant Pepper took you by surprise'. I thought it might be a song about *us*, the fans. Because I remember being blown away by *Sergeant Pepper*. It was a real surprise to everybody at the time. In retrospect, now – fifty years later, I prefer *Revolver* as an album. Blimey, what an album. I remember my sister bought it, actually. I would have been about 20 when it was released – she would have been about sixteen. And she didn't like it, even though she was a big Beatles fan – a member of the Beatles fan club and all that stuff. She thought it was a bit weird.

I remember listening to 'She Said She Said' and thinking *this is great.* And then 'Tomorrow Never Knows'. *What are these guys on?*

AP: Do you remember any moment of the studio dynamic between musicians?

KM: I mean, they were like musicians anywhere. Whether they're jazz musicians, classical musicians, rock musicians – whatever. They go, *what do you want us to do?* And if there's one guy leading it, the band leader, or the conductor, they take their cue from him. He may have sent a demo to George first, because George, when he arrived, started playing some ideas to John on this little battered Spanish guitar. I think – he might have said something like, "Here's some ideas for the solo." He was playing bottle neck on this beaten up old Spanish guitar. So maybe he had sent him something. I don't know if that's true, but looking back. I surmise that might be what happened.

But the other guys were literally being taught: 'Right guys, it starts in A minor and goes to F," or whatever it happened to be. And it sounds very rough and ready by comparison to the finished track, which has got a great sinister feel to it. It's really sinister, I think. Particularly the strings – there were obviously no strings at that point. There were the two guys from Badfinger playing acoustic guitar, with Nicky Hopkins, Klaus Voorman – who was another hero of mine. And obviously George. And Alan White. And they were just like *learning a song,* like any musicians do.

AP: And Phil Spector – do you happen to remember any particular direction that he gave, or any interaction between him and John or him and the musicians?

KM: He was very quietly spoken. Which I always think is a bit of a danger sign. Particularly in men. Guys who speak quietly tend to be very frightening. Because obviously we now know he's in jail for murdering his girlfriend. I may be overlaying all that. But he was very creepy. And he wore shades all the time, so you couldn't see his eyes. I don't remember much about him being there, other than that John began to fuss around him a lot when he appeared. John got him a chair – I think he may have even thrown someone off a chair.

But certainly, Phil leaned over to John at one point and said, "I think we should make a start." Which I happened to hear, because I was very close to the two of them. John literally *shot* into action. "Right lads – everybody into the studio. Phil wants to start – come on." Like they were a bunch of naughty school kids. And every so often he did appear in the studio, as opposed to the control room. I got one nice picture of John and Phil in the studio, actually. But I never heard anything he said in the studio. Either because he didn't say anything or because he said it so quietly. And maybe only said it to John. I don't know. But he was certainly a very big presence, even though he's quite a small man – and dressed very strangely. He had a real vibe about him. He was wearing a pinstripe suit with collar and tie and a waistcoat in the middle of summer. I thought, *what's with this guy?*

AP: Do you recall a moment of John's humor?

KM: I remember one time, when he was hustling everybody into the studio – this is a tiny, trivial little incident. There was a sort of corridor which linked the kitchen and the studio – like a hallway – and I was following some of the other guys, just walking behind because I didn't know where to go. I was walking along, and John came running out of a doorway to my right. He literally came charging out of the doorway and we crashed into one another – he nearly knocked me off my feet.

He said, "Oh, I'm sorry man – I'm sorry!" He gave me a big hug. "Well, I've got to run!" And he ran off again. And I thought, *he's okay*. But I was almost bowled over; he was running full speed. He just opened the door and came flying out – *bang!*

AP: And John invited you back a few weeks later to hear a press of the album.

KM: It seemed to me he was very insecure about it. He seemed genuinely insecure – *Okay, here I am presenting this to a member of the public, and they might think it's crap.* That's really stuck with me for whatever it is – nearly fifty years. He just seemed to be, *well, is it any good?* I'm paraphrasing slightly, but it was, "I've written this thing, I've recorded it – I just can't tell if it's any good anymore."

When I saw the film *Above Us Only Sky*, I'd actually forgotten how brilliant the album is. I'd kind of taken it for granted. I thought, *this is fucking amazing.* It's an amazing album. And he didn't get it – he didn't seem to get it. Or at least he was insecure about it. In my view – that could be just my interpretation, but I remember being quite struck by it.

AP: What was it about him that gave you this sense of insecurity?

KM: He just kept grilling me about every single track. I mean, he actually said when he put the vinyl on the turntable, he literally said, "I can't bear to listen to it anymore. You're the first member of the public to hear it. So have a listen and tell me what you think." I'm thinking, *oh, Christ almighty. I've got to give John Lennon some feedback.* I was 24. He was about six years older. And he was a world-famous person, and he was one of my heroes. And suddenly I'm in this position of, *well, tell us what you think.* What am I going to say if I don't like it?

I remember the first time I heard the previous album; it took me a while to get used to it – then I thought it was fantastic. But I thought the *Imagine* album was fantastic from the first few bars of the first song. So that's what really stuck with me. And also just getting that sense – you sort of get this after a while, meeting famous people – that they're actually real human beings. But he was *so* famous at that time, and I'd been such a massive fan of the Beatles right through my teenage years, that I was very star-struck meeting him for the first time. But after fifteen minutes or so, I did get – on some level – *yes he's incredibly talented, and he's a bloke drinking a cup of coffee. Eating bacon and eggs for breakfast.* So that really stuck with me, that he was actually *for real*, and also he was working very hard.

AP: What kind of feedback did you give him, when you did hear the album?

KM: It was all good. He wanted to go through the album track by track. And of course, as I said in that video, there was no information on the white label of the vinyl. Not even handwritten track names or anything. So I didn't know what the songs were called. The first song turned out to be 'Imagine'. I didn't even know the name of the song 'Imagine'. I said, "I really liked that first song – I think that's going to be a big hit." I remember saying to him at one point, "I think people will still be listening to this album in ten years' time." Which he thought was a ludicrous idea – *for fuck's sake, it's just a rock album.* And of course, here we are fifty years later still talking about it.

There's a song called 'I Don't Wanna Be a Soldier, Mama'. "Did you like that? What did you like about it?" He said, "We managed to get King Curtis to play on 'I Don't Wanna Be a Soldier'. I thought, *that's a really weird thing to say.* Because *anybody* would have – people would have been queueing up to play on the album. Maybe he meant, *we just managed to synchronize diaries* or whatever. But it was like he was in awe of King Curtis. In the same way that I was in awe of him.

There was something really lovely and warm about him, as well. I'm not trying to claim we became bosom buddies or anything – we didn't. I met him twice, for about six or eight hours each time. And a lot of that second time he wasn't even in the room – he was off somewhere else because he couldn't bear to listen to the album, while I listened to it about three times through. Eventually I just kind of staggered back outside, by which time it was nearly dark.

He said, "Wow – what did you think?" And there was little Kieron Murphy from Dublin, giving John Lennon some feedback about his album. And thinking, *what if there's a track I didn't like?* But of course, there wasn't. They're all brilliant tracks, every single one.

AP: So obviously something happened in the first session that you were taking pictures, that John said, "This Kieron Murphy fellow is going to be the first person to hear the *Imagine* album".

KM: I don't know what the answer to that is. I think it was just that I happened to be there taking photographs when they were recording the song, and I don't even remember leaving that night – 'cos it was the middle of the night by the time I left. I must have said something like, *thanks very much for letting me sit in the studio* – because I was right in amongst them. At one point I was actually sitting on George Harrison's amp – 'cos it was so cramped in the studio. It was a tiny studio. There wasn't room to move. I asked George, "Do you mind if I sit on your amp for a minute, while I take this shot?"

But John must have just said, "Yeah that's fine – great, wonderful. I'll give you a ring when the album's done, you can come and have a listen." And it must have just stuck in his mind. I don't know what the answer to that is. I had no idea that I'd be the first person to hear it. I've often thought, too – maybe he was just being nice in saying that. There might have been other people. I don't know. Obviously, all the musicians had heard it; he'd heard it; Yoko had heard it. But he said, "I need a member of the public to give me some feedback now. 'Cos it's only been people that have been involved that have heard it."

AP: Did you shoot photos in that second time you came back as well?

KM: Yes – the *Lennon Legend* album cover is from the second session. It was two or three months after the recording session. I think the recording was May, and the listening was July '71. The funny thing was, I wanted to ask him to take the shades off, because I couldn't see his eyes. But I was too nervous to say, *John, would you mind taking off the shades?* I thought – I don't want to push my luck. Because he also had – which he admitted to himself – a bit of a temper. He was quite likely to just turn around and say *fuck off.*

But that was something interesting about the cover for

Lennon Legend – the record company chose that one. It wasn't one that I had ever printed up. So when they said *Sheet B, 28B* or whatever it was, when I came to print it I thought, *I don't particularly like this picture, I don't think it's particularly great.* It wasn't what I would ever have chosen. But that's what they wanted, so I sent them off a print. When I saw what they'd done with it – they'd cropped it slightly differently, they put the typography on – I thought, *God, it looks fantastic, actually* – I would never have seen that. If they'd said *choose the one you think is best*, it wouldn't have been that one. But I'm really proud of it now – it looks good.

AP: I'm interested in terms of that shot – where did you go to shoot it? Is it natural light?

KM: It was all available light – I didn't light it at all on either session. The first time, a bunch of the shots were in the kitchen, 'cos that's where everybody's congregating; having a cup of tea and so on. Nothing stronger, interestingly enough, ahead of the recording. It was late afternoon, about five o'clock I think. There was plenty of daylight; it was summer. And then we all went into the studio which was all artificial light. But because I was there the same time as some of the camera crew filming some of what ended up in *Above Us Only Sky*, there was plenty of light. I was quite used to shooting in low light anyway. So that's all available light as well.

And then when I went back in July, we sat outside for *yonks*, talking for hours and hours. I didn't take any pictures then. I'm not quite sure why. I kept thinking *we're about to go and listen to the album* – 'cos that was the whole purpose of me being there. So I didn't take out the camera. So I listened to the album, came back outside – or did we go do the photographs in the bedroom first? I can't remember, it's all fifty-odd years ago. But myself, John and Yoko went to their bedroom. A lot of conversations with Lennon happened in his bedroom. And they were just talking on the bed. I said, "Can I take some pictures of the two of you talking on the bed?" They were very amenable to that. My favorite picture of the whole lot is one of the two of them just talking on the bed. I took some of John as well, just him on his own – sitting on the bed. One of which ended up as the *Lennon Legend* album cover.

But again – all daylight. And those ones are a bit trickier. I must have taken the photographs before we listened to the album, actually. Because it was a very bright summer's day outside, and John and Yoko were both sitting with their back to the window, lit by the ambient light in the room. The windows are all flared out, because it was so much brighter outside. So that was quite tricky, just getting the exposures right. I still felt a bit intimidated in terms of saying *could we move over here and do some pictures; could we try standing over here*, or whatever. I kind of, slightly meekly accepted whatever situation presented itself, if that makes sense.

AP: It makes so much sense that that shot is in the bedroom – it feels so intimate.

KM: John was yacking away at ninety miles an hour, and Yoko was just sitting there listening. I can almost hear her going, "Yes – yes dear, no dear." He certainly did most of the talking. And he was quite loud, and motormouth – boisterous, whereas Yoko was much quieter. She was a very quiet person, self-contained. She was a bit older than John, as well. He'd have been about thirty, then – which seemed very old to me.

AP: Do you remember what kind of things he was talking about?

KM: No, it's gone. I can't remember a thing. 'Cos I was so intent on taking the photographs, and they were just talking amongst themselves, about God knows what. It could have been a shopping list – I don't know. I was very much focused – no pun intended – on getting some decent photographs.

But the interesting bit was that here was the guy – who aside from being the great John Lennon, one of the most famous people in the world, he's still an artist, struggling with producing something that the public might hate – or be indifferent to. Like any artist in any field. Whether you're writing stuff and you give it to some friends to read – *what if they think it's crap?*

AP: It shows that he's a real person.

KM: And he was very funny. He was always – I can't remember a lot of what was said because it was so long ago. But there was a lot of wordplay – some of it very poor, actually. The sort of stuff you'd throw away – but because it was Lennon, you think *does it have some deeper significance?*

We did talk a bit about the similarities between Dublin accents and Liverpool accents, because I had studied English Literature and Language at college – and obviously I'm a Dubliner and he's a Liverpudlian, as we all know. I've always thought that the Liverpool accent – which is a real *one-off* accent, seemed to me to be a Dublin working-class accent, grafted onto a Lancashire English accent. And you get this very strange accent which is immediately identifiable as Liverpool. It doesn't exist *anywhere* else, apart from a 20-mile radius of Liverpool. He thought that that was a very interesting idea, and we joked around with that quite a bit – and how Liverpool people would say certain phrases. I'd say, "That's exactly the same speech rhythm as what they'd say in Dublin." So we spent quite a bit of time just talking about language and speech rhythms, which I've always been into. And the meaning of words and accents and all that stuff. I'm a real nerd around that kind of stuff.

The language that's spoken in Ireland is *as* different from *English* English as *American* English is. Its different speech rhythms; words with different meanings; phrases that Irish people use that don't make any sense in England at all. Like *more or less definite*, is a very Irish expression.

"Are we going to do such-and-such a thing?"

"Yeah, more or less definitely, yeah."

And English people go, *"Well, is that yes or no?"* There's kind of a different logic involved. So we did talk about that. I remember talking to him quite a bit about that. Other stuff is gone. And then there was the stuff about the album – the individual songs.

AP: Was there one song that he was really happy that you liked?

KM: I think 'Imagine'. Because I said – remember there was no information on the label, so I didn't know what I was looking for. I assumed one song was called 'Jealous Guy' – that was a bit obvious. But then I thought 'Imagine' was called 'Imagine All the People', because that's repeated. And I said, "I really like that song, 'Imagine All the People'.

And he said, "Yeah – it's just called 'Imagine'. That's going to be the single and the album title."

I said, "Yeah, I think it's really good. It's a classic – people will still be listening to it ten years' time." How wrong we both were. When you're 24 that seems like an awful long way into the future. And he was only 30 at that time.

AP: Given that you were a *fan*, getting to meet John Lennon – was there anything about him that really surprised you, that you weren't expecting?

KM: I realized quite quickly that he was a real human being, as opposed to being this icon who figured very largely in my adolescence and teenage years. It was really nice – this is going to sound really arrogant – to feel we were equals. You know what I mean? Not that I'm saying I've anything like the talent he had – but we were just two blokes in a room full of blokes, and Yoko. I've often found this before with people who are really at the top of their game. That he was completely – whatever the opposite of a *star* is. He was the least *star-y* famous person I've ever met. That was a real revelation, actually. I really enjoyed being in his company.

• • •

"Yes he's incredibly talented, and he's a bloke drinking a cup of coffee. Eating bacon and eggs for breakfast." As a fan of the Beatles, Kieron Murphy found himself at the epicenter of the post-Beatle world at John Lennon's dining table. Seated next to George Harrison. What followed was an insight into John's creative process: teaching the songs to the other musicians on-the-fly. John knew exactly how he wanted each piece of the musical puzzle to fit. And he was more than a little excited to have Phil Spector in the room. So excited that he nearly bowled Kieron Murphy over as he raced down the corridor. Then Kieron was invited back to hear the finished album and to take what became some of the most enduring pictures of John and Yoko.

John was clearly nervous to have Phil Spector co-producing.

Aside from Phil's own status as a genius songwriter and producer – inventor of the 'wall of sound' – Phil had produced George Harrison's *All Things Must Pass* the previous year. George's album was the first Beatle album post-breakup. It hit #1 in the UK and the US, plus Canada, Australia, Spain, Norway, Sweden and the Netherlands. John wanted to compete.

The track 'How Do You Sleep' was certainly a dig at Paul McCartney – John's right of reply. Paul had already taken a swipe at John with the song 'Too Many People'. Paul had said the line, *too many people, preaching practices* was directed at John – and Yoko. John and Yoko had become heavily involved in politics, from the WAR IS OVER billboards; returning the MBE; mailing 'acorns for peace' to world leaders; bed-ins – and Bagism.

Yoko had coined the term Bagism in 1964. The concept involved a person climbing into a large opaque bag, with the aim of removing their outward appearance. This allowed for the verbal sharing of ideas without prejudice – 'total communication', as Yoko called it. Between 1968-1971, John and Yoko made several public appearances and press conferences from inside a bag.

BBC television personality Michael Parkinson had to wear a bag in order to interview John and Yoko in 1971. He'd agreed that if he wanted to talk about the Beatles, he'd have to ask his questions in the form of 'total communication'. Sir Michael Parkinson politely declined to be interviewed for this book, but he did send a fabulous apology:

> "Paul was always the most approachable and enlightening
> of the Beatles and the one interview I did with John was
> only remarkable because of the absurdity of sitting in a
> sack asking dumb questions... I was delighted to have
> met him and known him but briefly, but whereas I could

**talk about Paul 'til kingdom come, John remains totally
unfathomable."**

Throughout 1971 John and Paul continued their feud in
the pages of *Melody Maker*. Paul said in an interview that
John was writing "too much political stuff" and that John
and Yoko were out to copy him and his wife Linda. John
wrote a reply to *Melody Maker*, criticizing Paul for being
too conservative: "Your politics are very similar to [religious
lobbyist] Mary Whitehouse's – *Saying nothing is as loud as
saying something*."

Of 'Imagine', John later told *Rolling Stone*, "It's an
anti-religious, anti-nationalistic, anti-capitalistic song – but
because it's sugar-coated, it's accepted." But in July 1971,
Imagine was not yet complete – the album would have to
be finished in New York. John and Yoko were about to go
on a manhunt.

DICK CAVETT
EARLY USA

AFTER A SERIES of confrontations spanning several years, Yoko's ex-husband Tony Cox took their daughter Kyoko to America in 1971. He cut all ties with England and disappeared. John and Yoko went after them in July, but their trail ran cold in New York. They checked into the St. Regis Hotel on East 55th Street and planned their next move.

American activists Abbie Hoffman and Jerry Rubin made an effort to befriend John while he was in New York, and John was quick to display his support for the left leaning Yippie cause. Rumors quickly reached the Nixon White House that John Lennon was to play a concert in San Diego during the 1972 Republican National Convention. The rumors were most likely false, but the Yippies had disrupted political conventions before – notably in Chicago 1968. The Chicago riots had caused an ongoing media circus around the trial of the Chicago Seven, which included Hoffman and Rubin. Nixon didn't want to risk the kind of publicity that John Lennon could add to this political arena. The Nixon tapes, when they were made public, revealed Chief of Staff H.R. Haldeman saying of John, "This guy could sway an election." In March 1972, the United States Immigration and Naturalization Service began formal deportation proceedings based on John's 1968 cannabis possession conviction in London. So began three years of court hearings.

But John knew how to whip up publicity. When he first arrived in New York he had made contact with producers at *The Dick Cavett Show* and arranged for the taping of a special show featuring only he and Yoko. The couple were largely un-gettable for television and the booking was seen as a major coup. It was their first US television appearance since the breakup of the Beatles. During the hour-long broadcast, John and Yoko were seen chatting jovially about Yoko's filmmaking and joking around with a stethoscope. But the crux of the program was two-fold: the immigration issue was front-and-center, as was Yoko's appeal to the national audience – *Help find my daughter.*

The Dick Cavett Show was an iconic staple of the American television landscape from the late 1960s through to the 1980s. A selection of Dick's guests include Alfred Hitchcock, Salvador Dalí, Groucho Marx, Katharine Hepburn, Marlon Brando, Ingmar Bergman, George Harrison, Jimi Hendrix, Janis Joplin, and a selection of star musicians on the day after Woodstock 1969. Dick Cavett continues to perform on Broadway, and he writes a regular column for the *New York Times.*

Dick was privy to John's trademark wit as well as his more serious side. After their two appearances on *The Dick Cavett Show* in 1971 & 1972, John and Yoko asked Dick to act as a character witness at their immigration hearing. Dick was backstage with John before the 1972 *One to One* concert at Madison Square Garden. And prior to all this, before taping his first show with John & Yoko, Dick Cavett was invited to their hotel to meet up with the Lennons and break the ice.

DICK CAVETT: I met John on a rainy day at the St. Regis

Hotel. On the bed was – not the Lennons – but a lot of projects they were working on.

John said to me, "Part of the reason you're here is that you have the only halfway intelligent talk show."

I said, "Well, why would you want to be connected with a *halfway* intelligent show?"

I felt that he laughed inordinately. I think he even quoted it back to me once. One thing that amuses me is an aspect of his sense of humor – some people would call it *naughtiness*, but you don't want to know those people.

At the beginning of my first show with him, somewhere in the first fifteen minutes or so, to many people's surprise, he suddenly said, *"Dick, what's your definition of love?"* And there was a sort of mild confused laugh, as I recall.

We had been talking about our mutual lack of admiration for David Frost. And that was one of those sappy questions that Frost used formulaic-ly every time he did a show. *"What's your definition of love?"* Now, having heard that, Alec Baldwin would sometimes call me in the middle of the night and say, *"Dick, what's your definition of love?"* But I guess – to confess – I have about the same amount of admiration for Frost as the *Beyond the Fringe* four get.

You know that when Peter Cook was asked what he regretted in life, he said, "I once saved David Frost from drowning." The funny part is that it was true. I hope that got around to John.

But John – I have two letters from John which could have been written by James Joyce, with puns and wordplay that was really high class. Unfortunately, I haven't seen those letters in some years.

AIDAN PREWETT: In the first show you taped with John and Yoko, my favorite moment is right at the start. John is very nervous – it's palpable that he's nervous. And then you turn to him and say, *"So you're Jack Lemmon."*

DC: Oh my God. Thanks for reminding me. Yeah, I remember that did get a laugh. It was a really pleasant, wonderful experience.

When I got to the hotel, where I first met them – weeks before they were on the show – John pulled me over to one side of the room, stood three people in a row, put me beside them, and said, "This is a thing where a joke passes among four people. So if you just stand here and pretend you're one of the people…" I've never seen the movie, but I'm told I'm in it. I don't remember the joke.

Oh by the way, I asked John who I would be in this movie with – jokingly. He said, "Just before you got here, Fred Astaire left." Yoko had danced with Fred Astaire. Improv – surely by accident. I guess they met in the elevator or something.

AP: Did you get much of a sense of – I mean, you must have – the relationship between John and Yoko? What was your take on what their relationship was?

DC: In the short amount of time that I was with them, they seemed extremely nice to each other; no trouble visible. There was no humor in the subject of her child, and her desire to be reunited. But I guess they had such a good time on the first show – during which, by the way, they seemed to kill an entire pack of Viceroys; they kept passing it back and forth. At one point, the two Lennons were holding three unlit cigarettes. And maybe a lit one, I don't know.

When they got over that, they said they'd come back. Well, we were stunned: they did come back. And they did a song.

They said, "We'll do our song now." They didn't say what it was. They walked up, got in place in front of the microphone, and John said, "This is a song that Yoko wrote, called 'Woman is the Nigger of the World'." *Oh dear.* And then they sang 'Woman is the Nigger of the World'.

It has just a touch of feminism, doesn't it?

AP: Just a touch.

DC: The audience loved it, but the network panicked. Now the show was supposed to air some days later, so there would be time – if I agreed to it – to put in a little segment just before the song that would be added to the show, saying – in effect – *some of you may be offended.* I know John found this funny. So the show aired, and I had to go in and tape this thing and say *some of you may be offended and we know that tastes vary* and all that crap. Then the song aired. There were – I think it was 362 complaints. None of them about the song – but, as one woman said – *"That cheesy mealy-mouthed thing you made Dick say before you played the show."* So that would have amused John to no end. It probably did.

A couple of weeks later, George Harrison and I did a one-on-one show. People had warned me, saying, "If you're expecting Beatle humor, you can get it from Lennon but you're not going to get any from Harrison." Well anyway I went ahead, and I did a 90-minute show with Harrison. He warmed up and got quite pleasant and quite funny. So much so that at one point I felt at ease to say, "You know, Yoko Ono sat in that very chair that you're sitting in." He instantly leapt out of the chair and brushed off his butt and his pants.

And then I went down and testified that John should

not be heaved out of the country by the Great Unindicted Co-Conspirator.

AP: Do you remember what you said at the hearing?

DC: I remember when I got down to that building with the wide broad steps that you see on crime shows everywhere, John was very solemn. First of all, I didn't see him. I went in, I walked around. I didn't see him anywhere. But I remember looking down a long corridor, and there was John – a lone, tall figure at the far end. It was sort of like something out of a Sidney Lumet movie or something. And we came together and talked. He was quite, quite serious. He just said, "Thank you – thank you for being here."

And I said, "I hope it helps." And I hope it got to Nixon that I said he shouldn't be thrown out of the country. That *John* shouldn't. Nixon certainly should have been.

I had a hard time with one question, which was: "What do you think the *value* of John Lennon is?"

I managed to stammer out something that I wasn't terribly proud of. But it was some, maybe not too awful, version of: "*His fans seem to look to him in some way to make their lives better*". And they printed it in the New Yorker, so I guess it wasn't that awful. I couldn't come up with anything else at the time.

I ended up on Nixon's hate list, and I'm still proud of that. But at the time that I wasn't *yet*, I met him at a reception at the White House – everybody in tuxedos. I didn't know what to say, except that I couldn't take my eyes off his nose. I used the phrase *its appalling width*, in writing about it. But it was wider than three fingers together. It looked like a Herblock caricature. But anyway, I thought *what's the great man going to say to me?* He'd obviously been told a little bit about everybody, I suppose.

He said, "Who's doing your show tonight?" With his face screwed up tight.

I said, "Joe Namath, he's sitting in for me."

Nixon: "How are his knees?"

A genius at small talk. I wanted to say, "Well, last time I caressed either one of them they seemed quite okay." Instead, I moved on to Mrs. Nixon.

AP: And your involvement with the Lennons got you a special mention in the Nixon tapes.

DC: It's like the beginning of a crime novel. Years later I get in the back of a car at L.A. Airport, and the guy who's picking me up opens a laptop. On the screen is Richard Nixon and H.R. Haldeman. It was a still image. But the sound: It's from the Nixon tapes. And there's *my name* in the dialogue.

> *Richard Nixon: What the hell is Cavett?*
> *Haldeman: Oh Christ he's, he's…*
> *Nixon: He's terrible?*
> *Haldeman: He's impossible. He loads every program. We've complained bitterly about the Cavett Shows.*

DC: But the best line of all is right at the end. It's only a few minutes… and it's a strange feeling to have the most powerful man in the world saying about you:

> *Nixon: Well, is there any way we can screw him? That's what I mean, there must be ways.*

DC: He came up with something. I found out years later – when two of my former staff members had happened to bring up the subject of being audited the same year – and then found out that other staff members had. Mr. Nixon had, in his favorite way of doing things – illegally – frequently used the IRS to punish people. And he decided, I guess, the way to get at me was to audit my staff – and me. But I didn't know he'd done it to the staff. And he hurt some people. Not for the first time in his life.

AP: I heard that you found yourself backstage at Madison Square Garden when John was about to perform, for one of the very few times that he did perform in New York. Do you have any recollections of that?

DC: I do – I went around behind him and said, "You'll be unusually good tonight." And I massaged his shoulders.
   He said, "You'll have to travel with us from now on."
   You're good at eliciting memories.

AP: Did you spend any time with John and Yoko in the dressing room before taping, or after taping?

DC: I think – I know I stopped by the dressing room to say hello, which I usually never did – I usually met the guests on stage. And I just said, "Don't worry John, it's a friendly country." And he was somewhat amused by that. We got along really well. They *were* nervous – as you can see from the consumption of Viceroys. It was endearing.

AP: In my notes I wrote down a very poignant quote from one of the things he said on your show. *"One day, Yoko, we'll be an old couple retired to the south of Ireland, and we'll say to each other: Remember when we were on the Cavett show?"*

DC: And tottering around with their canes. I liked that. I haven't seen the show in a long time, but certainly after he was killed – you just can't help thinking *God, we can't afford to lose this man.* But we certainly did.

• • •

The John Lennon that Dick Cavett knew during this time was an older, different person – a man with a tremendous weight on his shoulders. So much was at stake. John and Yoko needed to stay in America, and they needed to find Kyoko. Dick Cavett knew the John Lennon who was a lone, tall figure at the far end of a corridor of the New York Supreme Court. It was a figure that possessed a dignified solemnity, and a distinct otherness from the persona of Beatle John.

But Dick also saw the best of John's joviality. He saw it through his participation in one of Yoko's short films: *"Just before you got here, Fred Astaire left,"*. He saw it in the final reveal of the name of the song they were going to perform – and he saw it in the jittery couple anxiously consuming a packet of Viceroy cigarettes during the first interview. John continued to use humor to disguise his unease in any given situation.

John and Yoko appeared on *The Dick Cavett Show* a second time in May 1972. November of the same year saw Nixon's re-election in one of the biggest landslides *ever* in an American election. It was during the campaign for this election that the Watergate break-in occurred and led to Nixon's eventual resignation two years later.

On the night of the election, John and Yoko went to a 'wake' party hosted by Jerry Rubin. Attending guests were reeling from the shock of Nixon victory in forty-nine states. Nixon's opponent, George McGovern, had proposed an immediate end to the war in Vietnam and an embryonic version of universal basic income. Under Nixon, the war would continue, the poor would stay poor, and John would likely be deported.

The party got a little out-of-control and John lost his

cool. Already drunk, he then took some cocaine and ended up in one of the bedrooms with a female guest. So began the fabled 'Lost Weekend' period.

Yoko could see the downward spiral appearing in front of her and arranged for John to take a mistress – of *her* choosing. She selected May Pang, a young assistant at Apple who was now working for the Lennons. It is May's voice repeating the whispered "*John*" in the song '#9 Dream'. The new couple hit it off. John and May headed for Los Angeles on the proviso that Yoko would be able to phone to check in with both of them.

May Pang was unable to contribute to this book due to contractual obligations, but her kind response gave me a sense of a genuine, empathetic spirit. May stated in another interview that John's 'Lost Weekend' period was highly creative, but only the tabloid gossip made the press.

During 1973 & 1974, John completed *Mind Games, Walls & Bridges*, and recorded most of the *Rock 'n' Roll* album, while also producing albums for his friends Harry Nilsson and Ringo Starr. When John returned to Yoko in early 1975, he referred to this period as his 'Lost Weekend', after the Charles Jackson novel about an alcoholic writer.

In later years, disparaging comments from a tail-between-the-legs Lennon reinforced the tabloid image of out-of-control debauchery with his gang of miscreants, featuring Nilsson, Starr, and Keith Moon of the Who. Two ejections from the Troubadour nightclub are cited as indicative of the mood. On one occasion he was kicked out for drunken heckling of the Smothers Brothers – who were friends of John's; Tommy Smothers had played guitar on 'Give Peace a Chance'. Another incident saw John running around the venue with a Kotex pad stuck to his forehead.

It was during this period that Paul McCartney returned

to John's life. While John was recording at Burbank Studios, Paul McCartney casually walked in, sat down at the drum kit, and started to play. John and the assembled musicians joined in for a jam. The bootleg recording of the session includes a lot of fumbling around before John says, "Hey, who else has a mic besides me? I've been up here screamin' all night."

Paul's voice is soon heard joining John, and they begin playing through some of the old favorites, including Little Richard's 'Lucille', Ben E. King's 'Stand by Me' and a medley of Sam Cooke numbers. John and Paul took this opportunity to begin rebuilding their friendship. Walls were being patched up, bridges mended.

ELLIOT MINTZ
AT HOME WITH JOHN

ELLIOT MINTZ was working as a broadcaster in LA when he interviewed John and Yoko by telephone for the first time in 1971. They hit it off and began a close personal friendship. Elliot and Yoko remain close friends to this day, and Elliot continues his work as a media consultant. Over the years he has represented Bob Dylan, Diana Ross, Christie Brinkley, Melanie Griffith, and Crosby, Stills & Nash, among others. His interviews – many of which are available online – include names such as Salvador Dalí, Norman Mailer, Jayne Mansfield, Raquel Welch, Allen Ginsberg, Timothy Leary, Groucho Marx, Jack Lemmon, and John Wayne. In 1980 he was presented the California Associated Press, Television and Radio Association Award for his telephone interview with an Iranian occupier of the US Embassy in Tehran during the Iran hostage crisis. And he spent much of the 1970s with John and Yoko.

Together they would relax within the comfort and seclusion of their various New York apartments. There they would discuss the day's events as well as favorite topics including philosophy and history. Elliot was there when the FBI was making their presence known. Elliot was there for John's recording sessions in New York and Los Angeles. And Elliot was with John during his 'Lost Weekend'.

ELLIOT MINTZ: It was rare to spend 30 minutes with John without humor, satire, or wit being included in the dialogue. Yes, at times he became extremely cerebral. Sometimes emotional, sometimes angry and vituperative. I mean, he was also the person who wrote 'How Do You Sleep?' and 'Gimme Some Truth'. I don't mean to create the impression that he was this completely passive dreamer. That would not be an accurate portrayal. He was a man, he wasn't a saint. And he was prone to moments of anger, and raising his voice and saying unpleasant things, just the way everybody else was. That was not his predominant personality around me, but others can attest to other parts of his character. He peppered it, always, with wit and humor. Not in the form of telling jokes. I don't remember him ever – quote – 'telling me a joke'. But his commentary on things would be biting and witty.

He loved *The Goon Show*. It was an old British radio series. Yoko bought him a collection of all the *Goon Shows* as a Christmas present once, and he just loved that, and he loved Monty Python. So the humor was just built into the equation. And subtle, for the most part. And he rarely made jokes at the expense of others.

AIDAN PREWETT: Is there a particular prank that you recall?

EM: Well, one prank that I do recall – I told you that I'm not a musician, and I can't sing. I don't have any singing voice. It's bad – when I sing in the shower, the water goes off. I would never allow people to hear me at a karaoke bar – it would clear out the place. I just have no ability in that area. So he got a kick – sometimes – out of me trying, if we were discussing a song and I would say, "Do you remember that song with the lyric so-and-so?"

And he'd say, "I don't know – just hum it for me." And I would sing a little bit of it and he'd say, "Please, stop."

And Yoko couldn't stand it when I sang. Sometimes when we were together, I'd just – for no particular reason – would sing 'As Time Goes By', or something that I enjoyed. And to her it was really irritating. So I recall one Christmas, John and I went into the white room – the living room where the white piano is located – where he created 'Imagine' – and he recorded me singing 'Happy Birthday' to Yoko.

He said that on Yoko's birthday – which is two days after mine – he would take the tape and secretly, as she was half-awake-half-asleep, put it in a little cassette recorder, push the button, and she would awaken to me singing 'Happy Birthday' to her. And he said he would also record her reaction to it and send it to me. It seemed like a fairly good prank, and nobody would be hurt. So I recorded the song with his tutelage. He, on one of Yoko's birthdays, played it for her, and he sent me the tape of her reaction.

The first reaction you hear on the tape is her giggling. And then thirty seconds later she says, "Oh, he's *awful*. Oh, *please* turn that off – it's *terrible*." But she'd be half giggling. He would giggle at the thought of the prank, and then send the thing back to me. So I recall that as being mildly amusing to them, in the prank department.

AP: You were there in LA for some of the Spector sessions – is there a moment within that that sticks out?

EM: I was with him during the 'Lost Weekend', during all that time that he was in LA. And that was the lowest time in his life. That was the time that I saw John at his most depressed. He wanted to get back to Yoko. It was a time that she virtually told him to leave for a while. They needed a break from each other, and she sent him to La La Land. For a week or two he was having a good time, the way boys do when they come here. And shortly thereafter, his only wish was to get back to her. She wanted to wait until he was *ready*. So during that time, there was a copious amount of drinking going on, and maybe some substances. And he was depressed. He wanted to reunite, but I think he knew and she knew he wasn't ready. We talked about it all the time. I explained that I was friends with both of them; I would keep no secrets. I would be in touch with Yoko almost on a daily basis – she wanted to know how he was doing. She heard reports of him being thrown out of the nightclub with Harry Nilsson, and reports about how raucous the Spector sessions had gotten. And I was honest with her – that he was going through difficult times, and he was not always joyous to be with.

The one complaint – if it's a complaint – is that some people shouldn't drink. It's simple – that there are some people in this world who don't do well after they've had two or three beers, or two or three brandy Alexanders. And one of them was John Lennon. He could have *one* and be somewhat charming and witty. *Two*, and be slightly buzzed, but at the *third* he would become somewhat confrontational. And after that he was unpleasant to be around. Phil Spector drank *constantly*. The later *Double Fantasy* sessions did not resemble the Phil Spector sessions. So yes – some good music came out of that period, but at too high a price.

AP: I heard that Phil Spector at one point fired a pistol inside the studio – do you know if that's true?

EM: I never independently verified it. Which means – I was not present when Phil allegedly did that. Now, I've known Phil Spector since 1966. That's when I met him.

I went to the funeral of Lenny Bruce when I was 21, and Spector delivered the eulogy. So I met Spector years before I met John and Yoko. Spector and I spent a considerable amount of time together – at his home; at restaurants – we got to know each other well. I considered him a friend at the time. And obviously, a musical genius.

But among other things, Phil had a fascination and a preoccupation – as many do – with firearms. He *liked* guns. He liked *lots* of guns. And if you visited him at his home, there were guns everywhere. On the coffee table; in the kitchen; by the couch; wherever you were, there was a weapon. They were – to my knowledge – loaded, and ready-to-go. Phil carried a gun; he had a shoulder holster. And he wore a gun sometimes around his ankle. He was a very small man – five feet one or two. He sometimes had large bodyguards around him. He had guard dogs around his house. There's no question he suffered from some degree of paranoia, as well as perhaps other mental illness. And the guns were part of his life. And he was a huge drinker. Even at his size he had a tremendous capacity for drink. The legendary stories of him fueling alcohol with the presence of weapons was fairly well known.

Is it possible that at one of the recording sessions, when he was trying to get some order established among a very rowdy group – 'cos people dropped by all the time to observe these sessions – is it possible, to get their attention, that he discharged a weapon into the ceiling? In other words – firing a bullet *up*. It's possible – and I've heard other people who were there attest to it. I never saw any pictures of holes in the ceiling. I never heard any issue of a police complaint being filed. I don't know if the recording studio prevented them from ever coming back into the studio – which seems like it would be a match. So I'm aware of the story – and if you find people who will source and double-source that, it's not something that I couldn't conceive of. But in a direct question – I did not see him do that.

AP: Was May Pang – did you see a lot of May during this time?

EM: Yes – I wouldn't say a *lot*, because she was, of course, around John most of the time. And frequently I would be in the company of both of them. But when I spent my solo time with John – and there was a lot of that – May was not present. She was a good and stabilizing force for John. To the best of my knowledge, May did not smoke or drink, and I think she tried her best to maintain some order in John's life. She was able to interact with other musicians who seemed to like her, and she knew how to deal with them. She was somewhat of a gatekeeper. And of course, the very basic stuff that John just was not able to deal with, she *was*. I mean, it's not as if John could go shopping for groceries. I don't know if he had ever been in a supermarket. When I picked John and May up at the airport when they arrived here, the first thing he told me is he had some traveler's checks, and he needed to turn them into money. I said we could go to my bank and do that. I think it was his first trip to an actual bank. We sat down and he had, I think, ten thousand dollars in traveler's checks; got them converted, as half of my bank also wanted his autograph, *welcome to L.A.*

AP: Around about this time, Paul McCartney came back onto the scene and they recorded a short jam in a studio. Did you see that, or was there anything in the air about a potential reunion?

EM: I did not see it, but I know it to be true. John spoke to me briefly about that on tape in one of our interviews. He said, yeah – it was one of those occasions that Paul just happened to be in town, there were a lot of other musicians in the studio. It's not as if the two of them said *let's have a reunion.* They just went into a studio and started picking away at guitars. They were more conscious of the fact that other people who were present viewed this as some great union of sorts.

I haven't heard Paul speak about it, but from John's perspective, it just felt kinda comfortable. Jamming and playing – it didn't last very long, with Paul – but it was nothing more than that. You've got to keep in mind that these are two guys who knew each other since they were teenagers, and they were as close as guys could get and they traveled the world and they created the Lennon-McCartney experience. So whereby they had their ups and downs, John compared it to a marriage. Where occasionally there are arguments in the marriage, and threats of separation and divorce and all the rest of it.

When the politics of Beatledom are set aside, it was just probably comforting for him to sit and jam with Paul for a little. And if he had the opportunity to do it again, it wouldn't have surprised me if they had. That stuff is the easy stuff. The complicated stuff is when people come around and say, "Well, this is great – we should now call George and Ringo and see if they can come in. And now we should really do some tapes and we should think about some material to put down. And maybe even now, approach a record company, or consider going out and doing a concert." Once you get into all of that, then the conversation has shifted form casual dating to an eternal marriage. And it did not appear to me, toward the end, that any of them were interested in recreating an eternal marriage.

John, today, would be eighty years old. For those who think about a Beatles reunion and what it would have been like for them to have been together, well, imagine today, four men in their eighties, on a stage somewhere, singing. Does that sound like the kind of show you would attend *twice*? If they were in residency in Las Vegas, how would that play? I pose that question – people say *it would play really great, that's what Elton John does; that's what Paul McCartney does*. They're all older; they travel the world and sing songs and fill stadiums and people love it. Bob Dylan tours a hundred and fifty nights a year and fills venues. We're *all* getting older. Maybe it could have worked. Then again, maybe not. Could they have been in a recording studio together, creating their magic and just releasing music? To me, that would have sounded – if I were consulting with them; I'm not, I wasn't – but if anybody had asked me, I would say *that* would be the preference.

But when the subject came up with John and I, he voiced very little interest in the concept. In our last interview – our walk on Malibu Beach – we walked along the beach with a video crew; talked to him about the whole experience. The last question I asked him was about a Beatles reunion. It's on video. You'll hear what he says – which, to paraphrase, would be: "Well, I couldn't really say."

And I said, "If you could – is it something you'd like to see yourself doing?"

He said, "I don't know, Elliot – 'cos you know me – I go on instinct. If the idea hit me tomorrow, I might call them and say *'come on, let's do something.'* All the wounds are healed. If we do it, we do it…as long as we make music."

That's how we ended the interview. That was kind of his attitude. Music, *yes*. A bigtime reunion with a private jet flying them into hotels around the world? Well, what about wives and kids, and grandchildren? What about other interests? I don't think that the question is that realistic. The cowboys would use a phrase, *that's like trying to lasso a dream.*

AP: Is there a singular moment you shared with John that has really stuck with you more than any other?

EM: When most people think of *oh, what would it be like spending an afternoon with John, or John and Yoko,* just hanging out at the Dakota, or wherever we might be: *How spectacular an event of that nature might be.* People have expressed that to me over the years. And they view it as something that would be earth-shaking. That's never the way I recall it as being. Yes, the first time that we met, physically...keep in mind that I began a lengthy telephone relationship with John and Yoko as a result of a radio interview I did with both of them. So we'd spoken on the telephone for many hours before he actually got out of a car and shook my hand. It was as if, in the three months of our telephone relationship, where we spoke virtually every day, we got to know each other. We eased into it.

So when the moment came that we met, I knew what he looked like. At the time I think he had seen a picture of me. He knew what I looked like and we knew a whole lot about each other, so it wasn't as if *you spot somebody on the sidewalk that you've always had some kind of fascination with and suddenly there is that person.* It wasn't like a lightning bolt in the sky.

Once, I'd be in the Dakota, where I guess we had most of our lengthiest conversations. We used to talk in the old bedroom – he would get into his pajamas, and Yoko would get into her dressing gown. We'd come back from a dinner or something, and they liked to get into bed. He would turn the television on at the base of the bed, but because of his poor vision, the sound was off and he couldn't see the pictures. It was like an electronic fireplace. It was just there and present. And we would talk into the night.

Yoko would frequently fall asleep, as he and I would continue to talk – two, three, four in the morning. And then I would leave the building. During those occasions, it's not as if I sat there thinking *I'm here with Beatle John. I'm here with The Great John Lennon.* All that stuff just dissipated rather rapidly. It was just being in the company of somebody I was close to, where we could just talk about anything and everything. Not spectacular – just warm, accommodating, friendly and *real.* The only time that perception changed is when we would leave the apartment, take the elevator downstairs, the doors would open, and we would be in public.

Once we were in public, and the gate would open at the Dakota, there would be a group of fans outside already beginning to take pictures and looking for autographs. And getting into a cab and the cab driver asking when the Beatles were going to back together again. And trying to go to a restaurant or a store without being besieged and followed. In moments like that, I knew I was with the person who people thought of as *Beatle John.*

So – a long way of saying to you – there's no specific evening or moment that sticks in my mind. Just dozens of composite pictures in my brain of us in different places in the world, aware – we were just engaged in conversation and I was overwhelmed with his passion. For everything.

There was no *small talk.* There wasn't – although a part of him liked Hollywood gossip. He would sometimes call me and say "What's going on out there?" There were a couple of public figures he took an interest in. But most of the conversations – he had a great interest in history. He liked to discuss history, he liked discussing politics. He liked discussing human nature; religion, philosophy, things of that kind. We never talked about music, because I'm not a musician; I don't play an instrument. I think it's one of the things that made it a little easier for him, that I didn't profess an interest in the music aspect. Whereas I certainly was a *John & Yoko* fan, by the time the Beatles were here, I was a little too old for the Beatles. I was raised on Elvis. We talked about the Beatles during my interviews – but in person, things were much more ordinary.

AP: On the phone – the first time you spoke with John – did something change about your prior image of him? Suddenly you're speaking with the real man – was there something about him that you went *that's different to what I expected?*

EM: I was surprised at how little money he had when the Beatles broke up.

I said to him, "They're always interested in the money."

And he said, "Yeah – the Beatles were completely ripped off."

I said, "You must have made a hundred billion dollars during that period of time."

He said, "Yeah, I'm surprised that you still think that was real – it was all invisible money." He said, "When I got out of the Beatles, I think I was lucky to have a million dollars left – that I was able to hang on to a mil. And Yoko was able to invest it and we're okay now. And that was mainly from publishing – songwriting." You can imagine how it was for somebody like George or Ringo, who only had a handful of songs; who may have only had a couple of hundred thousand dollars. I was surprised by that response.

I asked him to do a word association with me, and some of the words came back in an unusual way. I like the fact that – I asked him if he dreamed in color or black-and-white, and he said he dreamed in vivid color. All of his dreams were very surrealistic, and he enjoyed dreaming tremendously.

I'd have to listen to the interview again to see if there were some surprises. But there usually were. And I asked him some political questions as well – if he was of draft age in America at the time of the Vietnam war, would he have gone to Canada, would he have gone to Vietnam or would he have gone to jail?

And he said, "I would have gone to Canada. I would not have fought." That didn't really come as a surprise. But during that time, it was unusual to hear a public figure speak with that kind of candor.

AP: Speaking of politics – were you ever in a room with John while Abbie Hoffman or Jerry Rubin were around?

EM: No – whereas I had met and interviewed both Jerry and Abbie separately during that particular period. It wasn't as if they were in a room with John frequently, although it appears that way.

But there were political things. I certainly was in a room, during the first time we met, in Ojai, California – when it was the first day that the three of us were together. John was changing into his swimsuit – there was a little pool that he wanted to jump into. They were renting a house. This is a small artistic community about a hundred miles north of L.A. While John was changing, Yoko asked me to follow her. We walked into a bathroom. She closed the door; she turned on the water. She asked me to sit at the side of the tub with her, which I did. Over the sound of the bathtub water, she softly said, "We're being followed by the FBI. Our phones are tapped; we're under surveillance. So I just want you to know that the house could be bugged."

Years later, we found out that was not paranoia. The FBI released all of the dossiers that they had maintained on John and Yoko. They're available online. You can read the FBI reports about them being under constant surveillance because of their association with Jerry and Abbie and their anti-Vietnam War feelings. But it was Jerry and Abbie who stoked that a little harder. They were more hard-core, far leftists. John and Yoko were peaceniks. So with them it was about bed-ins. *Grow Your Hair For Peace.* Things of that nature.

It wasn't about revolution; it was never about violence, and there was never any security threat posed to the government. But John had to resist deportation. The government tried to get rid of him. He fought for years, all the way up to the Supreme Court, wanting to stay in America. He loved America; he loved New York. It became his second city. He did not want to leave. So he had a profound love for this country; while never losing sight of his roots. Always speaking to me affectionately about Liverpool. But New York was home.

AP: Do you remember a time where it changed from a feeling of *threat* from the FBI – to relief, of the absence of a threat?

EM: I think once he went public with it – and he told that to Dick Cavett, he told that to Tom Snyder on the air, he told it to me on the air, he told it to others. He wanted people to know he was aware of the fact that he was under surveillance. And it could have been at a time that the FBI just realized there was no threat. During my phone calls with John and Yoko, I occasionally heard what I thought was interference on the telephone line. I never physically saw anybody following us. But the FBI usually does this stuff fairly obviously. As most intelligence agencies do. If you had somebody following you, you'd probably know about it. So I didn't personally see it, but the facts are, he was under surveillance. The facts are, the government moved to have him deported.

Of course, the government's position was that in England, years before, he was arrested for being in possession of a small amount of cannabis. John claimed that he had been set up, and indeed the police officer who found the cannabis was later found guilty of planting cannabis in the homes of other rock stars and was let go. But John pled *guilty* to that charge. Apparently when you're applying for your green card, if you had such a charge against you – this was a tiny little bit, probably less than a joint – *that* could be used as the pretense for evicting him.

And when I asked him on the radio, it took all those years; all that money; all that energy and effort and lawyers and depositions and court hearings. All of that stuff: "Do you have any ill feelings towards the FBI and the director of the FBI, J. Edgar Hoover, some of the people who surrounded Nixon?"

"Time wounds all heels."

AP: When John was allowed to stay; when he received that news – I believe it was around the time of Sean's birth – do you remember their reaction? Were John and Yoko both elated? Were they relieved?

EM: Overjoyed. There are photos the day that he's walking out of court, displaying the green card, wearing his suit and tie and smiling. I think they went out for a big lunch.

That was a major, major accomplishment. Most of the time when you fight the government, you don't win. He *won*. He was allowed to stay. It made him very, very happy. That burden was gone, and it was time to pursue the next battle.

With John and Yoko, keep in mind – there were many battles. There were many controversies. But they led, in the Dakota building, a very conventional, quiet life. I observed it; I was with them during that time. A *lot* of the time. Not all the time, of course – I lived in L.A. But that was what was going on inside. What was going on *outside* were all the battles and issues; people trying to get them to do things and support causes and contribute money. To march for various things. To get the Beatles back together again. To get them to pursue artistic projects. To raise a son. Of course, they had the gift that money provides in making some of that go away. But it was the celebrité that got in the mix. I think George Harrison once told his son Dhani, *it's okay to make music, and it's even okay to get rich. But don't get famous, because that's what imprisons you.*

• • •

Elliot Mintz gives us a window into John's world at an age when John was able to look back and reflect. From across the Atlantic, John could feel a kind of separation from his past. *Time wounds all heels.* In a later chapter, Elliot will provide further insight into John's world as a father, too: when he started looking *forward*. But for now, John was waiting on his immigration hearings and getting his latest albums together.

During this time, John found a kind of comfort in his semi-rekindled friendship with Paul McCartney. The two had known each other since their teenage years and, as a duo, immersed themselves in music and didn't look back until they were significantly older. In their wake fell the shadow of a world to which they could never return. But in each other they retained a sense of normalcy; of the old life. George and Ringo shared in this too – but John and Paul were songwriting partners from the very beginning. They kept in touch sporadically over the following years.

Sessions for John's *Rock 'n' Roll* album commenced in October 1973 in Los Angeles. Recording was soon curtailed as Phil Spector flew off the handle. He usually carried a gun; he may or may not have fired a round into the studio ceiling. This was the alleged breaking point. John has been quoted as saying, "Phil, if you're going to kill me, kill me. But don't fuck with my ears. I need 'em."

A&M Records ejected them, and John took his cue to leave LA. Phil Spector was later involved in a car accident and went into hiding, and with the *Rock 'n' Roll* master tapes locked in Spector's vault, John took *Walls & Bridges* back to New York instead. John and May Pang took up residence on 52nd Street, overlooking the East River.

During the *Walls & Bridges* sessions, Elton John performed backing vocals, piano and organ on John's track 'Whatever Gets You Thru the Night'. Elton saw serious potential in the track, but John was disparaging of it. They made a bet. If the song hit number one in the US, they would perform it together – live on stage.

SHELLY YAKUS

IN THE STUDIO

JOHN'S RECORDING STUDIO of choice was the Record Plant on 44th Street, one city block west of Times Square. He liked the studio's gritty, unpretentious vibe and formed a close friendship with the owner, Roy Cicala. With a close-knit team of engineers and musicians, they recorded, mixed, and mastered the bulk of three albums there: *Mind Games* (1973), *Walls & Bridges* (1974) and *Rock 'n' Roll* (1975). The same team put the finishing touches on *Imagine* (1971), the semi-live album *Some Time in New York City* (1972) and the compilation *Shaved Fish* (1975).

When John was first hit with Nixon's deportation order, Roy Cicala connected John with his legal team. Together they spent three years fighting the government. They shared in each other's good times and bad. Sadly, Roy passed away in 2014. He had a great many friends in the music industry, several of whom are represented in this book. Roy and his Record Plant team helped launch the careers of countless acts from the late '60s through to the late '80s – in many cases, studio time was given *pro bono* to up-and-comers when Roy believed in the music. Roy was also a great mentor to the many studio engineers, musicians and producers who came up through the ranks of the Record Plant.

Roy Cicala's Vice President and top recording and

mixing engineer at the Record Plant was Shelly Yakus. Shelly first worked with John Lennon and Roy Cicala on *Imagine*; he was heavily involved with recording and mixing on each of John's subsequent Record Plant projects. Prior to this, Shelly had worked as assistant engineer for projects with Frank Sinatra, Dionne Warwick, and Count Basie. He went on to become Chief Engineer and Vice President of A&M Records, working closely with artists such as U2, Tom Petty, Van Morrison, Dire Straits, Don Henley, Stevie Nicks, and Madonna, to name a few. In 1999, Bono nominated Shelly Yakus for the Rock 'n' Roll Hall of Fame.

With Shelly we're transported into the recording studio with John and his choice of musicians and engineers. We see John enjoying working with people who aren't necessarily set in their ways. And in some ways, John takes on the role of mentor. Here is John Lennon, bursting with enthusiasm and surprising humility.

SHELLY YAKUS: One of the things that was unique about John was that he was very comfortable working with new, younger engineers. He'd spent so much time in the studio with George Martin, and George had always liked working with people who were fresher; willing to try new things. Geoff Emerick, for example, was originally a mastering engineer. George brought him in on *Sgt. Pepper* as a recording engineer. His first album as a recording engineer was *Sgt. Pepper's Lonely Hearts Club Band.*

I worked for Record Plant in New York, and Roy Cicala was the owner. He was also my mentor from years before, and Roy and I worked on some of John's stuff together and separately. To get that opportunity to work with John — that he was comfortable working with me as a young engineer — that says a lot about John. He didn't feel that he had to have a guy that was older, or much more experienced.

He had a lot of trust in working with me, 'cos he had had that experience with George Martin. So that was the great moment – that he was willing to work with me.

On one of the albums we worked on, I remember driving in to work and hearing 'All You Need Is Love' on the radio. You hear all those instruments and the horns and how it's arranged; it's really amazing sounding. I tried to be really careful with John to not drive him crazy with, *Well, how did the Beatles do this?* and *How did the Beatles do that?* The press was already asking him that, and everyone he encountered asked those questions. I didn't want to have that kind of relationship with him – where I asked him about all the sounds the Beatles made. I shied away from that.

But I remember driving in. I got to the session and then John came in. Just before we started working, I said, "John, I've gotta ask a question. I never ask you this stuff, but I heard this song on the radio. In 'All You Need Is Love', with the horns playing *da da dadada,* and you have this big horn section – were those Mellotron horns?"

And he said, "No mate, it was the fuckin' London Symphony." He said, "No, no – those are the real horns. It was a whole symphonic orchestra…But I will tell you – there are no drums on that record. There is no snare drum. It was an upright bass being held by one of the Beatles, and Ringo hitting the strings of the upright bass with drumsticks, and another Beatle shaking a tambourine." And I'm thinking to myself, *how is that possible? I hear a snare drum.*

When I got home that night, because the drums were on one side of the record, I turned off one speaker. When you do that – when you know this information – you can hear that it's *not* a snare drum. It's a kind of clacking sound that really does sound like a snare. It makes a snare sound. But

I'm picturing one of the Beatles holding an upright bass by the neck, and Ringo slapping the strings with sticks. It was crazy. Those kind of moments – those are the things that were great with John – plus a few other things.

AIDAN PREWETT: I'm going to go listen to that track again. That's amazing. Other than that – is there another particular moment that stuck with you?

SY: Yeah, on the song '#9 Dream', he's singing these lyrics in the chorus – it's basically *ah böwakowa poussé poussé.* When he was running down the song with the band, he said to me, "Ignore these lyrics. I'm gonna write new lyrics for the chorus. I just don't have the song finished yet." He said, "I've got the verses and everything else, I've got the melody – but I haven't got the words for the chorus." By the time the song was finished, he said to me, "You know, I really like these lyrics. I'm gonna keep them."

And I said, "Well, John – that sounds good to me." What am I gonna say? He made those lyrics work. He sang them differently in the rundown of the song. It sounded quite goofy. But once he refined it, he got them to work.

There's another moment – I think it happens twice in the song, where the instruments stop. There might be an organ held over. The instruments all stop and there's a tom-tom fill, and then the song resumes. On the take that was *the take* for that song, I'm realizing that when those tom-toms were played, the meters on the tom-tom tracks weren't moving. That sound's just leaking into every other mic that was open in the room. So it's all in the distance. I was horrified. At the end of the take, on the playback, I'm turning around, and the take is playing – all the drums are there except for the tom-toms. What happened was, the tom-tom mics were going through a limiter – a Fairchild limiter. And the assistant engineer accidentally kicked the plug out of the wall. So when the limiter turned off, it killed the signal.

John said, "Okay – that's the take." Oh *man*, my heart dropped. Just imagine telling John Lennon you don't have some of the drums on the tape. And this shows you how cool a guy he is:

I said, "John, listen – something happened to the limiter. It got unplugged and the fills aren't there on the drum tracks. But they are there leaking in – they sound like they're in the distance."

He said, "Hey mate, it sounds perfect to me. Those tom-toms shouldn't be up front." It wouldn't work in the arrangement of the song to have big loud tom-toms. He said, "Actually, because they sound like they're down the street and far away, it's perfect for the lyric."

I said, "That's awesome, man – that you feel that way. But I could take them from the take before and fly them in to the two spots where they're missing."

He said, "No, no – this really works. It's a great accident."

It says a lot about John. I get asked all the time, *what was he like to work with?* And really, the truth is, he's about his music. It's about – it has to sound right to him. He's not doing it for other people. He's getting it to all work for himself. It's very interesting. I mean, he would say to me when he would play acoustic guitar on a song with the band, "Don't turn my acoustic up loud." Because normally you would take an artist who's singing a live vocal with an acoustic, it becomes *them and their acoustic*, and the band is *around* it, so to speak. In this case, when he played his acoustic, he wanted it to be lost in the band. It's unusual for me to hear that. I always thought, *well – you've got John*

Lennon, he wrote the song. He's a Beatle whose had all this phenomenal experience in the studio.

When we had a break from the session, I put it on the playback in private and I muted his acoustic guitar. The whole song just fell apart. Even though you could barely hear the acoustic in the balance that he wanted. It just had to be there. He looked at me and said, "You know – I'm not the best acoustic player." I almost burst out laughing. 'Cos you know – how do you keep a straight face when a guy like John Lennon says, "*I'm not the best acoustic player.*"

I felt like saying, "Are you serious? You're joking, right?" He was serious when he said it.

He said, "You know – it just has to be there because it's part of the song." I said *okay.*

But that also happens with other artists. Tom Petty was the same way. He'd play his acoustic guitar and say, "Now – don't turn it up loud, you know? Just keep it in the balance of the mix." With some of these songs that I did with Tom, you can barely hear the acoustic – but if you muted it, suddenly the song changed dramatically, and it wasn't for the better.

Every time I worked with John, it was truly an experience where it was he and I and the band and whoever else was involved, working *together.* You never felt you were working against each other. There was no – this may be hard to understand or even believe – but he didn't have an ego. He was the coolest guy to work with. He wasn't going to let anything go that bothered him arrangement-wise or playing-wise, or sound-wise. He just wanted it to be how he wanted it to be. But to get there, you felt like you were working together. It was never like, *I'm a Beatle and you're not.* You never got that sense or that flavor. He was really an awesome guy.

AP: With that in mind, do you recall a moment when you saw John at his happiest?

SY: He was the happiest in the studio. Let me put it this way: I didn't hang out with John outside the studio. It's not something I do with artists I work with. It tends to make them not be able to say, "Hey Shelly, I don't like the way this sounds." It changes the relationship in a way that makes it harder to make a good record. So I always try to avoid that. I saw early on in my career what happened with other engineers and what could happen if I hung out with artists I worked with outside the studio. Producers can do that, and it works quite well, but not with the engineers and the assistant engineers.

The point is, I didn't really see him outside the studio. In the studio, he'd walk in happy. He'd walk in with this enthusiasm about – *okay mate, let's get to work now.* We'd listen to a playback and he'd say, "Anybody hear anything – any mistakes?"

A player might say, "I missed this note here."

He'd say, "Okay, this might be the take – so if it is, we'll just punch that in."

He's like anyone else. He's the happiest when it goes well, and when it didn't go well, he made it go well, through his knowledge and his understanding of why the song wasn't working. I never once – in all the years on all the songs we worked on – saw him ever change from what I just described to you. I never saw him in a crappy mood. That stuff you read about in the newspapers where he did *this* in a nightclub, and he did *that* in a nightclub. *He did all this crazy stuff.* I never saw any of that stuff. It just didn't exist in my world with John, or in our relationship. I think a lot of it was blown way out of proportion.

AP: Is there a particular snippet of conversation that has stuck with you?

SY: In all the years I knew him, I can only remember a couple of times when I asked him about specific things, like 'All You Need Is Love'. One time I said to him something like, "John, when you and Paul wrote songs, and you wrote together and separately, how did you guys work together? What was it like?"

And he said, "Well, one day I called Paul. I said, 'Paul, I have a middle-8, and I'm trying to finish this song. What have you got?'"

Paul says to him, "Well I've got this verse that's been sitting in the drawer for a long time. I'll sing it to you over the phone – *Got up, got out of bed, dragged a comb across my head.*"

John says, "I'll take it." So he put it together with his bridge, and it became 'A Day in the Life'.

That whole thing – maybe it's public knowledge, maybe it isn't. The reason they always had Lennon-McCartney as writers, even if they didn't both write the song, was because their original manager, Brian Epstein, never wanted them to fight over the publishing and ownership and all that stuff. He was smart enough to know that Paul and John – even if one guy wrote the song, it most likely came from inspiration from something that the other said. He always felt that you couldn't separate them in that way. He wanted to avoid infighting. So that's why it always said Lennon-McCartney, where Paul might have written the song, but John didn't. But *indirectly*, he may have. So Brian Epstein didn't want them to ever say, "Well, wait a minute mate – I played you that six months ago. You didn't think of that!" "No you didn't!" He was very smart, setting an absolute: Lennon-McCartney. That's the way it stayed for life on those songs.

AP: Do you remember any moment with May Pang that stands out?

SY: All the moments with May stood out because she really had a cool personality. She was part of John's creative life in a lot of ways. I don't remember anything beyond that except that it was always a pleasure to have her there. There's a picture of me producing Johnny Winter's album, and John came in to visit the session. I'm turned around, so you really just see the side of my head, and I'm talking to Johnny Winter. Behind Johnny Winter and I, sitting at the console is John Lennon, May Pang, and Jimmy Iovine. Johnny Winter and I are sitting there; May came into the studio with John and Jimmy came to visit.

It was really a cool atmosphere to make records, especially in that day. Nobody makes these great records by themselves. It's always groups or teams of people. And I'll tell you what – you don't see any egos. That's the most unusual part. But it *became* usual. You don't see any egos. At least, from my perspective, I didn't see *any* egos. Everybody was just involved, making the best version of the song we were working on at the time.

AP: That's great to hear – there are definitely stories of artists that are *not* like that.

SY: Record Plant New York, where all the work I did with John was done, the atmosphere was great. Greg Calbi worked there – a lot of great people worked there and came out of there. Jack Douglas came out of there. Jay Messina. Really great engineers and producers came out of that place. There was a great atmosphere. I never felt – and I don't think anyone else ever felt – that somebody was trying to crawl over someone else to get an opportunity. That kind of thinking can happen in studios, but I never saw it at Record Plant. At most studios that I've worked in, you never saw anything like that.

Control rooms in successful studios seem to be a very sincere, honest places. I don't know how else to explain it. Outside that control room, I can't comment. But I know that in the control rooms where I've worked with really great artists, it's all about making the best record you can make. Nobody's trying to take over and push the producer out of the way or push the engineer out of the way or take control of the artist and get in his ear. Like I say, I don't know what happens outside the studio; I don't know what happens at the labels or the management offices or any of that stuff. But it was always noticeable to me that I was just able to go about my business.

AP: With that in mind, in the control room – was there a moment that comes to mind where you got a real sense of sincerity from John?

SY: Always. How about this – there was never a time when he was *insincere*. It was always about making the best version of the song and bringing it to the finish line. It was about what you were left with at the end of the day. You were left with all the blocks in the right place. You just had a really good feeling about working together and creating something that was on paper to start with. You take it from notes on a piece of paper – written notes and lyrics scribbled out on a piece of paper. To take it from there to a finished song, to something that John was happy with – and that the label was happy with. I can say for myself, and I know for many people involved – we all walked away with the same feeling – that it was all sincere and honest. Things you don't think about. You just feel good. There were no thoughts or actions that got in the way of that feeling of *wow – this was really cool.* We all worked hard – and at the end of the day and the end of the week and the end of the month, or two months – we came out with something that was really cool, and we all went on to the next thing. It would be easier to explain that there was nothing that came in to disturb that feeling.

AP: The first time you met John – do you remember that first moment?

SY: Roy Cicala was working with John, and Roy introduced me to him. I remember shaking John's hand and thinking to myself *holy shit. What a pleasure – what do you say to a guy like this?* What do you say – *I love your stuff? I think you're great?* What do you say? I'm thinking this to myself, so I said, "It's really a pleasure to meet you." I noticed he was different from his image – even his *hair* was a different color brown. And there was a presence.

If you saw him in a crowd of a hundred people – but you didn't know it was John – he would stand out. *Really* stand out. There was something about his presence. There's a lot of actors and actresses – when you're successful, you have that presence. But there are a lot of people who want to be actors and actresses and models. There are people – guys and girls –women who are very beautiful, men who are extremely handsome. I'm talking about some people who maybe haven't quite made it yet. But no matter how beautiful or handsome they are, they blend in with the crowd or they blend in with the wallpaper. They don't have that presence.

John had that presence. Marilyn Monroe, before she

started doing drugs, had that presence. She had that thing that stood off the page, and so did John. Actually, I think all the Beatles had it. Just talking about John – there was a certain presence – there was something about him that stood out – *way* out from the crowd.

Bette Davis had this saying – *Some women just have this thing. And if you don't have this thing, it doesn't matter what else you do have – it's not enough.* Everything else falls into place when you have that thing.

AP: Speaking of that – having a presence – were you there when Elton John came in to record on 'Whatever Gets You Thru the Night'?

SY: Yes, I was. I couldn't be there for all of it – at that time in the album, I had a previous commitment to another artist. So when Elton came in, Jimmy Iovine, who was really an assistant at the time, and just becoming an engineer, did the session.

I said, "John – over the next few days I have a commitment I can't change." I think it was Chick Corea who I was working with. I said, "I can't change this." But I said, "Jimmy can do this overdub for you, and do a really good job."

Roy told him too – *Jimmy can do this for you.* I remember Jimmy saying to me in private, "I don't know how to get that sound that Elton gets on his piano – 'cos that's what he's going to expect. How the hell does he get that sound?"

I said, "You know – if you just mic the piano the way we usually mic it here, and use a little EQ and just make a good recording of the piano, maybe it can be taken further in the mix. But you'll be fine. John's comfortable working with you."

Then I think Jimmy said to John, "John – I don't know

– how do they get that sound on Elton's piano? I want to make sure I get something you're both going to be happy with."

And John said to him, "*Elton* makes that sound." He said, "You'll see – when Elton sits down to play, that piano is going to have that sound." And it did.

AP: Was there a moment between Elton John and John Lennon that you recall?

SY: Yeah – they just had a lot of fun together. There was just this brightness in the room. I don't know how to put it into words – it's just when you're in the room with those two guys, it's pretty amazing. The talent is just dripping off the walls.

AP: Did you come across Phil Spector? I mean, you would have.

SY: Yes, when I worked on *Imagine* with John, we got the tapes in New York, and they were adding strings to the song. John and Phil were working with the strings to get them to fit the song that was already recorded. So there was this large string section doing the overdubs. Roy Cicala and myself, we were all working on this; and Jack Douglas. With those two guys in the room – Phil Spector and John Lennon – it's incredible because they both have this unbelievable history of making some of the greatest records ever made. These records reached millions and millions of people, because they were able to reach the deepest part of you with their music. And here's these two guys in the same control room – and I'm just hoping that the tape machine doesn't stop working that it doesn't eat the tape. Or *holy cow* – somebody knocks a coffee in the console, or – you know, you're just hoping that it goes smoothly.

We all knew we could capture the sound of the strings and make it work with the other instruments. I don't know what everybody else was thinking, but I know it was a happy and nervous time.

John and Phil were kinda quiet with each other during the sessions for *Imagine*, as if maybe they had some stuff they had to work out *outside* the studio. Direction – maybe there was some question about how much strings should be used in what places and arrangement. There's always different opinions and disagreements when it comes to creative stuff, you know? It almost seemed like outside the control room there was maybe something else going on. They were very respectful in the control room, but they were quiet with each other, other than just businesslike conversations about the strings or where they should play, or was it working in this section and that sort of thing. I didn't hear it, but you get the feeling that they weren't best of friends. I don't want to say that they *weren't* best of friends, but I'm trying to describe to you what it was like to be standing in that room. 'Cos I remember it like it was yesterday. They worked together, but it was almost from a distance. I still feel it to this day. Maybe a way of describing it would be that there wasn't a lot of laughing going on. They were both quite serious about working on these strings for the song, and the direction.

When Roy Cicala and I were working on *Imagine*, after the session – and this was always with John's permission – we would go to another room with John, or without John, and we would work on some of these songs. We'd try to make them come across stronger for the listener, just by reinforcing some of the sounds. That was done after hours, where nobody knew about it. There was even a work tape that we used that Roy made sure nobody was ever going to hear. Nobody wanted this tape in the tape library to get mixed up with anything – it could have been construed that *that* was the master.

So there was stuff going on in private, even after Phil left the session. We would play John what we came up with the next day. It was really a very cool thing. No one else knew about this except the three of us – Roy, John, and myself. I was really fortunate to be included in this. I don't take any of this stuff for granted – it's humbling, actually. It really is. To have a guy that was a Beatle – that had *all* this worldwide success – and was so popular. To be able to work with me, a mere mortal, and not ever act in a way that made me feel like I shouldn't be there or wasn't important to the project. He wasn't patting me on the back – but by what he *didn't* say, that always made me feel really comfortable.

We were able to just focus on what we needed to do, because of his *being*, so to speak. And how he saw it all. Imagine sitting next to John Lennon – and it's just the two of us – and I'm thinking to myself, *is he gonna figure out that I don't know what the hell I'm doing? If he thought that, he would have figured it out already. So I think I'm okay.* But I couldn't help thinking it – he's worked with the best in the world. I'm saying to myself, *I just want to give this guy what he came to me for, and more.* Am I going to be able to do this? Or is he going to figure out I don't know what the hell I'm doing? That's what I was thinking for a moment there.

AP: Is there anything I've missed – anything you feel that people should know about John?

SY: I would say that it was just an amazing experience. You can't have that with someone who – if you read some of the articles about John; the controversial stuff – I could never have had the experiences I had with him if that stuff were true. I'm not going to say it's *all* not true, but as an overview, he was just fabulous to work with and always made me comfortable. He made me feel comfortable that we were doing good work together, and that stayed with me. I was really fortunate to work with John. I learned a lot from him.

. . .

In his mentor capacity, it's clear that John enjoyed working with and spending time with his younger musical colleagues. We'll hear more of these kinds of stories in the next couple of chapters. John was open to change, patient, and accepting of the variety of hiccups that occur in a studio environment. And he celebrated the happy accidents, such as the one with the tom-toms and the unplugged limiter. And Shelly Yakus was a good student, taking those lessons with him through countless albums with other artists over the years.

John's ethos was to serve the song – to create the best version possible, egos aside. And John wanted the song to work for his own ears. He wasn't doing it for anybody else.

John had been up late with May Pang one night in 1974, channel-surfing, when they heard a televangelist utter the phrase, *it's whatever gets you through the night*. John quickly jotted it down – he knew a great title when he heard one. 'Whatever Gets You Thru the Night' was recorded in July/ August with some assistance from Elton John. The single was released in September 1974 and shot to #1 in the USA. Elton John had won the bet. Interestingly, the track barely cracked the Top 40 in the UK.

It was decided that John would join Elton on stage in a surprise appearance at Madison Square Garden for Thanksgiving in November. They played 'Whatever Gets

You Thru the Night', 'Lucy in the Sky with Diamonds', and 'I Saw Her Standing There.' John introduced the last song – usually led by Paul in the old days – with the words, "Here's a number from an old estranged fiancé of mine called Paul." The audience erupted. It was a public olive branch for McCartney and it kicked off rumors of a Beatle reunion. Nobody there that night could have known it would be John's final stadium performance.

Yoko attended the concert, bringing flowers for John and Elton. Another bridge was being mended.

GREG CALBI

MASTERING

"WALLS KEEP YOU IN, either protectively or otherwise – and bridges get you somewhere else," John said in promoting his new album. *Walls & Bridges* was released in September 1974 and became another #1 album in the US. John later spoke of the track '#9 Dream' as one of his favorite singles. Its unique vocal sound was achieved using a beat-up old microphone that had been discovered inside a bass drum – having been left there, forgotten, for years. Many of the tracks on the album deal with themes of loneliness and separation – John was now in limbo. Back in New York, still living with May Pang, he was also in closer proximity to Yoko.

John saw more of Julian during this period. The final track on *Walls & Bridges*, 'Ya Ya', is a duet between John and his then eleven-year-old son. John provided the vocal and piano part, while Julian contributed snare drum, keeping time in eighth notes with a single stick.

Greg Calbi was the mastering engineer for *Walls & Bridges* and John's other major Record Plant albums. Calbi's audio career started with Roy Cicala, where he mastered *Young Americans* with David Bowie, *Born to* Run with Bruce Springsteen, *Fear of Music* with Talking Heads, Patti Smith's *Easter,* Paul Simon's *Graceland,* the self-titled

Blondie and *Ramones,* among a great many others. Between 2014-2019, albums mastered by Greg Calbi earned 33 Grammy nominations. Recent acts The National, The War on Drugs, Lady Gaga, Kacey Musgraves, and St. Vincent have all won Grammys with albums mastered by Greg Calbi.

In 1974, during the mastering of *Rock 'n' Roll,* John left a handwritten note for Greg, which he signed off with the words:

I TRUST YOUR EARS

There could be no higher compliment – this was from John Lennon, the studio veteran. Greg has the note framed on the wall of his new studio, Sterling Sound.

If you've ever heard an unmastered or poorly mastered track, you'll know how important the mastering process is. The instruments and vocal don't blend so well, they tend to stick out in unexpected ways, cohesiveness is lost, and it sounds amateurish. Beautifully mastered tracks sound smooth and warm – each musical element seems perfectly positioned and balanced. It just sounds *right.* The mastering process smooths out the rough edges by carefully adjusting individual sound frequencies to allow for optimum play-back on a wide variety of stereo systems. Mastering has been described as the magic pixie dust that brings a track to life. Greg Calbi has that magic.

John would check in with Greg to see how the tracks were shaping up during the mastering process. These finishing touches were of great importance, but John's sense of humor was never far from the surface. John saw the way to get the best out of his colleagues – to make them feel comfortable.

GREG CALBI: There was a practical joke that John came up with. We were doing the *Rock 'n' Roll* album, and I was mastering it. With reel-to-reel tape, there's different ways of storing the tape. One of the ways to store it is not to put it on a reel, but just to put it on what we call a hub, which is just the center of the reel. If the tape machine is not winding properly, that hub is very insecure. Way before John was working with me one day, I had dropped one of these reels and I had it in a box. It was literally like a mass of confetti. What I would do is, when I had some time in between things I was doing, I would wind it back onto a reel. Very slowly – it was going to take all year. But it was an old jazz tape and there was no urgency. I just had to return it to its correct form at one point.

John came into the room and he saw the box. He just looked at me and said, "What is that?" And I told him exactly what I just told you, and he looked at the tape that we had on the machine I was playing and listening to – his mix. And he said, "Is there any way that we could make that look like it's my tape?"

And I said, "Yeah, it's actually pretty easy – I could just cut the tape and I could attach it to the tape on the machine and put it on both sides, it would look like the machine jammed up and flew off the reel."

He said, "Oh, that's fantastic, that's perfect." So this was all his idea. He called up Roy Cicala, the owner of the studio, and he started screaming at him. I had never heard him raise his voice before that. He's saying "This fucking kid doesn't know jack shit – he doesn't know what he's doing. He just ruined my whole mix. I can't believe it. How'd you stick me with him? He doesn't know anything!" I was laughing really silently in the back. So Roy walked into the cutting room. I had never seen him like this – he was petrified. He was completely white – he was as white as a ghost. And he came over to the machine and he looked at it; he was confounded. He was trying to figure out *how the hell does this thing jump off the machine?* And then I think John might have snickered first. And he might have got the laugh going, and then I started laughing. And then we both started howling and crying, laughing.

And that's when Roy turned to me and he said "I'm gonna get even with *you*. I'm never going to forget this."

And John was like, "Oh, forget it – don't worry." He was so happy.

He was very easy. He wasn't *blamey*, you know. He wasn't the kind of person that would blame you – particularly blame *me*, as a very young mastering guy and machine operator, cutting engineer. John spent a lot of time trying to perfect what he was doing. I knew that because in those years, in order to listen to mixes at home, you'd have to cut them on the lathe – he wouldn't take a tape home, you'd have to cut him a record and he'd listen to that on his LP player.

So day after day, we'd be working. '#9 Dream' was the one I remember – day after day I'd get a call at six o'clock that *we have another mix of '#9 Dream'*. Like, *oh my God they haven't finished this yet*. It would go on for days and days and days. He just kept trying to get pleased with it, you know. I'm not saying that he was insecure in the studio, but I think he was very open. I don't think that he was tortured by it. He enjoyed playing in the studio and I think he liked getting out of the house. And I know he liked being with May, because I witnessed the two of them being very affectionate many, many times.

May would be sitting on his lap, and he'd be laughing. May was just great. I mean, the other thing that happened with May, was when they insisted that they saw a flying saucer coming down the East River. They *insisted* that they saw it. John said, "It was unbelievable. We looked out and it went right down towards Brooklyn, and then it made a left turn. We weren't high." He was insisting.

And I was like, "John, what can I tell you? Were you the only one that saw it? Wouldn't that have been in the newspaper?"

He said, "No, no – it happened so quickly. You had to be looking at the sky at the time."

So, *"Okay, well..."* And recently, in the last couple of years, I saw May and I said, "May – this has been bothering me for forty years. Did you guys really see a flying saucer?"

And she said, "Absolutely."

AIDAN PREWETT: Could you tell me a little bit about the note that you got from John where it said *I trust your ears.*

GC: It was a very gracious thing for him to say. When I do the work, the clients react to the work. And he reacted to what I told him. This is before the days of text messages and email and everything. He wrote the note, and in the note he said he trusts my ears. When I read that, I was really flattered, 'cos the communication that we had about the cutting would be: If we had the bass loud enough; is the vocal loud enough. You know, the basic stuff about mastering. What the mastering person does is to evaluate certain balances and things. So it was very sweet of him. And the other thing that John did – that May did – and she was very, very careful with this – was that she'd get John to sign albums for everybody. So I have a *Walls & Bridges* album which is signed to me from John, with a cute little cartoon. May had actually gone to college for a few years with one of the guys at the Record Plant. She knew him from before

John & Yoko. She was just a very bubbly, young, gorgeous woman who everybody got a kick out of. May was really a believer in tying everything in, like a community of people.

There were a lot of great artists in that studio all the time, so it wasn't like everybody was star-struck. We had everybody in there. I mean, the history of that place is really legendary.

I'd come in one day – "What am I doing today?"

"Well, Allen Ginsberg is in Studio A." And I'd be working with Allen Ginsberg. Or I'd get a call – "John is doing a TV show, you gotta go down and help John with some engineering on the TV show". Or – you know, it could be anybody. Lou Reed doing *Berlin*. Todd Rundgren and the New York Dolls. I mean, it just went on and on. The place was amazing.

So John was – I think he liked it too because he'd run into people from the biz. In a very casual way, a very non-threatening way. It wasn't open to the public, so he wasn't going to get a lot of fan problems. But the fact that he was murdered was so typical of how open he was. You know – I would see him during the late '70s, when I hadn't seen him for three or four years, I'd see he and Yoko walking around the West Side of Manhattan.

And my ex-wife – one time I remember she said, "Just go over and say hello".

I said, "You know what? He doesn't need any professional connection people to come and say hello to him. He just wants to see New York." So I never – even though I was only fifty feet away from him one time, he didn't see me. I didn't go and say hello to him. I felt like he needed his privacy. And he got his privacy in those years – unlike today, where everybody's trying to take a picture with a celebrity, running up to them with a phone. He would not like that – that I guarantee you. His life would be so different if he was alive now in New York. I don't know if he would enjoy New York the way he used to because he could be under the radar. He'd just be walking around. People would turn their head, but they wouldn't approach him. It's interesting.

AP: Could you give me a kind of portrait of the vibe at the Record Plant, and John's coming in…

GC: John used to go into one of the big rooms and work on arrangements of songs. It was just to keep him in performance shape, or something. But there was a room in the studio that we used to play ping pong in, and when John was coming in to rehearse, the guys used to fold it up. That was what the atmosphere was like in the studio. John was living in New York – the studio is on 44th Street, he's on 72nd Street. So he basically has a ten-minute cab ride to get out of his apartment and go to a fantastic recording studio, where he was always welcome. And he was very close friends with Roy Cicala, who would have some great John stories, but he passed away about five years ago. So John and Yoko, and May, were around the studio frequently, either working, or just hanging. At this point I'm about 24 years old. And John, I guess, is about 34 years old. This is in 1974-1975 – just to give you that background. So when Sean was born, then John kinda didn't show up anymore and he did that retirement thing until *Double Fantasy*, which was obviously at the time that John was murdered.

AP: Was it a different feel when he came in on his own, or when he came in with May, or when he came in with Yoko?

GC: I don't remember any times when Yoko and John were together in the room with me. With John I did *Walls &*

Bridges, Mind Games, Rock 'n' Roll and *Shaved Fish*. And the Harry Nilsson album that he did called *Pussycats*. But he was rarely in the room with me one-to-one, except for – with each of those albums, maybe two hours. John wasn't a *hands-on with mastering* guy, but he would show up.

One time we were working on the *Rock 'n' Roll* album, and I don't remember which song it was – I wish I did remember. But there was one song where his vocal was mixed way, way back. It was just too low in the mix. And I questioned him about it. I said, "I have to try to EQ this to get the vocal to be a little louder."

He said, "Oh, no, no – that's rubbish. I don't want it loud. Don't make it loud."

I said to him, "I don't understand that, John." And it was ridiculous that I said this, as a 24-year-old, but I said, "You know, you're one of the greatest singers in the history of rock 'n' roll, and you don't want your vocal loud. I don't get it."

And he just shook his head and said, "It's rubbish. It's rubbish."

There were also a couple of songs in that mastering that didn't end up on the album – which were used on that album that he mistakenly offered to Morris Levy which came out on a TV ad. It became a big John Lennon story, and then there was a whole big lawsuit about it. It might have been 'Be My Baby' – he just didn't like what he did. There's a whole lot of stuff about that album which is atypical of John's creative process. But I did always remember that he said that.

He was very humble with people who were working with him. He wasn't – you know, I've read so many things about John being arrogant, and being crazy drunk and all these different stories about his lost weekend and all that stuff. But to be around somebody who was so famous, and for him to make you feel comfortable – he knew he had to make people feel comfortable. And he did. He didn't pull rank, there was no *star* feeling. I think that's one thing he loved about working in a New York studio with New York guys. Because everybody was pretty down-home, ex-hippie, kinda grubby. It *was* kinda grubby. It was a great studio, but it was in Times Square in the 1970's. It was pretty funky down there.

AP: How did you come to be at the Record Plant? What was that journey for you?

CC: I've told this story, and it sounds like something out of make-believe, but I went to a party for my friend from high school and college; my best buddy at the time. His sister was dating a guy – Richie – who I heard was a musician, and so I talked to him at the party. Then a month or two after that, I get a phone call, and it was this guy Richie, and he said, "Let me ask you a question – do you know how to drive a truck?"

And I said, "Yeah, I actually drove a truck all during college, 'cos my father-in-law is a water proofer and I used to have this big water proofing truck with all the ladders and the ropes and everything on it. So yeah, I can drive a truck, you know?"

He said, "Well, we need somebody to drive down to Duke University in North Carolina to record the band Yes. And Yes, at that time – the album *Fragile* – I mean, Yes was huge.

I was like, "Holy smokes. No problem!" Fifty dollars a day. Fifteen dollars meal money. I said, "I am there. I'm so there."

So, I lived in Queens at the time, I took the train. This

is absolutely stone-cold truth. I took the train and I got there on a Sunday morning, and when I got to the studio, the door of the studio opened, and who walked out of the studio but John and Yoko, together. And I almost – I literally had to catch my breath. I almost fainted. I mean, I was so… I had never seen… you can just imagine! I came from *nowhere*, and now I go to the first recording studio, and the first person I see is one of the Beatles? Gimme a break! Crazy! So that's how I got my foot in the door. In this particular instance, I had a tremendous amount of luck.

It was a fantastic period, and all the folks who were around that studio – having to do not only with John but with all the other great people that were in and out of there. John was a wonderful, pivotal person for me. And even hanging that letter in the studio for years has helped me. So even after his death, he helped me – just with that one little kind word, that he trusted my ear.

• • •

Working with John Lennon would be a career highlight for any engineer or musician – let alone for young people who grew up listening to the Beatles. But the Record Plant was the top studio in New York City, and Roy Cicala had his pick of the best engineers and musicians in the world. Working with John at that time had little to do with luck – it had to do with hard work, perseverance, talent, and what potential Roy Cicala could see.

They say that you should never meet your idols. But to have that chance, and to experience working with John as a regular guy – no *star* feeling…. to witness the Lennon humor first-hand, playing pranks on his friends – albeit at Roy Cicala's expense – must have been exhilarating. And the written note, *I trust your ears…*

Paul McCartney called John in January 1975 to invite him down to New Orleans, where Wings were working on a new album called *Venus and Mars*. May Pang and Art Garfunkel both tried to convince John to take up the offer. John was seriously considering it, but eventually decided against it. Instead, he went to the Dakota, to see if Yoko would take him back.

JON COBERT
ROCK 'N' ROLL

JOHN LENNON kept a diary during his 'Lost Weekend'. Yoko never read it; they symbolically burnt it together when they rekindled their romance. John moved back into the Dakota, and the couple renewed their wedding vows in early 1975. May Pang remained a friend of the couple and would continue to see John and Yoko over the course of the year and sporadically thereafter.

John was contractually obliged to deliver a final album for EMI/Capitol in 1975, and *Rock 'n' Roll* would be it. EMI retrieved the master tapes from the now-reclusive Phil Spector, and John produced the final sessions himself. After that he had a more important role to undertake – namely the raising of Sean Taro Ono Lennon, who was born on John's birthday, the ninth of October.

John's final gig was at the New York Hilton Hotel in April 1975. *A Salute to Sir Lew* was a televised variety tribute show in honor of television impresario Sir Lew Grade. On the surface it was a chance for John to promote the new album. Underneath, John knew he would do well to play nice with Sir Lew, who held a controlling interest in Northern Songs – the entire Lennon/McCartney publishing catalogue. The television broadcast was also a very public way to show that John was able to kowtow to the upper crust. His final immigration hearing was soon to follow.

Despite the 'tribute', Sir Lew Grade would hardly have been one of Lennon's favorite people. In 1969 he had purchased his 34% share in Northern Songs from music publisher Dick James and had then launched a campaign to secure control of the company. Lennon and McCartney held 15% each. John's public behavior back in '69 had grown increasingly erratic, and it wasn't long before Sir Lew convinced the other major shareholders to sell to him.

In characteristic Lennon style, his 'salute' to Sir Lew was performed with an underhanded gesture: Each member of the backing band appeared with a molded cast of their own face applied as prosthetics to the backs of their heads. They were, both physically and metaphorically, *two-faced*. The band played three songs, although only the first two were televised: 'Slippin' and Slidin', 'Imagine', and 'Stand by Me'. The opening number, written by Little Richard, was first heard by John nearly 20 years earlier on Michael Hill's 78rpm record player. It was the B-side to 'Long Tall Sally'.

Present throughout this period was Jon Cobert, keyboard player with the house band at the Record Plant, who accompanied John on many occasions including the *Sir Lew* performance. Cobert has since worked with Bruce Springsteen, Jackson Browne, Dion DiMucci, Tom Chapin, Harry Chapin, Dionne Warwick, B.J. Thomas, Chubby Checker, and Al Green, among many others. His work with Tom Chapin has been nominated for five Grammy Awards. Cobert was the musical director and pianist for a sold-out Lead Belly tribute festival at Carnegie Hall in 2016. He currently runs his own recording studio in New York.

With Jon Cobert we catch a glimpse deeper into John's

life as one of the most famous people in the world. John was grappling with his desire to live a more normal life – to revisit his days as a young musician jamming with his friends, or to take some buddies out to lunch. Jon Cobert experienced all of this first-hand, as John Lennon ventured a bit further down the studio corridor to make music with 'a bunch of teenagers'.

JON COBERT: John was like a little kid in the studio. I was surprised about how he had not lost his wonder. So when he was in the studio, he was always very excited about what was going on. You know – just like a little kid, and happy. And I think he was at his best in the studio. I kind of feel that way myself. It's a special place to be creative and be with other people who share what you have going on. There's a kind of a special bond that you have with people when you're in the studio making music. So that was number one. I never felt – from the minute I met him, I never felt like *oh my God, this is a Beatle.* You know? He never made me feel that way.

I was nineteen years old at that time. So I felt comfortable right away, right from the very beginning. And he was just a regular guy. I think that's what he moved to New York for. So he could just be a regular guy, just walking around the streets and shopping, and going to lunch and taking a cab, and doing all those kinds of things. Which he really loved doing. I went to lunch with him a bunch of times. It was always a very interesting experience, because we were just having lunch. And I'm sure – he didn't notice it as much – but I'd look around and just see everybody at all the other tables looking over: *That's John Lennon at that table.* So it was fun. It was just exciting. It was always exciting.

And in the studio, the first thing I ever did with him in

the studio was I watched a session for the *Walls & Bridges* album. We were basically the house band at the Record Plant studio. So when he was doing *Walls & Bridges* we'd get to sit in and watch while they were doing the sessions. And I watched Elton John play piano on 'Whatever Gets You Thru the Night'. And afterwards, we were back in our rehearsal room, which we called the BOMF Room – the name of my band was BOMF. We were just in there, and he came into our room, and he said, "Hey guys, you wanna come and clap on 'Whatever Gets You Thru the Night'?" So we did that, and I had a little Sony Walkman recorder with me, that I had just bought. And I took it with me into the studio. And I turned it on. So I captured the whole session.

AIDAN PREWETT: Oh my God.

JC: All the – in between the takes, and everything that was going on, and all his comments and everything like that. I went up to him afterwards, and I used it like a reporter. I asked him a couple of questions and he was having a great time, pretending – in his voices that he used to use.

AP: Wow.

JC: So yeah, he had a really good time. So we clapped on 'Whatever Gets You Thru the Night'. It was a lot of fun. He was leading the session; Jimmy Iovine was the engineer. And then later on he did the *Rock 'n' Roll* album. So we got to go in and sing background vocals on that record. 'Cos it had already been – almost all – completed, by Phil Spector out in LA. Then he brought it back to the Record Plant to finish it up. So we sang background vocals on it, and then John said to me, "I want to put strings on 'Stand by Me'." It had already been recorded and mixed. So he didn't want to go back to the two-inch master and overdub strings; re-mix everything.

He had me get my Arp String Ensemble, which was a synthesizer that I had that simulated strings. I brought it into the studio, and Jimmy Iovine was in the booth. So it was the three of us in the studio. And what they did was – they put the mix, which was on half-inch tape, already mixed – they put the tape on the tape recorder. Jimmy opened up the head of the tape recorder and disconnected the erase head so that we could overdub on top of the mix, without erasing what was already on there. Normally when you record, you're erasing what's there already. So he actually pulled the wires off the tape machine that were connected to the erase head, so it was just going to record on top of the mix. So we had one shot to do it.

AP: Oh God!

JC: 'Cos you can't go back and – you know. Now you're playing new material on top of the mix. So, before we recorded, John and I went over to the keyboard that I had set up. And I tried all different types of voicings for the strings at the beginning. What he liked was a very low note, and a very high note, and another note in the middle. Which I couldn't reach with my two hands, because it was beyond the reach of two hands. So I had him stand next to me, and I put his finger on the note in the middle.

I said, "Just keep your finger on that note in the middle, and when I nod to you, then you move it to *that* note." So we did it. It came out perfect, and it ended up on the single 'Stand By Me'. So that's how we recorded the strings on 'Stand By Me', with John and myself playing the String Ensemble at the same time.

AP: That single is one of my favorites.

JC: It's a great single. It's an interesting story. You know, because it was back in 1975. When that happened, there were no cell phones. Nobody had cameras in their pockets, so there are no pictures of that. That's the part that bothers me – is that all of these interactions I had with him – I was nineteen, and then twenty years old for those two years. And I never thought *oh my God, I should be taking pictures all the time, because one of these days he's not going to be around anymore.* No – I thought this was going to last forever. I thought, *oh, this is my life now. Here I am.* And why should I take pictures? I'll see him tomorrow.

There's another interesting story. We did this TV show called *A Salute to Sir Lew Grade*, and that was the last time he ever performed in public. So we were the backup band behind him when he did that for that TV show. 'Cos after that, he kinda went into fatherhood and stay-home-dad land until he did the next album, and then he sadly was assassinated.

When we were doing the prerecord for that TV show, we weren't actually playing live behind him – for technical reasons at the time. So we went into the studio to record 'Imagine' so he could sing it on TV. And we're in the studio about to record and John comes over to me.

He said, "Let me show you exactly how I played 'Imagine' on the record, so you can do it the same way." He sat next to me on the piano bench, and he played 'Imagine' for me. And then I played it for him – to make sure I was doing it exactly the same way he did it on the record. And that's another thing I don't have pictures of.

Speaking of pictures – when we taped the TV show, we were wearing masks of our faces. John had taken us to an artist down in the East Village, who molded our faces a couple of weeks before the TV taping. So we sat in her loft; she put plaster on our faces. We sat there for an hour while it dried, and he came with us and sat with us. So before the TV show was taped, we all went into makeup together – John came with us too – and we had the masks put onto our heads. We had bald wigs on top of our heads, so we looked like alien creatures with two faces. We were in makeup for about two hours, and one of the guys in our band brought his friend to be the photographer and take pictures of us that morning. And none of the pictures came out, because he used the wrong kind of film.

So I was really bummed out. For years, I never had pictures of that. John had been posing with us, and kissing me on the cheek, and all these beautiful pictures like you see in the Beatles' pictures. I never had any pictures. Until about the year 2000. My friend Ira called me on the phone and said, "Jon, I just saw your picture with John Lennon in the newspaper."

I said, "What are you talking about?"

He said, "Apparently, when you did that TV show there was a photographer there from a magazine. And he took a whole bunch of pictures of you guys. And now he's having a show at an art gallery of all of his John & Yoko pictures – and you're in them."

So I immediately got in the car and drove to his gallery, met him, pointed to my face and said, "That's me."

And he said, "Oh, come up to my loft – I have more." And he gave me all these prints of pictures that he had with me and John, and stuff like that. So now I have them. For years I didn't.

AP: Of all of the time that you spent with John, is there one conversation, or one moment that has stuck with you more than anything else?

JC: Yeah, I think so. He used to call me the Bearded Wonder. That was his nickname for me. That's just an extra thing. But there was one time when we were just hanging out in the lobby at the Record Plant, and I had been writing poetry at the time. Just kind of nonsense poetry. I would stick a piece of paper in the typewriter and just type – making up words. Things that just sounded good to me. Stream of consciousness kind of stuff.

I had it with me, and I said, "John, would you take a look at this poetry and just tell me what you think?"

And he said "Sure." So he read the poetry and he said, "You know – I love this. And it reminds me a lot of my own poetry. I'm going to bring you a book."

So the next day when I came to the studio, he had a book for me. It was a paperback book of his two books – *In His Own Write* and *A Spaniard In the Works.* I was so thrilled. I brought it home and I told my sister about it and she said, "Did you get him to autograph it?" And I said *no*, and she said, "You idiot!" So the next day I brought it back in with me, and I was a little embarrassed to ask him because I was in my head thinking *oh, we're colleagues, we're contemporaries – I'm not going to ask him to autograph things. A fan would do that.* But he made me feel really comfortable.

He said, "No, don't be silly," and he opened it up and he autographed it for me and he drew a little picture of a dog taking a dump, just next to a little picture of his face. So yeah, that sticks out.

AP: That's beautiful. When you said John was like a kid in the studio, can you think of any specific moment that would illustrate that?

JC: I just remember him always coming up with ideas. He

would always have the tape rolling from the minute he walked into the studio so that any idea that came off his head would be captured. And he was always going over to Kenny Ascher – who was the piano player and arranger on a lot of dates – just singing him ideas. You know – he would just pop up out of his chair in the control room and he would just run into the studio and just say "*I have an idea for a string line, and it goes like this.*" And he'd sing it to him, and Kenny would write it down. It was those kinds of things that illustrated how enthusiastic he always was when he was in the studio.

AP: When you took the tape recorder in and listened to it back later, is there anything that really stuck out as being – *that thing that John said was really interesting...*

JC: He was just silly. He was being silly. I held it up to him and I said, "John, would you say something for posterity?" He said, "Hello there, Posterity. How are you?"

AP: Do you recall the first time you met John?

JC: The day I met him there was an article in the paper about this fifteen-year-old Perfect Master, who had seventeen Rolls Royces, and there was a picture of him with all his Rolls Royces.

I just said to John – I said, "Hello, it's nice to meet you. Did you see that article in the paper?"

And he said, "Boy, it's very funny all those cars."

It was kind of my way of breaking the ice with him and being a regular guy. It illustrated to me at the time that some people have it in their heads that people that famous can't just be normal people and you can't just have a normal conversation with them. But you could.

He was very charming. Very friendly, very charming. If

anybody ever asked him any questions about specific things about the Beatles, and lyrics – he just wouldn't – he didn't know. He just wanted to be *in the moment*.

There's another interesting thing – when we did the taping of *Sir Lew Grade*, he had the lyrics to Imagine written on an index card, taped to his guitar. Which I found very amusing. And he was nervous before the show. Kind of nervous.

AP: Tell me about that – what does a nervous John Lennon look like?

JC: Just – just kind of staying in. We shared a suite at the Hilton Hotel when we were taping it. And he went into the bedroom with Yoko, and she kind of had to calm him down. He watched a little *Galloping Gourmet* on TV, which he loved. And she made sure to come out into the other room, where the rest of the band was, and say, "John's a little nervous, so if you don't mind letting him stay in the room with me for a little while before we go on."

AP: I read somewhere that there were times when you would go out walking with John, just around the block of the studio – is that right?

JC: Oh yeah. We would do that. We went to lunch a lot at a restaurant on 8th Avenue called Downey's. The Record Plant's on 44th between 8th and 9th. The restaurant was on 8th Avenue and we would just go outside the studio and walk around the corner to the restaurant and have giant crabmeat salads. There was one time when we were about to do the *Sir Lew Grade* show that we went in a cab with him up to a boutique near Bloomingdales, to buy the jumpsuits that we ended up wearing on the show. So that was interesting. Here we are, riding in a cab with

John Lennon; we get to the store, and they just let us in and chased everybody out and locked the door. They let us walk around the store by ourselves, looking at all the merchandise. And he ended up picking out the outfits that we ended up wearing.

It's amazing – because like I said – in the restaurant, you just notice everybody is looking. And nobody is really bothering him or coming up and approaching him and asking for autographs. They would just let us go. But you'd see everybody whispering to each other, and looking and pointing, and there he was.

AP: Did he pay any attention at all to that?

JC: No, not really. We were just talking, and he wouldn't pay much attention. Just a normal day. I can't imagine what it was like.

AP: So you're in the restaurant and you're having a beautiful crab salad sandwich – what do you talk about?

JC: We talked about a lot of things. We talked about the record, we talked about music, we talked about the show that was upcoming. Actually, he produced some songs for us, that we ended up recording with my band. He wrote a song with Roy, the owner of the Record Plant – Roy Cicala – called 'Incantation'. So we would talk about that; the lyrics of the song. He actually gave my band the name Dog Soldier. And then we realized we couldn't use the name because it was already used by someone else. So we ended up changing the name of the band to BOMF. Bunch Of Mother Fuckers.

AP: That's so great. What made him choose 'Dog Soldier' for you?

JC: I don't know – I just think he liked the metaphor. I remember asking him sometime about lyrics. And he would just tell me that he liked the way the words sounded together sometimes. So sometimes there was no deep meaning when you were looking for a deep meaning in some lyrics. It was just a combination of words that sounded good together.

AP: I'm very interested in terms of music – was there any… what was his philosophy toward music?

JC: I'll tell you what – here's another illustration of how I know he was a little kid in the studio, when it came to that. We had our own room at the studio. The BOMF Room, our rehearsal room. We would hang out there at night sometimes, just writing new songs and rehearsing and getting ready to record. And John – after he finished recording down the hall – he would come into the studio with a bottle of wine, and just jam with us. Can you imagine, a guy that's played all of the Beatles shows that he's played, all the famous people that he's played with and just spent the whole day in the studio recording his record – just going down the hall and jamming with a bunch of teenagers. You know – he loved it.

AP: What kinds of stuff would you jam with?

JC: Sometimes we would just pick a blues; 'Johnny B. Goode', or some old Beatles songs just for fun.

AP: Wow. Hang on – so you've… was that just, someone

in the band was like *hey, let's do 'Love Me Do'* and then suddenly you're there with an actual Beatle...

JC: Yeah, exactly.

AP: So would John... in these situations, would John go straight to the mic? Would he be the leader in that sense – or would he take a back seat? What was the dynamic?

JC: No, he wouldn't be the leader. He would just want to jam along. He would just pick up a guitar and just jam along. He really liked just being *one of the guys.* That was the big impression that I took away from my time with him.

AP: Jon – how did you find yourself in the Record Plant to begin with?

JC: Well, we were all a bunch of guys from Brooklyn, and I joined a band that had a bass player named Jimmy Iovine. And he decided instead of trying to be a bass player, he wanted to be a recording engineer and a record producer. So he left the band and got a job at the Record Plant studios as an intern – basically unpaid – in the beginning. And he decided he wanted to learn how to record. So since we were all his friends, he'd take us in there at night and record us. That's how he learned to be a recording engineer. And he played the tapes for the owner of the studio – Roy Cicala – and he liked what he heard, and he signed us to a deal. He gave us our room, and we were there every day after that – for years.

AP: Could you paint a picture for me – what was the atmosphere within all of that?

JC: We were there every day, and it was always a special day when John was at the studio. He was there a lot when he was doing those albums. So there'd always been a little buzz, like *oh, John's here today*. We would just see each other walking up and down the hallway, just, "Hi." I can't say that it became run-of-the-mill, because it never did. It was always special – *there's John. We're hanging out with John.* You're always aware of it. But it was just – I always felt like *this is it. This is what I always wanted to do. This is where I always wanted to be.* Just a sense of specialness.

AP: Was there a particularly poignant moment that you had with John, that you look back on as being really quite special?

JC: A poignant moment. Well, when we did the video for 'Stand by Me', our guitar player was sick that day. I'm the piano player, so we did the main scenes – we shot the scenes where I'm playing the piano, and you can see me in the video. And then there was a time for a close-up of the double guitar solo that happens in the middle of the record. So John said to me, "Why don't you pick up a guitar, since the guitar player's not here? And we'll do it." So the two of us stood there, face-to-face – probably six inches apart, with our guitars facing each other, and the camera just shooting down the guitars at our hands. And we shot that scene a couple of times. That was amazing to me.

AP: I'm going to have to go and watch that clip again. That's – I mean, when you think about who the *other guy* is that stood six inches from John, for all those years. And you got to be that guy. Jon, is there anything I've missed? Is there any particular moment with John, or something that we haven't covered that you think people should hear about John?

JC: I remember in our hotel room, the day we were taping the *Sir Lew Grade* show, and there was a knock on the door. And I opened it up, and there was Goldie Hawn. She was so nervous. She said to me, "Do you think there's a chance that I could say hi to John?"

So I knocked on the door – I knew that Yoko had said that John was a little nervous – and I timidly went over to the door and I poked my head in and I said, "Goldie Hawn is here – she wants to say hi to John."

And John immediately got up and said, "Oh, no problem." And he came out, and he said hello to her. And she was so happy and giggly – you know the way she is. So that was one moment. 'Cos he was always very, very generous.

• • •

It must have felt freeing for John to spend time in a safe space where outward display of admiration was minimal. He enjoyed the anonymity of '70s New York and he enjoyed working at the Record Plant for the same reason. He was able to feel, for the most part, normal. He was one of the guys.

But there were times when normality wasn't possible – people staring at him at restaurants; the need for certain stores to close in order for John to browse – and his nerves before live performances – taping the lyrics to his guitar.

For those involved there was a feeling of specialness. Recording on 'Stand by Me'. The hand claps on 'Whatever Gets You Thru the Night'. The sense of excitement when John came running into the control room with a new idea. And finishing up recording for the day only to grab a bottle of wine and spend the evening jamming down the hall with a bunch of teenagers. *John never lost his wonder.* To illustrate this further, a transcript of Jon Cobert's personal recording of John Lennon with BOMF in the studio is included as an appendix to this book.

John intended the *Sir Lew Grade* performance to be his last for 1975 – Yoko and John were busy preparing for the birth of their son. Two days before Sean was born, the US Court of Appeals made the decision to overturn the deportation order. John could now apply for a green card. John was granted permanent residency on July 27, 1976, and he had no intention of defacing his new status as a valued member of society. Instead he removed himself from the professional world almost entirely and threw himself into fatherhood with vigor.

By this time, the Beatles' dissolution had finally been decided on by the British court, and royalty back-payments from the last half-decade flooded in. About the newly dissolved Apple management contract with Allen Klein, John told *Weekend World,* "Possibly, Paul's suspicions were right." John now had everything he needed: family, freedom, and the money to do as he pleased.

During this period, Paul McCartney and John Lennon started hanging out when they were both in New York. One night in '76 they were watching television at the Dakota when, by chance, *Saturday Night Live* host Lorne Michaels declared he wanted a Beatles reunion on the show. The pair briefly considered showing up at the 49th Street studio and surprising the world. But they had another glass of wine and forgot about it. Another time, at Christmas, Paul and Linda McCartney turned up at the Dakota singing Christmas carols.

In these pre-paparazzi days, John was free to take Sean out while Yoko largely stayed in her downstairs offices and managed the finances, investing their wealth and making more of it. John took great pride in teaching Sean to swim down at the local YMCA, which they frequented several times a week. The family kept a staff of housekeepers, nannies, and assistants as they enjoyed each other's company and that of their three cats, Sasha, Misha, and Charo. John even learnt to bake bread.

ELLIOT MINTZ
THE PRIVATE YEARS

JOHN IS OFTEN DEPICTED as having lived as a kind of recluse between 1976-1980. But a more accurate picture might show that he didn't *need* to be seen. He certainly didn't chase the spotlight. John's priority was simple, and of great importance: He was raising a child. John also started phoning his Liverpool family more frequently. He asked Aunt Mimi to mail him his old Quarry Bank tie, which he wore frequently in the seventies, and he asked Julia Baird to send a stack of old family pictures.

With his own young family close by, John took the time to enjoy the little things. He could take Sean across the street to Central Park and enjoy the expanses and the little trails. Passers-by generally left him alone – asking for autographs and photos mainly around the arched entry to the Dakota building. John's friends from the wilder days, like Harry Nilsson and Keith Moon, found it harder to communicate with John during this time. Mick Jagger even expressed frustration – his phone calls weren't being returned. But Elliot Mintz was invited to stay whenever he was visiting from Los Angeles.

In 1977 John and Sean took a trip to Hong Kong on their way to meet Yoko in Japan. Other exotic destinations followed. The world was opening up and John found he was able to travel quite discreetly. They invited Elliot Mintz to join them in Japan to meet the extended family.

In June 1980, John decided to try sailing. His father's side of the family had been seafarers, and John discovered a love of the ocean. He embarked on a week-long voyage with some professional yachtsmen from Rhode Island to Bermuda. Along the way, treacherous conditions – and a 40-hour squall – provided John with an opportunity to prove his value as a competent sailor. One by one, each of the yacht's crew succumbed to seasickness and crawled below deck. John found himself unaffected and took the helm. He was alone for six full hours, screaming into the wind and contemplating the fragility of life.

John later told *Playboy:* "Once I accepted the reality of the situation, something greater than me took over and all of a sudden I lost my fear. I actually began to enjoy the experience, and I began to sing and shout old sea shanties in the face of the storm, feeling total exhilaration. I had the time of my life."

Safely in Bermuda, John found himself brimming with new material.

Elliot Mintz was a close friend to John and Yoko throughout the 1970s and saw John come into his own as a father to baby Sean. Together John and Elliot continued to enjoy their philosophical discussions and ruminations on life. It was during this period that John was at his most comfortable and contented.

ELLIOT MINTZ: We took a little sailing trip in the harbor of New York when John was learning how to sail. There are photographs of us sailing around the harbor. You'll see John and I on the sailboat, where he is practicing getting ready for the infamous trip to Bermuda. But thank heavens I wasn't on *that* boat.

AIDAN PREWETT: Was he a natural sailor?

EM: Yes. Now, I don't know much about sailing – I'd never sailed a boat. I was a passenger on this little boat. I don't do terribly well on them. But keep in mind, his father was a merchant seaman. Although his father left him when he was very young, I don't know how much of those recessive genes stay with you. He was raised in a city by the docks, of course, where boats and sailors predominated the population. And he always seemed to have had an affinity with the water. He married a woman whose name translated from Japanese means *Ocean Child*. So he seemed to have a natural feel for it, and was very comfortable behind the wheel when we went out sailing for that memorable afternoon.

AP: In amongst all of this, when John came back from Bermuda, had something changed about him?

EM: Yes. Prior to going to Bermuda, there was certainly a creative block. He wasn't writing. He had been so involved with Sean, and house-husbandry. Of course, there was an acoustic guitar around that he would play. I would come to New York, and on a number of occasions he would play a song or two for me on the guitar, or something he was working on on the piano. So music was still part of his life – not professionally.

But *direction-wise*, Yoko felt that a trip to Bermuda would help stimulate the creative juices and be a good protective tool for him. She was the one who suggested he go. He wrote virtually all of the songs for *Double Fantasy* in Bermuda, within a very short period of time. He would call Yoko in the evening and sing her stuff he was working on. I listened to the 'Bermuda Tapes' when he came home – fifteen or sixteen cassettes where he's just sitting there with a guitar working out the songs. But he told me that they all came to him in succession. They arrived very quickly, very spontaneously. And Yoko, alone, in New York, was working on her songs. 'Cos *Double Fantasy* was going to be a dialogue between a man and a woman. So when he returned, a) he was returning with the music, and b) he was returning with a burst of enthusiasm for returning to the studio. Even very briefly flirting with the idea of maybe going out on the road. Not for some big massive tour, but of just the two of them. And maybe a band – playing some of the songs from *Double Fantasy*.

And I would go to New York after that and go to the recording sessions. And these sessions were very sedate; very calm. Above the control board there was a large monitor, and the monitor was usually used by other musicians to watch TV shows or videos when engineers were doing technical stuff. John and Yoko pasted a large picture of Sean over the monitor. In a little room adjacent to the engineer's booth, they set up this little white room that the two of them could go into, where a fellow who worked for them – I think his name was Toshi – prepared tea, where there was fresh sushi. It was a little decompression room. The crew who worked on *Double Fantasy* – when it was time to eat, fresh sushi was sent in for everybody. We all ate together. There wasn't any alcohol permitted in the studio. He had his favorite little collection of candies or licorice sticks or some peanuts at the board. I've been to a lot of recording sessions in my life – I don't remember one quite as peaceful – laid back – as that one. And it's reflected, of course, in the songs.

I also attended the Phil Spector sessions in LA – which were the most raucous sessions I had ever attended in my life. And the contrast between the two: The Spector sessions were *before* Sean. *Double Fantasy* was after. The Spector sessions were about early rock 'n' roll; about looking into the past. *Double Fantasy* was a preview of what was to come in the future. So *Double Fantasy* was far more nurturing. On the *Rock 'n' Roll* sessions, as much as I enjoyed the music – you heard John singing 'Stand by Me' – probably the most powerful version ever done of that song. But by the time it was *Double Fantasy*, he had the two beings that meant most to him, already now standing with him. He had his son, and he had his wife back. He wasn't *alone* anymore. He wasn't talking about the mountain crumbling to the sea. He had reached a point beyond the demons, beyond the hauntings and beyond *yesterday*.

He was extremely at peace during the last time I saw him, which was probably – give or take – September of that year, 1980. He was a man in his own skin.

AP: I wonder if you could tell me about your travel with John and Yoko – I was fascinated to see that you went to Japan with them.

EM: We spent three or four months in Japan, where we were, for a very small amount of time, in Tokyo – for a longer time in a place called Karuizawa, which was about a hundred miles outside of Tokyo. It's an ancient Japanese place, where people took bicycles instead of cars, where westerners don't usually travel, where virtually everybody speaks Japanese. And we went from there to Kyoto. And Yoko of course was the best tour guide we could have had.

John was at peace in those places. He was at peace in any place where the name Ono meant more than Lennon. Yoko came from a very, very well-known banking family. The Ono family was like the Rockefellers – on that level. She was a very recognizable figure in Japan. John, on many occasions, could get by walking down the street without people pointing at him. If he was wearing the hat, and his hair was up, and if it was just *us* and not Yoko. He was comfortable in his skin with anonymity.

We were going to go someplace together in New York, to pick something up. I think we were going to look for some old 78rpm records for a jukebox that Elton John gave him as a birthday present. And we were preparing to leave, and he was thinking about what he was going to wear and which sunglasses to put on and the rest of it.

And I said, "It must be really inconvenient to try to make yourself less conspicuous."

He said, "Well, they're going to know me wherever I am anyway." He made an interesting comment. He said, "Elliot – I was famous when I was in *Liverpool*. When I was 16 and 17 years old, people knew who I was in the local town. We played at the Cavern; we had our group. And ten, twenty, thirty, forty people who would say hello to me on the street, or point and say, "There's the guy with that group, and they have the haircut." He said, "I kinda got used to people staring at me and looking at me – strangers approaching me. The only thing that really changed is the stage got larger." So he learned the expectations of the public, and to some degree he learned how to cope with it. During the height of Beatlemania, it became impossible to cope with it, outside of just being locked away in rooms.

But in New York, with the New Yorker mentality, he felt a sense of freedom about walking around in the street. And, for the most part, not being annoyed. Although I was conscious of the fact that wherever we went there were people on the other side of the street who were about to cross over – that if they weren't approaching him for autographs and the like, they were still looking or pointing or whispering. By then, he considered *that* the relief. You or I would feel encumbered by that. A single woman walking down a sidewalk, who is noticed or approached by four or five strangers for conversation, or wanting to take a picture, would be very intimidated. For him, that became the new norm.

In traveling – when we left Japan, Yoko arranged the travel route. It's hard to explain, but some travel agencies in Japan had something like a numerologist or an astrologer – called by different names – that determined the best and safest route that a traveler should take. In which direction they should go, and what day they should fly. And when it was time for us to leave Japan, Yoko's numbers were such that she was able to take a direct flight from Tokyo to New York. When she ran our numbers – John and I – we were not as fortunate. For us to go home, we had to fly from Tokyo to Hong Kong, Hong Kong to Dubai, Dubai to Germany, Germany to New York – and I had to then fly on to LA. Surely the longest flight of my life.

But it was in – I think it was Hong Kong to Dubai, could have been twelve hours, or something like that – in the cabin of an airplane, when you're seated next to somebody for endless hours, you get to know them even better. I got to know him very, very well. He didn't have to do his autobiography to me.

He also took an interest in my life. John was a naturally curious person. If you were sitting alone with him at the Dakota, having a cup of tea – and that's about all he had at the Dakota, because Yoko doesn't drink alcohol and there wasn't a bar. He liked tea. He would take an interest in others. *He* already knew the John Lennon story and became impatient with those who wanted to ask more. So it didn't matter who you were or what you did. If you were a handyman or a worker who came to the house, John would ask questions: What did the guy use on the tree leaves that made them look so green?

AP: During the time that John was not in the public eye, was there a moment *then* that you could say summed him up – as a father?

EM: I probably spent more time with them during what's referred to as the secret years, the quiet years – the first couple of years that Sean was born – I probably spent more time with them *then*, than during any other period. They called me within a week of Sean's birth to come and meet Sean, and I got on a plane and went to meet Sean when he was a week or two weeks old – a situation I remind Sean of all the time; he has no recollection of the visit. That was forty years ago. In fact, two days ago I got an invitation from Sean to come to New York on February 18 to celebrate Yoko's birthday together. That's something I've done in recent years, and I'll be there in two weeks again. I was there when he would play with Sean, when he would bathe Sean.

When it was nighty-night time for Sean at seven o'clock or whatever the hour was, and John would put Sean over his shoulder and start, almost in a fairytale-esque way, repeating some of the things they did during the day, as he would carry Sean to his bedroom. And Sean would be decompressing. John would lay next to him, and Sean was a fairly rapid sleeper – it only took a few minutes. Maybe that's true of all children at that age. But Sean would go to sleep, John would come back inside, and then he and Yoko would say to me, "Let's go in the old bedroom and just have a talk." And we would.

That time after Sean's birth brought out the most quiet

and reverential side to him. The cornerstone of John's life is what took place before Sean, and what took place after. He no longer had to hang out with the mates after he had his child.

AP: Is there a particular day you spent with them as a family that evokes a strong memory?

EM: After Sean's birth, *all* the time we spent together was as a family. I spent Christmases with them. I spent holidays and New Year's. We went to birthdays. John and Sean were born on the same day, so they would celebrate their birthday on the same day. And Yoko would throw birthday parties at a little restaurant called Tavern on the Green in Central Park, across the street from the Dakota. Or we would have a little gathering at the Dakota building itself. Keep in mind, Sean only knew his father for five years. In conversations I have with Sean, he remembers his father in these images – the images that a five-year-old might retain.

There was a man who had a beautiful duplex apartment in the Dakota, and on one level had a screening room. When Sean was three or four years old, he said he was going to screen *Yellow Submarine*, and would Sean like to see it? So I went with Sean. We watched the movie, and Sean kind of got the picture. In that cartoon-esque way, he saw his father with those signature glasses, singing those songs. And it was *then* that he came back to the main apartment, and he asked his daddy if he was a Beatle. And John explained that he *was*, and that was a long time ago. I believe that he once sang 'Yellow Submarine' for Sean on the guitar. Before seeing the movie, I don't know if there was any reference, and I don't know if there was any consciousness on Sean's part about his father's history. In the Dakota there were no gold records on the wall. There was no souvenir case or anything like that. And little has changed.

AP: Was there ever anything that John mentioned that has stuck with you in terms of philosophy?

EM: Yes. Philosophy and religion occupied a lot of our time because I was a believer – and he was *not*. I recall one time, talking to him about the song he wrote called 'God' – *God is a concept by which we measure our pain*. Whereas we hardly ever discussed Beatles songs, from time to time there was something that he wrote that impacted me in a certain way, that *was* up for discussion. And I said to him one evening – he had a little night table by his bedside. And on the night table was his stereo, his ashtray and cigarettes, and a small collection of books, that he would look through before he would fall asleep at night. The books that were in his little night table were mainly philosophical, and – I call them – 'religious-in-nature'. I don't remember him having a bible, but stuff that referenced the subjects he wrote about in 'God'.

I said to him, "I love the power of the song – the impact of it. I love the way the song ended, with your declaration of what you believed in." But I said, "You know, based on my feelings and knowledge about you, I would probably would have eliminated the word *don't*. 'Cos I think a part of you believes in all of it. Or did at one time or another. On some level, and in some way."

He says in the song, "*I don't believe in Elvis*". Well, I think the record would indicate that there was a time when he *really* believed in Elvis. He may have let those belief systems go. But his response to me was fairly curt, and a bit testy.

He said, "Well, next time you decide to write a song,

you write it your way." And that's how we kind of ended that subject.

When I would come to New York and he would ask me who I'm going to interview, on one occasion I told him it was going to be Baba Ram Dass. I remember that clearly because it was in January '76. I did a lengthy interview with John and Yoko at the Dakota, and the following day I was going to go to Ram Dass' apartment to talk with him. John and I had discussed Ram Dass before.

He said, "Look, you and your Ram Dass; Ram Dass all the time. It doesn't impact me the way it impacts you. I'd been fooled by the Maharishi."

I said, "Well, Ram Dass isn't the Maharishi. He's somebody different. I'm not asking you to be impacted." I just gave him a quote. Ram Dass said, *"Nothing is ever learned, only remembered."* Nobody ever teaches you something that you don't innately know. You're simply reminded of things.

His response was something to the effect of: "Everybody knows that. That's easy. Do you think he's the first person to make that observation? Haven't you heard that expressed in a thousand different ways – that you're always looking for affirmations of your own belief systems?" He said, "I want to go with you tomorrow, to the interview."

Yoko was half-awake-half-asleep, and she said, "Yeah, let's go with Elliot." And I thought *well, this is not going to work out – bringing the two of them to an apartment when I'm trying to tape an interview. They're just going to be a distraction.* They had done it with me once when I interviewed Salvador Dalí, and they knew him from a long time ago. They asked me if they could travel along. They insisted upon going to seeing Dalí and they insisted on seeing Ram Dass. Neither of those interviews worked out very well because they interjected themselves in the interview. They weren't quiet bystanders, they were very vocal.

So, when I say we discussed religion and philosophy, it was in that sense that John didn't believe in idolatry. In 'God', he says *I don't believe in kings and queens* and in the video you see a picture go by of Dr. Martin Luther King, Jr. Well, of course he believed in the teachings of Dr. Martin Luther King, Jr. Of *course,* he did. You see a picture of Bob Dylan go by, and he says *I don't believe in Zimmerman.* Well of *course* there was a time early on when he certainly appreciated the poetic delivery and wisdom in Bob's music. What he was saying in essence, to me – in many of our conversations – was *don't place your faith in leaders.* Don't look for daddy figures in the sky. That was a recurrent subject of discussion with us. And whenever anybody kind of emerged and appeared to be, quote, a 'daddy figure', or a leader – John would have an aversion to it.

It's one of the reasons, when I talked to him about his own fame, and his own celebrity – how people looked to him as somebody with all the answers – he said, "They didn't *get* me. I told them that I was the *working-class* hero. I told them that we *all* shine on. I didn't say or do anything to prop myself up as being superior to anybody else. Ever. I never told them who to vote for; I never gave them any instruction. Except maybe in 'Imagine'."

But when people sat with him quietly and talked about things – just *stuff* – the stuff you talk to your best friend about. He was, in many ways, like every other smart, creative, and down-to-earth person. The moment that flipped a little, and he felt that somebody was coming to meet *the Great John Lennon*, it would be a turn-off to him. It's the pretty girl who you take out for the first time to dinner, who really thought that you were interested in what she had to say. And somewhere after appetizer, she notices that your eyes are no longer focusing on *her* eyes, but perhaps other attributes. And it's a turn-off.

AP: Lastly, I would love to hear if there's a moment that you recall where John and Yoko were at their happiest.

EM: There is something that definitely comes to my mind. It was New Year's Eve or Christmas of 1976, or thereabouts – where I tell the story about the two of them at the Club Dakota. The Club Dakota was simply – in addition to their primary residence at the Dakota, there was an adjacent apartment. In the adjacent apartment, they placed a Würlitzer jukebox which I believe was a gift from Elton John. It was a vacant apartment; they just wanted to expand the space that they occupied. And that evening – it was in December – John said that he wanted to have a little gathering for Christmas Eve or New Year's Eve, to celebrate the opening of the Club Dakota. We went to the downtown area that sold vintage stuff, where we found the old 78's. And we found some pink flamingoes, and an old Rattan couch – just kind of minimalist stuff that we found. And we hauled it back to the Dakota that day.

"Let's dress up, you and I," he said. "Let's get dressed up – lets both wear ties. And I want you to take this handwritten invitation to Mother." Which is how he referred to Yoko – who was in the main apartment. It was a simple note saying that *your presence is requested at 10pm at the grand opening of the Club Dakota*, which was the next apartment. So I delivered the message.

She said, "What's this about?"

I said, "All I know is what I read."

John put on a tuxedo jacket. I believe he wore his old Liverpool school tie with a white shirt. I think he had a cane. We got all the 78rpm records, loaded them into the jukebox; moved a little bit of furniture around; lowered the lights. And at 10pm Yoko appeared, dressed and ready for whatever was going to follow. He ushered her in. They sat down together; the three of us talked for a while. He played some of his favorite old recordings on the jukebox. They were mainly 1940s songs. Blues singers – Billie Holiday; that kind of thing.

The apartment had floor-to-ceiling windows – the Dakota is a 100-year-old building in Manhattan, the oldest apartment building. The view was spectacular – and it was snowing. The '40s music was playing; the bubble lights of the jukebox were reflecting over this living room. He handed me a polaroid camera and he said, "Snap some pictures of Mother and I." And the two of them stood up and danced. They danced the *slow* kind of dance, holding each other. And I watched them for a few minutes, in silence. I snapped some of the Polaroid pictures of them doing just that. And in answer to your question, that was the single most romantic moment I recall sharing with them.

• • •

"Let's dress up, you and I," says John, echoing his younger self – wearing an old fox-fur and drawing stares at the bus stop with Michael Hill and Pete Shotton, or his disguise when meeting Tony Palmer at Cambridge University. Not to mention his changing appearance from the Quarrymen years onward – John's desire to reinvent himself was never far from the surface. He grew quickly bored with himself.

But John had a natural curiosity and interest in other people. He would find ways to glean insights from *outside*, as he had always done with his songwriting. In this later period of his life, his interests were no longer professional

– they were for his own development as a person, and as a father. Normality became fascinating.

Sean's birth heralded a new era. Fatherhood brought out the best in John the second time around, and he became focused in a way that had previously eluded him. For five years, John didn't feel the need to write songs. There were more important things happening in his life.

Then in July 1980, after spending time writing in Bermuda, John was feeling good about returning to the studio. He and Yoko sought out producer Jack Douglas and a new group of musicians, this time recording the bulk of material at New York's Hit Factory. The Hit Factory was a major competitor of the Record Plant, and Roy Cicala was disheartened that his friend John had moved on. But John wanted a fresh start.

The new album would become *Double Fantasy*, named after a variety of Freesia that John encountered in the Bermuda Botanical Gardens. John told BBC Reporter Andy Peebles, "I just thought, *Double Fantasy – that's a great title!* There's two of us… and it just sort of says it all, somehow. Without really saying anything – it says everything."

ALLAN TANNENBAUM

DOUBLE FANTASY

JOHN AND YOKO returned to the studio on August 7, 1980. In just ten days they had recorded 22 tracks – enough for *Double Fantasy* and the bulk of a follow-up album. They wanted *Double Fantasy* released quickly so they could move on to what they were already calling *Milk and Honey*. Geffen Records won the album contract. David Geffen embraced the idea of each track alternating between John and Yoko. Other more traditional labels had offered more money but baulked at the idea of a shared album. Geffen also took a leap of faith and signed the deal before hearing any of the music. His gamble paid off.

Double Fantasy was set for release on November 17, 1980. Publicity needed to be organized, which of course involved photography. In this regard, both John and Yoko seemed well disposed toward the idea, having pleasantly avoided the spotlight for several years. Through the *Soho Weekly News* they connected with photographer Allan Tannenbaum, whose rock photography of the gritty 1970's New York scene had already featured Andy Warhol, Blondie, Patti Smith, Led Zeppelin, Dolly Parton, Michael Jackson, Talking Heads, the Rolling Stones, Bob Marley, The Cure, The Clash, The Ramones, James Brown, David Bowie, Mohammed Ali, and Salvador Dalí. After working with

John Lennon, many more would follow, as well as time spent in the political arena and on international features in Iraq and Kuwait. Tannenbaum's work has been exhibited all over the world and has appeared in all manner of publications from *Newsweek* and *New York Magazine* to *Paris Match* and *Rolling Stone*.

As a photographer, Allan Tannenbaum witnessed several intimate moments between John and Yoko. The couple were thrilled with the pictures from Allan's first shoot and invited him back to photograph another project – a nude scene. In the presence of a tiny film crew and Allan's still camera, John and Yoko disrobed and climbed into bed.

ALLAN TANNENBAUM: I first photographed John in 1975, during rehearsals for *A Tribute to Sir Lew Grade*, where John is wearing a red jumpsuit. So I met him then – I don't remember anything specific except that he was very cool, very friendly. He posed with the band for me, which is something I set up and he just did.

And then of course when I did the session with Yoko Ono for *Double Fantasy*, when we got in touch with her, she came to my studio for a cover shoot. The idea was to do Yoko – because everybody was trying to get to John. So the music editor of my newspaper had the idea just to do a shoot just with Yoko. She came to my studio, and after the session I said, "We've got some great shots, but I need some black-and-white photos for inside the newspaper."

And she said, "Come up to the Dakota tomorrow." So I met her up there, we had breakfast together outside. And then we did some shots around the building, and then we went back to her office.

I said, "You know, it'd be great to do some shots with John and Sean."

And she said, "Well, not Sean, but I'll call John." So

John came down from their seventh floor apartment and I reminded him that I met him in 1975 at the Lew Grade thing.

He said, "Yes, I remember you." I don't know if he really did, but he was nice enough to say that he did. There were bits of conversation. And then after that there was the walk around the park. We did some shots in front of the Dakota – they're both wearing black leather jackets. And then we went back into Studio One, and Yoko was talking about the film that they were going to be doing for the *Double Fantasy* album. So I suggested that they have me there as a stills photographer.

And she just said, "We'll see."

So five days later I get a call that they're in the park, and to come and take pictures of the shoot. And after the Central Park session, he's wearing this silver jacket; she's wearing a black fur. They invite me to go have coffee with them at their favorite café, right around the corner from the Dakota. So I went and sat with them and had coffee. I don't remember the conversation at all, but Yoko said, "Okay, John feels comfortable with you, so you can come with us to the studio." So I thought *wow – great!*

So they did these scenes of getting undressed – first from their street clothes and then the kimonos and getting in bed, and being nude and pretending to make love. And I'm thinking to myself *I don't fucking believe this.* That was amazing. There were conversations between takes and I remember John just being like a regular guy. He just seemed very easy to be around. And he'd be talking with everybody like just one of the guys. So that was a very nice feeling.

So the idea was that I was going to bring the materials to them. Right after that session I dropped off my color film at the lab, and then I went back to my darkroom and developed the black-and-white film. I was so excited; you have no idea. A few days later I brought the film – the color slides and prints that I had made to the Dakota to meet with John and Yoko. So she sent the prints upstairs, and I was setting up a slide projector in her office.

John came down – he didn't see me at first – and he's holding the prints. He's kind of waving them. He goes, "Yoko, these are *great*!" And then he sees me and he goes, "Oh, there you are." And he comes over, right in front of me, and he's looking at me and saying, "These are wonderful. You know what I like about your photos? You really capture Yoko's beauty." That was just wonderful. He was so happy with the way I photographed Yoko. What could be better than that? That's the thing that he said that sticks with me the most. And really – almost gives me a chill when I think about it. It still cuts my heart.

AIDAN PREWETT: I've got a chill just hearing about it. That's just phenomenal. In all of that time that you – 'cos there's so many moments there that you got to experience with them – is there a moment that would illustrate John's sense of humor?

AT: Oh yeah, absolutely. Well, you know the classic film *Ben Hur*? With Cecil B. DeMille, and the huge production – or even the later *Ben Hur*, with Charlton Heston. Classic film – huge production. And endless scenes, endless takes. So anyway, they were doing this scene – John's on top of Yoko. They're nude – they had the covers over them, but you know – they're naked in bed. All the non-essential personnel were cleared out, so it was just the 16mm film cameraman and the sound man and the director and the producer. And me – fly-on-the-wall.

So John is kissing Yoko, and she's kind of tilting her

head back – raising her chin higher and higher. And John's kind of reaching up, trying to keep the kissing going. And the camera's rolling, and it seems interminable. And all of a sudden, he turns away and he goes, "What is this, Ben fucking Hur?" And everybody just cracked up. You can see that photo – I snapped it. You can see him laughing, and Yoko's laughing; he's on top of her.

AP: It's a beautiful shot.

AT: So that was the funniest thing I remember hearing him say. I mean, he was always joking, but that was the funniest thing. And the way it just *cut* the tension of the whole thing.

AP: As a subject for your photography, what was his approach to being photographed?

AT: Well, he was very used to being photographed, of course. Let's say, like walking around the park and the Dakota – I didn't really tell them very much what to do. You know – maybe *look here*, but they were also interacting with each other. So they – it was a very kind of documentary shoot. Not staged at all. And so I'd say *oh, let's sit on this bench*. And they would look at me – they both knew what to do. So it really wasn't hard to get good images at all. I didn't really have to pull teeth, they were just used to it. And then when we started crossing the street to go back to their building, I asked them to turn around and pose, and that became a classic shot in front with the Dakota building in the background. That was actually used about this time last year on the cover of the London *Sunday Times* magazine. It's become an iconic image.

The scene in this studio with the *Double Fantasy* shots – that was basically being creative and shooting what they were doing. So I didn't have to do very much there either. But there are some shots between takes, and I could shoot John doing this, or John doing that. And I just tried to be as unobtrusive as possible.

And a lot of times he would have an idea. *Let's do something.* So in terms of a subject, it was pretty easy to do. And a lot of it, again, was that he knew that they were there to do – in the case of the first shoot – to do press, and in the case of the second they were making a film. So they were in a *being photographed* frame of mind.

AP: Speaking of the Dakota, I'm wondering if you could sort of paint for me an image of what it's like to walk through those giant gates for the first time, and know that you're going to end up in their apartment.

AT: The first time, I didn't know I was going to end up in their apartment. But I did – I think I was up in that apartment with the two of them. But just to go through that kind of a driveway tunnel – you go to the reception and it's all this old dark oak. It's pretty intimidating. So I was very excited. It was a kind of adventure – to see Yoko. 'Cos when I went there the first time, to meet Yoko, I didn't know if I was going to meet John. So it was great that I was able to. They had a very big apartment. They had converted two apartments into one apartment.

AP: When Yoko said to you that John felt comfortable with you, what was your kind of thought process?

AT: Well, it was nice to hear. I mean, at that point I'd been photographing celebrities for many years – important people; famous people; especially in the rock 'n' roll world. Like Debbie Harry, for example – she's a pal. She wrote something for my book about me being this tall kind of laid-back guy. So I could relate easily to people who didn't want to be bothered by certain kinds of people. People who weren't nervous or edgy, or who acted like – maybe a lot of these people, they don't want somebody who acts like they're too impressed with them. Somebody who's just normal with them, that's all – just like a normal person. That's all. I mean, of course I was happy that John felt comfortable with me.

AP: How would you describe his personality? Was he affable? Charming?

AT: Oh totally. Absolutely. He could talk – he'd talk about a variety of subjects. The Beatles would be the last thing that he would talk about. Although, when we were viewing the pictures and going through the slides, he did make a comment about how when he was with the Beatles, they would have to look at pictures. One person would like *this* one, but then the other person didn't like the way they looked in that shot. So there was always this kind of back-and-forth between the Beatles, in terms of choosing pictures. But other than that, the way he acted and the way he was with the crew, and with me and other people, he was a really, really charming guy. Because he was very natural. And of course, *funny*. Not everybody who's natural is as funny and witty, and could keep the jokes going.

• • •

Intimacy and humor were often intertwined for John. *Most* aspects of life intersected with his humor in one way or another. And at his most vulnerable – naked in bed with Yoko – John managed to cut the tension and keep the crew feeling comfortable.

John was appreciative of the crew's work. He knew the

impact that his praise would have on people. But Allan Tannenbaum received the highest praise before John even knew he was there. *"Yoko, these are great!"* And then: *"You really capture Yoko's beauty."*

Double Fantasy was supposed to be just the beginning. Within days of its release, John and Yoko were back in the studio laying down tracks for new projects. News of the album opened the floodgates of old friends and acquaintances. John started catching up with many of them as soon as the album was announced. He spent five hours enjoying Ringo Starr's company at the Plaza Hotel, where they had first stayed together in 1964. He buried the hatchet with George Martin, with whom he had not spoken since Phil Spector was brought on board for *Let It Be*. And in celebration of the new album, John sent his Aunt Mimi a matching pearl necklace and brooch. His thoughts were returning to Liverpool.

STEVE MARCANTONIO
FINAL RECORDINGS

ON DECEMBER 1, 1980, John and Yoko returned to Roy Cicala's Record Plant to work on a new single for Yoko, 'Walking on Thin Ice'. The track was arranged as a disco piece and its complexity called for an eight-day stretch in the studio.

Steve Marcantonio was their recording engineer. Prior to this, Steve had already recorded Aerosmith, Kiss, Heart, and the Blues Brothers album with its cast of luminaries. In more recent years Steve relocated to Nashville, where he has worked with many artists including Rosanne Cash, Rodney Crowell, Vince Gill, Steven Tyler, Cheap Trick, and Taylor Swift.

In their eight consecutive days in the studio together, Steve got to know John and Yoko in that pressurized closed-quarters studio way. The atmosphere was celebratory – John was back at the Record Plant. It was a kind of homecoming. They shared in-jokes, they told old stories, and they put in hours of hard work. And at three o'clock in the morning on Monday, December 8, John joined Steve on a stroll around Midtown Manhattan.

STEVE MARCANTONIO: I started working at the Record Plant in New York City in 1978, and Roy Cicala took me under his wing. He had recorded most of John Lennon's solo career. *Walls & Bridges* – which I think is his best record; he mixed *Imagine*. He didn't record it, but he mixed all that. He and John were pretty close. And he had almost all of John's recordings up in a vault on top of the building – on the tenth floor. It was called the Lennon Vault. When I first started working with Roy, he used to go through those tapes, and I would hear all these outtakes. It was great. I learned a lot about him by what he did through Roy.

There's this picture of him and Yoko in front of a really big guitar. Guild Guitars built him this 20-foot tall guitar, and that was at the Record Plant. We had his jukebox, we had the Beatles' Mellotron, so you know – there was definitely a presence of John there. But I started working there in '78 – those are the years that he was at home as a dad. And 1980 is when he went back in the studio with Jack Douglas, but it was at the Hit Factory, it wasn't at the Record Plant. So that was kind of a drag that he went to our competitor instead of coming back home.

But in December of that year, 1980, John and Yoko came back to the Record Plant. We started on this one song, a single for Yoko – 'Walking on Thin Ice'. It was kind of like, almost a disco track – that kind of vibe, a dance thing. If John ever wanted to sound disco… which I'm sure he didn't want to, it was Yoko's song. It's a very haunting kind of dance song.

So they came in on a Monday, the 1st of December, and we worked eight straight days just to finish that one song. You know – we took out a lot of the instruments recorded, and John replaced things. Yoko sang, and then we spent probably two- or three-days mixing. And then on that Monday the 8th, they came in and listened, and I said goodbye as they went down the elevator – and an hour later he was gone.

AIDAN PREWETT: Wow.

SM: So I didn't really share a beer with him, but I worked with him and Yoko for probably like 12 hours a day that week. And I'd rather that than sit in a bar for an hour. You know – the first day there, I didn't even want to look at him 'cos I was so afraid. I'd just spent a year working with the Blues Brothers, so I wasn't star-struck – but how could you *not* be in the presence of such greatness.

I remember the first day, he and Yoko met with a couple of reporters who were doing a story on him, I think they were from the BBC. And I was going about, listening to the producer and setting up gear and this and that, but I could overhear what they were saying. And he brought up his song 'Love Me Do' – *"Yeah, when we recorded Love Me Do…"* and as soon as he said that, that's when it hit me. I was like, *okay – that's one of the Beatles sitting right there.*

And when they were done with the interview, they said they were going to go and John said, *"No – you guys can hang out as long as you want."* He was by far the nicest artist I've ever worked with. *Ever* – in my 40-year career. *So* down to earth. The last night there was Sunday night, Monday morning. I was getting tired and we took a break.

I said, "Jack," Jack Douglas was the producer. I said, "I'm just going to take a walk around the block real quick; get some fresh air."

And John says, "Hold on, I'll come with you." So it was just him and I walking around the street – together, alone on a Monday morning in New York. It was better than getting a trophy or an award, you know what I mean? You can't get enough Grammys to go through that again. And he was just very, very nice to me. Very nice. We hit it off really good, I could see that we had a little bit of a bond going.

And of course, when it happened, we were all shell-shocked. I had to bring tapes up to the vault, and it was just a very weird, bizarre feeling.

AP: I love the idea of walking the streets on a Monday morning in New York. Do you remember anything that you guys spoke about during that time?

SM: Yeah – it was like three o'clock in the morning. That's like the most barren the city ever gets. The only thing around at that time of the day are garbage trucks. And it was *freezing* cold, and we were bundled up and walking. And he was telling me a story about when the Beatles first started out, they were in neighborhoods where all the girls went after them, 'cos they loved them so much. So therefore, the gangs in that area didn't like them coming into their neighborhood and taking away all the girls.

At one point, this one gang started chasing them. John said he threw his hat down and when the gang got to his hat, they just stomped on it. That gave him enough time to run away and get away from them. So I thought that was so cool, man. Just out of nowhere. I can picture John, like 18-19 years old…

AP: Oh my goodness.

SM: And Yoko took to me, too. Yoko was very quiet – to herself. She had a reputation of being very aggressive, but she warmed up to me and she was very cool.

AP: Is there a moment that might illustrate her warmth toward you?

SM: No, she really didn't have any – I didn't have much interaction with her. All I know is that she was fine to me. I performed my duties well enough for her not to get angry at me. But she was fun – she cracked up at something I said once, that was silly – and she laughed. So I knew that she liked me.

One thing that I would say is that she was definitely kind of in charge, but it *was* her song. She was the singer. John did a vocal – it was very interesting – and her chants were pretty interesting. But he used to call her, 'Mother'. I'm sure he called her Yoko a couple of times – but I remember hearing him say, 'Mother'.

I will say that ten years ago it was the 30th anniversary of his passing, and I recorded a John Lennon tribute record for a local charity here in Nashville. A lawyer friend of mine knew her lawyer, and she OK'd the project and let us use all the songs without licensing fees. So that – I need to give her a lot of credit for that.

AP: Steve, when you're sitting in the studio – with John Lennon – could you paint for me a little portrait of what that feels like, what that looks like?

SM: Well, you know – I'll tell you one thing – if you go back to the song and listen to the solo. It's such a – it's so John Lennon. A signature solo of his. I forget the guitar he used. I can't recall. But it was a very cool sound, and it was just one-hit strokes for the solo. I remember, after he did the solo, I started playing air guitar to it. Every time that part would come up, we would play air guitar to each other, for that solo.

AP: What was it that drew him to the Record Plant, specifically, when he was recording there?

SM: Well, it was Roy. I don't know how he got connected with John in the first place – and then Roy knew a lawyer, and the lawyer helped John get his citizenship. Remember that problem – they were trying to kick him out of the country? Roy knew a lawyer and got him help. So Roy took him in when he first got to New York. They did a lot of work together.

Oh – there's another story. I'm pretty sure he had a lot of studio equipment in one of his apartments at the Dakota. But there was this device – this is 1980 – there was a device called the Clap Track. I believe it was a box that had a button on it – and it sounded like hand claps. And I did some research, and I found a company in New Jersey that sold it. So John gave me two hundred-dollar bills and said, "Can you pick it up for me?"

I said, "Yeah, sure." I took the money and I thought to myself, *I'm going to go get this Clap Track, and I'm going to have to bring it to him at the Dakota. I'm going to go hang out with him at the Dakota.* You know what I mean? It was like, *shit, man!*

AP: Wow.

SM: Wow is right. Yeah – that was pretty cool. And one last thing that I can tell you is that – I remember it was December, so we were talking about Christmas. 'Happy Xmas (War Is Over)' – that was done at the Record Plant, just downstairs in the studio where we were.

I said, "You know John, that's my favorite Christmas song."

When that song comes on the radio, it gets my attention. It makes me incredibly sad. It's just a sad song. It's sad for me, you know what I mean? 'Cos I think of him. And the video is just so sad. But when I said to John *that's my favorite Christmas song* – saying that phrase to him, I choked up. Because here I was – I was able to tell him right to his face, that that's my favorite Christmas song. You know – it can't get any better.

• • •

In the evening of December 8, John gave the money for the Clap Track to Steve Marcantonio and headed home to the Dakota building.

How I wish that the ending could be different this time. Sadly, every biography of John Lennon must come to the same conclusion. There's a sense of foreboding in the chapters leading toward the thin end of the book. But this is a story about how John *lived*. We don't have to focus on anything else. This book is a celebration.

On December 9, 1980, Steve Marcantonio returned the money John had given him for the Clap Track. He gave it to Roy Cicala, who passed it on to Yoko. A little while later, Yoko sent Steve a *Double Fantasy* platinum record. He still has it.

JULIA BAIRD

CODA

WHAT'S IMPORTANT at this point in the story is to note how *loved* John was and still is. John's music is being played at this very moment by more than a thousand stereo systems and portable music devices simultaneously. His lyrics are still being quoted by our most celebrated writers and his political efforts have inspired countless others to stand up for themselves and the less fortunate. And his influence can be traced through every piece of popular music since 1963.

In his later life, John continued to look back to his early days – the time before he was famous. Mimi sent his old school tie to him and his sister Julia sent the old photos of their mother and the happy times they had spent together as a family. He surrounded himself with visual clues to his childhood; even the architectural style of the Dakota building bore a distinct resemblance to the Strawberry Field mansion, as he saw it over the back fence of Mendips. As much as John loved New York, he was homesick.

Liverpool was still his hometown. All his most important formative moments happened there. He met his first wife there; his first child was born there – and his mother had lived there. He learned about music there. His natural ability as a sailor stemmed from the history of his family in the old shipping port. And Liverpool was where he *made it*.

Some part of John remained there — frozen in time as the isolation of stardom and Beatlemania set it.

Julia Baird still lives in Liverpool, where she has retired from teaching and now enjoys frequent travel as she works to preserve an accurate depiction of John's early years. Julia's book *Imagine This: Growing Up with My Brother John Lennon* has become the cornerstone from which present-day Beatle biographers develop their understanding of John's childhood. The earlier books worked from Hunter Davies' original 1960s interviews with Aunt Mimi — a simplified version of history, to say the least.

In his childhood, John's rebellious nature came to the fore as he butted heads with Mimi. John honed some of his creative skill in keeping many of his childhood activities secret from her. But after Mimi died in 1991, John's sister Julia discovered that Mimi had some secrets of her own.

AIDAN PREWETT: There's this beautiful phrase, and every time it pops up it makes me laugh. Of all the times that you heard the words *don't tell Mimi*, is there one incident with John that you still think back to?

JULIA BAIRD: Well, when he started phoning again in 1974, the first thing he did was send us some money. He said, "I'm going to sort everything out for you. Go and get a farmhouse — you and Jackie — in North Wales." We'd always loved North Wales.

I said, "Oh, that sounds brilliant, John. Would it be ours?"

He said, "What do you mean?"

"Would it be ours, or would it be a company house?"

He said, "Oh, it'd be an Apple house."

"No thanks," I said. "My husband works really hard,

and we pay a mortgage and we've got children here. I'm not giving that up to live in a house that doesn't belong to me."

So he said, "Well, we'll get this sorted." And that was it.

In the meantime, he sent me a check to share between me and Jackie – and he forgot to put a stamp on the envelope. A registered letter with no stamp! With a check in it.

And his last words that day were *"Don't tell Mimi."* Don't tell Mimi.

AP: Mimi had a few secrets of her own, though.

JB: The biggest shock of all was when another of my aunts, Nanny, was talking to me before she died. I was in and out of her house all the time. She started to talk – things she wouldn't say before. She said, "There was something going on in that house, Julia. *Something.*"

She never lost her marbles – she got weak, physically. And I said, "Oh I don't know, Nanny – I don't know."

She said, "I'm telling you – you listen to me. There was something going on in that house." She kept saying it. So when she died, I just thought – I wonder… Did Mimi have some sort of relationship? 'Cos she painted herself as white as the driven snow. And I phoned Michael Fishwick. He lived there as a student lodger for eight years. He ended up big in government scientific research – space research.

I rang him just to say, "Who was Mimi's boyfriend?"

AP: I wonder what went through his mind.

JB: There was a gap – and he said, "What made you think Mimi had a boyfriend?"

And I just said, "I have no idea – I'm just asking you a question."

And he said, "What are you doing next Tuesday?"

"Meeting you?"

"Yes."

And I thought, *he's going to tell me the story…*

AP: Of who it was.

JB: I didn't know it was bloody *him*! You could have knocked me down. And they were together for years. She lied about her age; they were going to go to New Zealand together.

AP: It really is – the truth is stranger than fiction.

JB: A story about Mendips – I used to go and see the man who lived there. He was a retired doctor; he was quite old. When he died, his son Rodney rang me straight away and said, "My dad wanted you to have first choice on the house."

I said, "Well, that is so kind of him."

He said, "Yes, you've got to get back to Julia. The family have to have the first choice if they want Mendips." Because he knew about the fans turning up and everything.

I said, "Well, thank you very much – but I wouldn't touch it. But thank you."

That wasn't a happy house. I said, "Do you know what? Before I do anything else, would you give me a minute to phone Cynthia?"

He said, "Yes, of course I will. I won't do anything until I hear back from you."

As it happened, it took me a week to find her. She was always on the move. And I said, "Hi, Cyn – Julia here."

"Oh, how are you, love?" She used to call me 'love'.

I said, "I'm fine – but this is a bit of a surprise: the old fellow in Mendips has died. He was a lovely old man. I used to sit with him." She said yes and I said, "Do you want the house?"

She said, "What?"

I said, "Do you want the house? We've been offered the house."

She said, "What do you mean, we?"

I said, "Well, Rodney, the son, has phoned me and offered me the house. And I said I didn't want it – it wasn't a happy house. But I did think that you might like it."

And she said, "Oh, I wouldn't touch it. No way – that was a desperately unhappy house. I don't want it." And then she said, "Would you and Jackie like it between you?"

I said, "I don't think we would, Cynthia."

She said, "I'll get Julian to buy it for you."

And I said, "We don't want it, Cyn – but thank you. I just wanted you to have the choice as well." And I got back to Rodney, and said no. And we all know what happened in the end.

AP: In your book, there was a point early on where you would ask John *what's it like to be famous?* I would love to hear what one of those conversations was like – what did he say?

JB: Well, he was locked away. The thing is – I originally loved – I still do – love languages. So – the travel. Saying to John, "Oh my god, you've been everywhere and done everything."

He said, "Julia, we're in a hotel room – we never get out. You will see more of anywhere than I do."

And do you know what – I'm so aware of that. I've done lots of travel, and I can do what I like. I can stay in a hostel if I want to. I can stay in a five-star hotel – *if I want to*. I can go to the cinema – this is before lockdown, of course – I can go to see a play, I can go to see a band, I can have a drink. I can make friendships without them thinking *oh this is John Lennon's sister* because that's the death knell for me, if they didn't know me beforehand. And maybe I'm not right − but I never would trust that relationship right away. Whereas if I meet people around the world, and I'm just talking to them, they've met me as Julia.

But John never had that, did he? When he had his lost weekend in Los Angeles − and I've been past the Troubadour a few times − the place where he very famously danced on the tables and hit people and did stupid things, when he was free for the first time in his entire life. *Entire life.* He was free. So of course, he went crazy with it.

Wouldn't it have been nice if nobody had known he was a Beatle? He couldn't even strike freedom properly. Everything he did was highlighted and in the press.

AP: But of all the crazy stuff that celebrities do... I couldn't figure out if he even hit anyone properly, to be honest. In my research − you hear about this Lost Weekend all the time, and I've been scouring everything to try and figure out the truth of it. It's all this allusion to things, but for the life of me I can't confirm anything beyond drunken heckling of the Smothers Brothers and running around the Troubadour with a Kotex stuck to his forehead.

JB: I agree with you completely − what I've said for the book − I only put in the book what I could verify. And if I couldn't verify it, I didn't put it in. Because people would only find one thing, and that would be it, wouldn't it? *"That's wrong. So the whole book must be made up."* And that's why I've had no comeback − and that's why I interviewed Paul McCartney. Because no one's going to come back on him, are they?

AP: Absolutely. I tried to get in touch with him. I had to go through several layers of gatekeepers. They were all very polite.

JB: Paul is quite down-to-earth, and I like to think that John would have ended up like that. Paul takes his dogs out, and he gets the tube – he goes on the underground and walks back to his house in St John's Wood. And people, on the whole, are kind enough to leave him alone.

AP: Wow. I'm sure that John would have – 'cos that's what he enjoyed so much about New York, getting out and going around and doing day-to-day things and people leaving him alone.

JB: I love that story that I did put in the book about, only in the days before he died, or the month – he met a young student jogging in the park. John was jogging in the park and the student said, "Hey man, you can't jog in those." And he took John to a trainer's shop and John bought a couple of pairs of trainers. And I like to think he would have bought the student a pair as well.

AP: I'm sure he would have. In your conversations with John – is there a particular moment where you can remember the actual words, specifically, in the tone of voice and the way that he said it?

JB: Probably not. It'd be a paraphrase, wouldn't it? I do have a sharp memory, still. But I wouldn't make it up. People do come to me now and say *when was this? When was that?* My cousin David, when they were restoring Mendips, would say, "Go and ask Julia." I can remember exactly what the house looked like.

When I went to Mendips, for example, when they were re-opening it, I said, "Oh, you've taken the cherry trees down. Why on earth did you do that?" I was upset that they had actually cut the trees down. I really was. I can't understand anyone cutting a cherry tree down.

And my cousin Michael said, 'There weren't any cherry trees."

I said, "For God's sake, Michael. There was one on each side of the gate here. Massive cherry trees. Don't you remember the pink carpet – regularly, for a very short time every year?"

He said, "No – there were never any cherry trees."

Simon Osborne – the director of the National Trust – said, "Yes, there were. We took them down." We scraped away some of the soil on one side of the gate – and there's the root. Beautiful.

Michael just looked at me. I said, "How could you not remember the cherry trees?"

AP: That's amazing. Memory is such a funny thing.

JB: And not only do they not remember, they deny it! "No, no, no, Julia – there were never any cherry trees here."

There were. All the way up. And I'll tell you what – I think this is a coincidence. Two cherry trees – beautiful cherry trees. And all the way up the middle of Menlove Avenue. And John ended up marrying a Japanese woman.

AP: Yeah…yeah! That's so true.

JB: I think there's some sort of strange thing going on there. I'm not anti-Yoko by the way. I say: John found love a second time. What a lucky man. What I'm saying is, he didn't find love for the *first* time when he was 26. He had already married, he had a son, and he had the most beautiful wife. But he was a rock star, so that ended that.

The cherry trees – I think there's a Yoko link here

somewhere. All his life, he had seen cherry trees. Right over the gate. 'Cos Mimi used to moan about, "Oh, the leaves have been trodden in." It was a carpet. And it's only for a short time, isn't it? Only for a short time.

AP: That's beautiful. Julia, we've covered so much ground, and with the breadth of experiences that you've had – I think perhaps this cherry tree story might be a nice closer for the book.

JB: One of the nice things – here we are – here's an ending for you... You're the first one that's going to publish this. 'Cos I haven't said it before.

AP: Oh my goodness.

JB: On November the 17th in 1980, as usual I had gone down to see Nanny after work. Now, Nanny became, for me, my surrogate mother. And if you remember in the book, I said she wouldn't have chosen it. But she had no choice. I had decided that this was my go-to adult.

I was actually teaching in a school nearby her house at one time. I did a year – and I went to her house every single day for lunch. It would have been better for me, as a teacher, to stay in the school and do a few things. I was teaching French; I could set up the lab. But *no.* Nanny said, "Well dear, you come to lunch."

And it was a dinner. You know – it wasn't a sandwich. It was *dinner.* In the middle of the day – where, you know, you didn't really want it. I would not have *not* gone, not for all the tea in China. So we made a relationship. A really nice relationship. And at the end of her life, she used to phone Michael, her son – the denier of the cherry tree – and say, "Where's Julia?"

And Michael would phone me and say, "Mother's asking for you."

I'd say, "I'm going tomorrow."

I was working as a school psychologist with troubled adolescents. I'd come away – there was never any time to come away – and go *phew*. Stressed. And I found myself turning left instead of right. *Left* to go to Nanny's instead of *right* to go home. Twenty-mile drive. I'd phone her in a phone box on the way – no mobiles or anything. I'd phone her and say *I'm on the way*.

"Oh good dear, I'll put the kettle on."

I'd go and spend a couple of hours with her, and then wait until she went to bed – which was quite early. And she'd go up the stairs in this humongous big house on her own. And I'd shout, "Night-night, Nanny. God bless."

She'd say, "Night-night, dear. God bless."

And I'd worry about her all the way home. A little old lady in this big house.

Now – come to John. It was Nanny's birthday on November the 17th, and she was the other one with the memory – really and truly. She never forgot a birthday. You always got five pounds, which was a fortune. An absolute fortune. You got a card and you *knew* what was in it. You couldn't wait to open it. She did all that.

And with Nanny, on her birthday of course, I'd taken down a cat card and a present. And the phone went – and it was John, to wish her a happy birthday.

So – this is it: your nice ending. I don't know why I'm being so nice with you.

Nanny spoke to John and then she said, "Julia's here." And I went to speak to John.

And he said, "I'll be back soon. I'll be back in January. We'll all have to meet in Ardmore." That was the name of

Nanny's house. It was a huge house, with servants' quarters. We all loved that house. A colossal garden.

So we spoke, and he said, "We'll all have to meet in Ardmore to begin with, so I can say hello to everyone all at once."

I just said, "And about effing time, John."

He said, "I can't wait. I can't wait to see you all and meet everybody, and all the children, and I'm going to sort you all out."

I said, "And we can't wait to see you, John."

OUTRO

There are so many what-ifs. What music have we missed out on hearing over the past forty years? What songs would John have written and contributed to that we will never hear? And would John have ever composed with Paul McCartney again? With their reconnection in the late 1970s, surely John could only have held out for so long. They could easily have gate-crashed *Saturday Night Live* at the suggestion of Lorne Michaels.

What John would have done in his later life is anybody's guess. But one thing to consider is the way Paul, George, and Ringo embraced their careers since 1980. Each followed their own path, reconvening intermittently, but gradually becoming more comfortable in the shadow of their 'ever-present past', as Paul puts it. I'd like to think that John may well have embraced old age, in the way he described to Dick Cavett:

> **John Lennon:** I have a sort of longing for that. I think everybody does. I dream of us being an old couple on the south coast of Ireland or something: *"I remember when we were on Dick Cavett"*, you know, and being a nice old couple like that.

George Harrison was able to say so much during the two decades he lived beyond John's time. And of course, Paul and Ringo continue to create music and carry the torch that they were handed when they were first turned on to rock 'n' roll. In their own ways, each Beatle is still connecting with new generations of music fans.

One thing is clear: throughout their solo careers, John and Paul still benefited greatly from their rivalry. When Paul was having hits, John wanted to have hits too. It was the same with Paul. They continued to push each other, even while apart. When John and Yoko were shopping around the labels for *Double Fantasy*, the asking price matched the huge advances Paul was getting for albums at the time. Is it possible that the Lennon/McCartney bond – forged once in Liverpool, then again on their countless tours – held so tightly that they could only look to each other for real validation? We have a chance to explore this question a little further in an Appendix over the coming pages.

But John's character is our central focus. And one thing stands out to me as his most telling quality: The generous nature of his friends. Without fail, every person who agreed to speak with me did so with a generosity of spirit that I found quite overwhelming. They took a chance on a writer who just wanted to find a way to get to know John a little better. Forty years after his passing, chances are, we all want to get to know John a little better. When it comes down to it, that was my entire motivation. But as I mentioned in so many of these interviews, I was born much too late.

Conducting the interviews for this project brought many surprises. Firstly, I was shocked by the number of untold stories that are still out there. Everyone who met John has a different one. The people in this book knew John in very distinct ways – they were falling asleep on trains with him. And hiding in cupboards. But there are still plenty more stories out there for anyone who wants to start their own search.

In several interviews, I asked what John might think of the world today, if he could see it. His former bandmates set a kind of example here, too: Paul and Ringo continue to support and champion a wide variety of charities and causes. Both artists are fully aware of the goodwill that their presence invokes. After 9/11, Paul McCartney pulled together a plethora of artists at Madison Square Garden in the Concert for New York City. Ringo holds frequent charity concerts – including his online 80th birthday celebration, conducted during the covid-19 pandemic.

John would have been involved. He would have evolved, too – continuing the metamorphosis that began so early in his life. But the question is, would John be working continually to bring awareness to the humanitarian issues of today? Would he be doing everything he could to work toward a more livable planet for his children?

I can only imagine the answer. You may need a ladder and a magnifying glass.

YES

APPENDIX I

ANTHONY DECURTIS
THE OTHER BEATLES

THE FOUR BEATLES were the only ones who experienced that bond – who *knew* what it was really like to be one corner of the square that constituted the most famous band in history. From 1962-1970, they lived in each other's pockets and were rarely able to socialize outside each other's company. For this reason, it is difficult to develop an understanding of John without getting to know the others.

As a Contributing Editor at *Rolling Stone*, Anthony DeCurtis has interviewed Paul, George, and Yoko on numerous occasions. DeCurtis' writing has received some of the music industry's highest accolades: he won the Grammy for Best Album Notes for his essay accompanying the Eric Clapton box set *Crossroads,* and his co-written Clive Davis autobiography *Soundtrack of My Life* is a New York Times bestseller. Anthony DeCurtis is also a member of the nominating committee for the Rock and Roll Hall of Fame, and a frequent judge for the Independent Music

Awards. And he has gleaned insights into the Beatles' lives that nobody else has.

ANTHONY DECURTIS: The first time I interviewed George Harrison, I was in a guest house at Friar Park. He came and picked me up at the train station. We're sitting there – he hadn't done an interview for *Rolling Stone* or pretty much anybody for twelve or thirteen years. We're smoking cigarettes in this room. It's in the afternoon; it's starting to get dark. I remember I asked him a question, and he responded.

And then I was just looking at him. I don't know what he must have thought. I was looking at him, and I literally thought, *his lips have stopped moving – you have to say something.* I had no idea what he had said. I was sitting there thinking, *my God, that's George Harrison. He's right there.* It really had that feeling. It was just like, *settle down, bro. You've got a job to do.* It really seemed magical. It just seemed like *how did this happen?* My looking at all those performances and all those magazines. All those stories. And suddenly, there we are. We're just sitting there in the same room.

AIDAN PREWETT: My understanding is that George was a beautiful soul – do you have any specific moment that could illustrate that?

AD: I interviewed him a couple of times. It was extraordinary. It was the twentieth anniversary of *Rolling Stone,* so it was 1987. We did four special issues that year. One of them was *the best concerts of the last twenty years;* one of them was about style over the last twenty years; one of them was the *best hundred albums of the last twenty years.* And one was just interviews with everybody that we felt was important.

And so for that issue, I was going to do interviews with Paul McCartney, George Harrison, and Jackson Browne. Jackson obviously said *yeah sure, I'll do it.* McCartney said *yeah...sure, I'll do it.* Harrison... just *finding* him was, like, a problem. Just getting a hold of him. I was leaving messages everywhere. You know – back then I was sending faxes, leaving phone messages and all this this other business, and calling up people who I thought might know him.

So I'm sitting there in my office at *Rolling Stone*, and the phone rings. I pick it up, and it's Olivia Harrison. She was saying, "I wanted to give you a call, I know you've been trying to reach George. George said the other day *you've been very persistent.*"

So I had a chat with her. I think she was supposed to size me up, you know? Later it occurred to me, maybe George was on the other line. But we just chatted. She told me George was working on *Cloud Nine*, and I broke that news. I did a story for *Rolling Stone* about it – I just said, can I write about this? And I did a nice piece, using her quotes.

So she said, "Well, look – he might want to do this, so let's just stay in touch about it." I said *great.* So every once-in-a-while, I would phone her up. When I set a date to go to England to talk to McCartney, I said, "I'm going to be in England around the end of June. I'm going to be in London right around then."

She goes, "Oh, okay – well, that's good to know. Let me know when you get to town, and where you're staying and how I can reach you." They never said yes. I mean, that was the fuckin' thing. It was driving me crazy.

Rolling Stone just said, "Look – stay there until they say *no* – or they do it."

So I went and I interviewed McCartney. It was good. He was very polite, very smart. I got a reasonable amount of time – maybe an hour and twenty minutes, something like that. Which was pretty good.

AP: Does Paul kinda stick to the party line now?

AD: There was a little bit of that element of him at that time. But yeah – at this point – yes. Which is sort of a shame. I mean, I think there are reasons for it. One of the things which he spoke fairly compellingly about – I don't think he said that much about it before that – he was talking about when John died, the kinds of things that people said about *him*. You know, that John was the genius, Paul was the craftsman. All sorts of stuff. Which I think was ridiculous. They both did arguably their best work *together*. He spoke about that with a lot of feeling. One thing that was funny was – he had these offices on Soho Square, this leafy little area in London. When I walked into his office, he was listening to Elvis on a jukebox. Which was kinda cool. He certainly was in a chatty mood.

My interview style is more-or-less to let people talk, and not interrupt – but to direct them if necessary. After twenty minutes or half an hour, I thought *man, you're going to have to take the wheel here. Yeah, some of this is good, but you're going to need to really direct it more.* Which I did do, which he seemed amenable to. So on the whole, I felt good about it. Again, it was kind of a thrill – amazing to just meet Paul McCartney.

So I go back to my hotel, and I call Olivia Harrison.

I said, "Hey, I interviewed Paul today – so I'm at my hotel, and obviously I'd love to speak to George, while I'm here."

She goes, "Okay, great." It was a Friday. She said, "I'll call you tomorrow morning."

I said *Okay.* This was obviously pre-cell phones. I was

in some English hotel room which was *tiny*. I remember I wanted to take a shower – but I didn't want to get in the shower and not be able to hear the phone, you know? So I kept the door open, and I dragged the phone as close to the bathroom as I could. Happily, it didn't ring – I was able to take my shower.

Afterward, she said, "Oh well, George will be free for a bit this afternoon. You're welcome to come out and speak to him then if you'd like." Just like that.

So I said *great*. I got the directions; I was taking the train out to Henley-on-Thames. So I get on the train and I go to Henley. Henley's kind of this very leafy suburb-type place.

Olivia had said, "Someone will pick you up." So I'm looking around for somebody holding a piece of paper that says DeCurtis on it, or whatever. So with everybody going to their cars and whatnot, I'm thinking *oh fuck*. Like, *nobody's here* – I'm going to have to find a phone and call again, and find out what's going on, figure out the money to make the call.

And then I heard behind me:

"Well, *you* look like you might be visiting from New York."

I turned around and there was George. He was just standing there.

He said, "God, I'm sort of surprised – I mean, they wouldn't pay for you to take a car out here?"

Which was kind of interesting, he'd obviously never worked as a music journalist. Honestly, it didn't even occur to me to ask. I mean, I probably could have gotten it.

So we get into this swank car. He loved cars. I'm practically lying prone in this car. It's sleek. And he goes, "Well, I understand you spoke to Paul yesterday. How's he doing?"

And I thought – *wow* – *this is what the Beatles have come to. George asking me how Paul is doing.*

AP: That's amazing.

AD: It was fuckin' incredible. 'Cos they were going through that period where they – well, they weren't speaking. And I was like, "Oh you know, he was okay." And I told the story of having the meeting with Paul. I said it just felt like an interview – that if I was going to get what I wanted to get, I needed to take hold of it. George just looked over at me and smiled. His look was like, *well – that's dealing with Paul.* He completely had that sense of *that's why I'm asking you.* He was very wry about it.

But that interview was one of my favorites – the one with George. It was incredible. It came out extremely well – I'm very proud of it. It was a thrill. And flying home – now I had these tapes – and I swear to God, every time I moved five feet, I looked at my bag to make sure the tapes were there. *Oh my God, I still have them. I still have them.* I was just petrified. I've only felt that one other time – the first time I interviewed Keith Richards. I was just beside myself. I was just terrified that I would lose them.

So yeah – George was amazing. He was very thoughtful. And then a month or so later I interviewed him in Los Angeles again, when *Cloud Nine* was just about to come out. That was for a *Rolling Stone* cover. When I walked into the room, he just saw me and he goes, "*Next* time, Japan." We'd been moving – London, Los Angeles…

There was another great thing that happened on that trip, which was incredible. Because it was a cover, we had to do a photoshoot. I was taking the opportunity to spend as much time around him as I could, so I went to the photoshoot. The photographer was this guy named William

Coupon. He was a very nice guy, and a very talented photographer. He took beautiful pictures of George. But you know, it was *Rolling Stone*. So he was asking Harrison to *do stuff*. You know, like, "Would you move your arms? Would you jump around?", and all of this. Which Harrison was like – at best – tolerating.

It was sort of interesting – Coupon had brought his wife, who was also very charming, but a little naïve. And she had a little baby with her. She was sweet, but she kind of didn't get it.

Harrison was a little grumpy, and she just said to him – I swear to God – "Don't you want to be on the cover of *Rolling Stone?*" And Harrison *stopped the show*.

He just said, "Do you have any idea how little that means to me?" And he went into this long jag – it was pretty incredible. He just said, "You know, when I was in the Fabs, we travelled all over the world. I met *everyone*. The only person who ever impressed me of all of them was Ravi Shankar, and the various people in that world that he introduced me to." He goes, "The rest of it – I don't care about it. I certainly don't care about being on the cover of *Rolling Stone*." And he was just – it was just like, *wow*. And then he was cool.

I was like, "Alright, let's get out of here." We were leaving – I was kinda walking ahead. And Harrison came up behind me and put his hand on my arm. He sort of took my arm, really. He said, "Look – I hope you were okay with that." He goes, "That wasn't for you. That was for their benefit." It was just amazing. Truly unbelievable.

AP: To take that moment to check that you were okay – I mean…wow.

AD: Oh, I know. Exactly... I mean, if you want to hear it I have another great McCartney story.

AP: Absolutely.

AD: This is actually very moving. It was shortly after 9/11, and I was interviewing McCartney in New York. It was October, maybe three weeks after 9/11, and the city was still shaking. It was unlike *anything*. People were really whipped up – just tense and nervous. And fuckin' celebrities were beating it out of here. Nobody wanted to be in New York. They seemed to just be *let me get outta here*. Like, fuck you – you know?

But McCartney wasn't. McCartney was great. He organised a concert; he was there. So I went to his office, which was in Midtown. It was a beautiful October day. We were going to do the interview at a restaurant that was about four or five blocks away. And usually with somebody like McCartney, there'd be a car to take you.

But McCartney said, "Why don't we walk, you know? Let's take a walk – it's a nice day."

I really think he wanted people to see him in New York. He wanted them to know – *I'm here*. And it was astonishing. Just walking down Sixth Avenue with him, in the middle of the day, on a work day, right after 9/11. It was like those cartoons where somebody stops and their jaw just drops and hits the floor. It was like that. And people were saying hello to him, like, "Hey Paul!" They were so happy to see him.

You know, it's McCartney, man. *Take a sad song and make it better.* That, to me, was what that was about. Greeting people – everybody was cool. It was like, "Hey man, how are you?" and, "Hey Paul, man – great to see you." It was so sweet.

As we were walking, I had seen that the night before he had gone to a Yankees game. They put him on camera just for a minute, just in his seat. He was having a beer, and he held it up and everything. It was one of these moments where you realise who you're with. 'Cos I'm walking down the street with him and it was amazing, but you know, we're walking together, we're going somewhere. It was like you're talking to a friend or something.

I just said, "Oh, I saw you on TV last night at the Yankees game."

He goes, "Oh God, yeah – it was so great. I mean, it was too bad they lost. That was disappointing, but the game was great. It was just so much fun to be at Yankee Stadium."

Again, very generous – people were wary of crowds, or going anywhere. And there's McCartney drinking a beer at Yankee stadium. It was incredible. There were 65,000 people there. Yankee Stadium is a pretty iconic place. So the question you would ask anybody at that time, who had just been to Yankee Stadium, is – and I started to ask him, "Yeah, Yankee Stadium is great. Have you ever been to Shea – ?" And I stopped myself, and he just looked at me and laughed.

He said, "Yeah, I've been to Shea Stadium a couple of times." I just thought, *right – you were one of those guys. There were four of you, and there was everybody else. We all watched it, but you didn't.* The idea that I asked him if he'd ever been to Shea Stadium was just hysterical.

But he was generous, man. There was really a desire on his part to reassure people. And it worked, you know? It meant something. It meant so much to people that he was here.

AP: More so than like, a visiting statesman, I'm sure.

AD: Without a fucking doubt. Totally.

AP: 'Cos who's had that kind of impact on people's lives? I mean, over that span of time, as well.

AD: Nobody else has that kind of standing – that just showing up would have meant something. I mean, if John was alive, certainly he would have had it. But who else? Who else?

AP: I have to ask about Yoko as well, because you've obviously spent a decent amount of time with her.

AD: I've spent a lot of time around Yoko. She was good friends with Jann Wenner at *Rolling Stone*. We covered her a lot, and I was on that beat for a long time. So I kinda got a picture of her. What I would say to people, which I think is true, is to whatever extent that she broke up the Beatles – which is kind of a ridiculous idea – that was her job. I think that's sort of what John wanted.

Nobody – I mean, Lennon was such a force, that nobody was going to *get over* on him. I think he wanted out. He didn't really know how to do that. I mean, despite his kinda acerbic nature – he was still English. There was a kind of non-confrontational thing. So I think that was kind of Yoko's job – to extricate him from that band. I think that's what he wanted.

She's a pretty compelling figure. This is maybe TMI – but I once had an erotic dream about Yoko. I think they had a pretty powerful sexual connection, to be blunt about it. If you ever look at those erotic drawings that Lennon did of her, you know? There's something going on there.

AP: *Definitely* something going on there.

AD: And all of that New York avant-garde stuff... If you ever talk to Mick Jagger, in particular – but Keith too. They talk about the Beatles like they're these country bumpkins or something, honestly. It's like, *we were from London, they're from the provinces somewhere.* As Mick once said, "Of all places – Liverpool." Just dripping condescension. So I think they felt a lot of that, even though they were the Beatles.

Underneath – certainly for John – some of that was still going on. So to meet Yoko, who knew all these fancy New York avant-gardists, and who had these avant-garde credentials. I think that was meaningful to him. It sounds like a cliché, but I think that meant something to him. And I think it freed him to do stuff that he wanted to do. For better or worse.

I'm kind of a big pop fan, myself. I mean, I can make my way through the avant-garde stuff, but for the most part, if you give me any early Beatles record, I'm perfectly happy. But I think he kind of got tired of it. And his problems too, with his own mother and his Aunt Mimi and all this other business. There was a lot of psychological stuff going on there. But Yoko is a presence. Yoko is *no joke.* I mean, she has a kind of force. I mean, that was the thing about the erotic dream. I sort of felt like, *fuck, man – she got into my head.* I'm just hanging out, doing an interview or chatting with her about a project. She's a pretty compelling person.

AP: Is there a moment with Yoko that would sum up her character? In terms of who she is as a person, I'm so interested. I really want to know.

AD: Oh, God. I don't know what this sums up, but it's something I remember. I was writing liner notes for the John Lennon box set. And I would go over to the Dakota and listen to stuff with her. She would show me this room that John liked to go into – there's a bed, and his little tape recorder and stuff. It was incredible. And we would talk. She would explain what these tracks were, and I would interview her and whatnot.

We were leaving together, and she goes, "Can I give you a lift downtown?" She had a driver there, waiting.

And I just said, "Oh God, I wish I could, but I've got to go back up to my apartment. I've got a bunch of work to do, I'm really busy."

And as we're walking out of the Dakota – right where John was shot – she just said, "You know, it's good to be busy. It's good to work – it keeps your mind off things that might otherwise be troubling you."

I'm thinking like, *this woman walks past the site where her husband was murdered – every day.* There's a kind of strength of will to that. I mean, somebody else might have moved, or somebody else might have done whatever. I feel like there's a kind of stoic quality to that, like – *I'm not moving. This is where we live. This is my house. A terrible thing happened here, but we live in a world where terrible things happen, and I'll deal with it.* So that sums up something.

APPENDIX 2

JON COBERT'S RECORDING

JOHN LENNON IN THE STUDIO –
'WHATEVER GETS YOU THRU THE NIGHT'

20 August 1974, at Record Plant, Studio C

In the studio are John Lennon, Jon Cobert, and other members of BOMF. Jimmy Iovine is in the control booth. Sound from the recording is taken from Jon's Walkman cassette recorder, which has been left in the booth with Jimmy.

John: [Inaudible...] That fuckin' pair of headphones.

John puts on the headphones and listens.

John: It's no good as soon as you're behind. You have to all be in a line. Come on straight, get in there.

John listens again.

John: I'll try and give you *one two three four* if I'm alive when it's happening. To come out, then to go in. Or I'll just wave on the way out.

Jimmy laughs.

John: The line we come out, the track goes *listen to me, come on listen to me,* then it goes *listen, listen.* After the second *listen to me* we go back to the one.

John claps twice.

Jon Cobert: That's both times?

John: Yeah, yeah.

Jimmy Iovine: You got your headphones on?

John: Well, we'll find out when we blast our head off.

Jimmy plays the tape. The reel winds up to the correct speed. The first bar of 'Whatever Gets You Thru the Night' plays. It stops abruptly. The voices in the studio groan.

John: Woah! Ours aren't on. [Funny voice] *Ours aren't on!*

Grumbling from the band.

Jimmy: It's too loud.

Somebody chuckles. Somebody lets out a *whoo.*

Band member: Ours aren't on either.

John: It's too loud in the ones that are on. And the ones that are off are off.

Band member: This is so criminal, man.

Jimmy: I'm working.

John: Oh, you're on?

Band member: Uh oh.

Band member: I think if I push this button.

John: Yeah.

Jimmy: Mine's on.

John: Man of the vole.

Somebody giggles. Somebody coughs.

John: Oh it's nothing.

Jimmy: [Funny voice] We'll break through the shield!

John: You mean these earphones are bust, or what?

Jimmy: These work.

John: So who else isn't on? Just us two?

Band member: This is directly into the wall.

Jimmy: Are you working now? You wanna go into the wall? That's alright, yeah. Yours doesn't work?

Band member: No, it's just us. Some of them are working.

Jimmy: It is now.

John: If you get the sound on this, you can get it right away. It just changes twice. So just one second to warm up here.

Jimmy: It's almost taken care of, we'll be right there.

John: Alright, *James*?

The tape winds up to speed: 'Whatever Gets You Thru the Night'. John and the band clap in time with the track. After a minute, the track increases in volume and suddenly stops.

Jimmy: I'm ready.

John: Just run through the change again.

The tape winds back up to speed, with John and the band clapping. After a minute it drops in volume. Continues under dialogue.

Jimmy: That sounds good to me.

John: Okay. [Louder – funny voice] *Alright?!*

The tape stops.

John: Alright. You get it? It goes *come on listen to me, come on listen to me* – then back to one.

Band member: Do it.

John: Do it man, let's do it. It hurts.

The band chuckles.

John: Is it alright, Jim?

We hear the sound of (John's?) hands rubbing together.

John: [Cowboy voice] *I mean, does it sound like one guy?*

• • •

Later:

Jimmy: I don't think the board will handle it if you can hear the count-in.

John: Yeah, remember those days? You hear it in the distance. *Two, three.*

The tape starts. We hear a very faint count-in. John and the band clap along. It hits the change for two claps and the tape stops.

John: Just drop us in there. After the second.

Jimmy: Just clap along.

John: Yeah. And maybe the very first one was a bummer, but we'll deal with that later. Okay.

The tape winds up to speed. After about 30 seconds it stops.

John: You're rushing. It's just – [demonstrates one clap – two clap pattern] That's all.

Jimmy: Clapping – here we are.

John: Yeah, well bring us in on that horn bit, we're alright.

The tape winds up to speed for the sax solo. It stops before the next section.

John: Forgot to tell you.

The band laughs.

John: I was listening to the sax.

The tape starts. They clap along and make the change between the one and two-clap sections. It stops abruptly.

John: That was in – after the break?

Jimmy: Yeah.

The band chuckle amongst themselves. Somebody lets out a whistle.

Band member: Wow.

John: [New York accent] *No easy work, huh?*

Jimmy: That didn't sound like one – it sounded like thirteen hand-clapping guys.

John: The very first one was like that. We'll do it after. Okay so… okay.

The tape starts, the track plays through to the final sax & piano solo.

• • •

Later:

(John?) whistles the end of the sax riff. The tape slows down as Jimmy returns it to the start. Somebody (John?) claps a few times, increasing in speed.
The track starts again. We hear John's count in a little clearer this time – a quick *one, two, one-two* preceding the sax riff's lead-in. Two claps – one bar – and it stops again.

John: Alright. Maybe just check it.

Footsteps – John walking into the control booth?

John: [Now clearer] Was it alright in the other bits, too?

Jimmy plays the tape back. This time we hear the count-in: *One, two, three, four*

John: Move on a bit, just to…

Jimmy: This guy's so good. [Referring to tape operator?]

John: They're red hot, man. Red hot.

We hear the tape scrubbing forward. It plays a section, then stops suddenly.

John: [Impresario voice] *Alright, good night and thank you. You were shit.*

Everyone laughs.

John: [Yelling upstairs?] *Alright, Roy – let's mix it!*

Jimmy: (to band) Go rehearse and you'll be famous one day, too.

They laugh.

• • •

Afterward:

Jon: Hey, John – would you say something for posterity?

John: [Funny voice] *Hello, dear Posterity – how are ya?*

Jon: That was –

John: *That was Doctor Posterity.*

Jon: That was Doctor Posterity.

John: With boobs!

FURTHER READING

Due to the interview format of this book, some areas of John's life have had to be glossed over rather quickly. If you are looking to fill the gaps, I can most highly recommend Ray Connolly's *Being John Lennon: A Restless Life.* As you can see in Ray's interview in this book, John was very fond of Ray and the two spoke at length about a wide variety of topics over the course of many years. Ray has written extensively about the Beatles – also very useful for this project were *The Ray Connolly Beatles Archive* and *Sorry Boys, You Failed the Audition.* Ray's Elvis Presley biography *Being Elvis* is similarly magnificent.

Julia Baird's book *Imagine This: Growing Up with My Brother John Lennon* provides a deeply personal look into their life together with their mother Julia. This book is the definitive story of John's early life – told with wit, pathos, and humor. *Imagine This* sets the record straight about these early days – and some later ones – and provides a poignant portrait of John, Julia, and their family.

For John's school days, the most essential reading is Michael Hill's book, *John Lennon: The Boy Who Became a Legend.* This book is a very recent addition to the Beatles literature and brings with it some startling revelations that were previously unknown to Beatles researchers. It paints a brilliant, down-to-earth picture of John at Dovedale and Quarry Bank, written by one of John's good friends.

The Beatles years are covered in a very personal style by Tony Bramwell in *Magical Mystery Tours: My Life with The Beatles.* There are many great stories in Tony's book that you won't find anywhere else.

Ivor Davis provides a wonderfully entertaining portrait of his time travelling with the Beatles in America in *The Beatles and Me on Tour*. Ivor features plenty of fantastic and hilarious tour stories, including when the Beatles met Elvis and Bob Dylan, and he doesn't shy away from the moments that are left out of the PG-rated Beatles books.

Leslie Cavendish's book *The Cutting Edge: The Story of the Beatles Hairdresser who Defined An Era* gives the reader a glimpse into the world of Apple Corps and the glamorous world of Vidal Sassoon in the thick of swinging London. Leslie shares some great stories about each of the Beatles, including some wonderful times at Paul McCartney's house.

Dan Richter has written two books, both of which I found fascinating. For this project, *The Dream is Over: London in the '60's, Heroin, and John & Yoko* was extremely useful, hard-edged, and heartfelt. The Kubrick fan in me also loved *Moonwatcher's Memoir*, about Dan's time on *2001: A Space Odyssey* with Stanley Kubrick.

Dick Cavett's books *Cavett, Talk Show* and *Brief Encounters* are filled with wonderful anecdotes about his time spent with near every celebrated figure of the second half of the 20th century.

Allan Tannenbaum's *John and Yoko: A New York Love Story* is a wonderful visual story, filled with intimate portraits and casual documentary images of the couple. Allan's striking pictures provide a rare perspective on their relationship.

Anthony DeCurtis' book *Rocking My Life Away* contains more wonderful moments with George & Paul, as well as the Rolling Stones, U2, REM and many others.

Jenny Boyd's *Jennifer Juniper* is named for the song

Donovan wrote about her, after their trip to India with the Beatles in 1968. *Jennifer Juniper* provides a wider portrait of the era, with plenty of stories of the fashion industry, Pattie & George, and Jenny's former husband Mick Fleetwood.

Of the great many books and articles that were consulted during research for this project, the following is a list of those which I found to be the most helpful, interesting, and insightful.

Baird, Julia. *Imagine This* (Hodder & Stoughton, 2011)

Boyd, Jenny. *Jennifer Juniper: A Journey Beyond the Muse* (Urbane Publications, 2020)

Bramwell, Tony. *Magical Mystery Tours: My Life with The Beatles* (Thomas Dunne Books, 2005)

Brown, Peter and Gaines, Steven. *The Love You Make* (Penguin, 1983)

Burger, Jeff. *Lennon On Lennon* (Chicago Review Press, 2016)

Cavendish, Leslie. *The Cutting Edge: The Story of the Beatles' Hairdresser Who Defined an Era* (Alma Books, 2018)

Cavett, Dick. *Talk Show* (Times Books, 2010)

Cavett, Dick. *Brief Encounters: Conversations, Magic Moments, and Assorted Hijinks* (Henry Holt & Co, 2014)

Connolly, Ray. *Being John Lennon: A Restless Life* (Pegasus, 2018)

Connolly, Ray. *The Ray Connolly Beatles Archive* (Plumray Books, 2018)

Connolly, Ray. *Sorry Boys, You Failed the Audition* (Malignon, 2013)

Davis, Ivor. *The Beatles and Me on Tour* (Cockney Kid, 2014)

Davis, Ivor. *Manson Exposed: A Reporters 50-Year Journey into Madness and Murder* (Cockney Kid, 2019)

Davies, Hunter. *The Beatles* (Heinemann, 1968)

Davies, Hunter. *The Quarrymen* (Omnibus, 2001)

Davies, Hunter. *The John Lennon Letters* (Little, Brown, 2012)

DeCurtis, Anthony. *Rocking My Life Away: Writing about Music and Other Matters* (Duke University Press, 1999)

Du Noyer, Paul. *Conversations with McCartney* (Hodder & Stoughton, 2016)

Etchingham, Kathy. *Through Gypsy Eyes: My Life, the Sixties and Jimi Hendrix* (Victor Gollancz, 1998)

Flippo, Chet. *McCartney: The Biography* (Pan McMillan, 1988)

Green, John. *Dakota Days* (St Martin's Press, 1983)

Gruen, Bob. *John Lennon: The New York Years.* (Abrams, 2015)

Hill, Michael. *John Lennon: The Boy Who Became A Legend* (Michael Hill, 2013)

Kirchherr, Astrid. *Yesterdays* (Vendome, 2007)

Lennon, Cynthia. *John* (Three Rivers Press, 2006)

Lennon, John. *In His Own Write* (Jonathan Cape, 1964)

Lennon, John. *A Spaniard in the Works* (Jonathan Cape, 1965)

Lewisohn, Mark. *Tune In: The Beatles All These Years, Vol. 1* (Little, Brown, 2013)

Lewisohn, Mark. *The Complete Beatles Recording Sessions: The Official Story of the Abbey Road years 1962-1970* (Harmony Books, 1990)

Norman, Philip. *John Lennon: The Life* (Harper Collins, 2008)

Ono, Yoko. *Memories of John Lennon* (It Books, 2005)

Richter, Dan. *The Dream is Over: London in the 60s, Heroin, and John and Yoko* (Quartet Books, 2012)

Richter, Dan. *Moonwatcher's Memoir: A Diary of 2001: A Space Odyssey* (Carroll & Graf, 2002)

Tannenbaum, Allan. *John and Yoko: A New York Love Story* (Insight Editions, 2007)

Seaman, Fred. *The Last Days of John Lennon* (Dell, 1992)

Wildes, Leon. *John Lennon vs. The U.S.A.: The Inside Story of the Most Bitterly Contested and Influential Deportation Case in United States History* (American Bar Association, 2016)

A NOTE ON THE COVER

This book's cover photograph and back cover photograph are courtesy of the Mark Naboshek collection.

The front cover features John's self-portrait, circa 1960. As it was taken in an instant photo booth, no negative exists for this picture – the small imperfections are unique to the original print. On the back, in John's handwriting, is written:

ME CROSS EYED

The back cover of the book features an original Polaroid of the Beatles at Harold's Café, Hamburg. The photograph was most likely taken by a roving photographer, and is dated September 28, 1960 in a caption handwritten on the reverse side by original Beatles bassist Stuart Sutcliffe. Stu also details the names of those featured in the image, for the benefit of his family, to whom he mailed the picture.

From left: Stuart Sutcliffe, John Lennon, Helmut (a waiter), George Harrison, Paul McCartney, Pete Best.

Mark Naboshek was also of great assistance in connecting me with Michael Hill – from whom further contacts flowed.

ACKNOWLEDGEMENTS

To my wife, Schy, and our little ones, Felix, Parker & Quincy, who are my constant inspirations.

For believing in the book, pushing for it, and working through many hours of edits, Lewis Slawsky and Alex Wall at Political Animal Press, who have rallied around this project to make it as groovy as possible.

Thank you to Debbie Golvan of Golvan Arts Management, who pushes for these books – and more to come!

This book was a major research task – and any mistakes in the text or interviews are solely my own.

For their generosity of spirit, Julia Baird, Mike Hill, Rod Davis, Tony Bramwell, Tony Palmer, Ivor Davis, Leslie Cavendish, Ray Connolly, Dan Richter, Kieron Murphy, Dick Cavett, Elliot Mintz, Shelly Yakus, Greg Calbi, Jon Cobert, Allan Tannenbaum, Steve Marcantonio, and Michael Pittard.

For their assistance in liaising with the artists: Mark Naboshek, Mike Hill, Lisa Troland, Plastic EP & Sharon Agnello.

For their ongoing support: Durham Prewett, Vicki Prewett, Natasha Prewett, Sam Hodson, Mitchell Prewett, Martha Prewett, Simon & Nancye Thomas, John Lewis, Matt Dowling, Timmy Byrne, Anne Leighton, Stuart Coupe, Mick Wall, Plastic EP, David Bedford, ChaChi Loprete, Siân Llewellyn, Andrew Massie, Tim Caple, Martin Kielty, Belinda Peterson, Rod Peterson, Amelia Peterson, James Hallal, Verity Edris-Peterson, Emran Edris, Arnold Prewett, Jan Wright, John Wright, Bruce Thomas, Cindy Farrell, the Sumner family, all at South Oakleigh College, and all my students past present & future.